From Practice to Praxis:
A reflexive turn

In the *World Library of Educationalists* series, international scholars themselves compile career-long collections of what they judge to be their finest pieces—extracts from books, key articles, salient research findings, major theoretical and/or practical contributions—so the world can read them in a single manageable volume. Readers thus are able to follow the themes and strands of their work and see their contribution to the development of a field, as well as the development of the field itself.

From Practice to Praxis is an exploration of the development of ethical practice as it applies to the meaning of quality within the tradition of practitioner inquiry and participatory research. Chronicling some of her most important works, this is a compelling overview of Susan Groundwater-Smith's contribution to the evolution of the nexus between thinking and theory as it stands between the academy and the field. It traces the steps between instrumental reasoning towards a more liberatory and challenging stance.

The book selects from a number of publications, each representing the genesis of the nascent ideas that have informed Susan's practice as a scholar and researcher. Taking a praxis stance draws attention not only to procedural concerns, *how things are done*; but also substantive issues that are associated with different forms of dialogue and trustworthiness, *why things are done*.

In addition to the assemblage of articles and chapters, the book is prefaced by a long essay that reveals those features of the writer's self-understanding as it is illuminated throughout the selection. The work is situated within a professional life-history, as well as relating to extant writings on theory and practice within a complex cultural and ever-changing professional educational environment.

From Practice to Praxis will appeal to initial teacher education students in both primary and secondary settings, as well as post-graduate students with an interest in action research/participant research with both practitioners in the field and young people.

Susan Groundwater-Smith is Honorary Professor at the Faculty of Education and Social Work, University of Sydney. She has over fifty years of teaching and academic experience in both mainstream and special education.

World Library of Educationalists series

A full list of titles in this series is available at www.routledge.com.

Recently published titles:

Educational Experience as Lived: Knowledge, history, alterity
The selected works of William F. Pinar
William F. Pinar

Faith, Mission and Challenge in Catholic Education
The selected works of Gerald Grace
Gerald Grace

Dysconscious Racism, Afrocentric Praxis, and Education for Human Freedom: Through the Years I Keep on Toiling
The selected works of Joyce E. King
Joyce E. King

A Developing Discourse in Music Education
The selected works of Keith Swanwick
Keith Swanwick

Struggles for Equity in Education
The selected works of Mel Ainscow
Mel Ainscow

Faith, Mission and Challenge in Catholic Education
The selected works of Gerald Grace
Gerald Grace

Towards a Convergence Between Science and Environmental Education
The selected works of Justin Dillon
Justin Dillon

From Practice to Praxis: A reflexive turn
The selected works of Susan Groundwater-Smith
Susan Groundwater-Smith

From Practice to Praxis:
A reflexive turn

The selected works of
Susan Groundwater-Smith

Susan Groundwater-Smith

LONDON AND NEW YORK

First published 2017
by Routledge

2 Park Square, Milton Park, Abingdon, Oxfordshire OX14 4RN
711 Third Avenue, New York, NY 10017

Routledge is an imprint of the Taylor & Francis Group, an informa business

First issued in paperback 2018

Copyright © 2017 Susan Groundwater-Smith

The right of Susan Groundwater-Smith to be identified as author of this work has been asserted by her in accordance with sections 77 and 78 of the Copyright, Designs and Patents Act 1988.

All rights reserved. No part of this book may be reprinted or reproduced or utilised in any form or by any electronic, mechanical, or other means, now known or hereafter invented, including photocopying and recording, or in any information storage or retrieval system, without permission in writing from the publishers.

Notice:
Product or corporate names may be trademarks or registered trademarks, and are used only for identification and explanation without intent to infringe.

British Library Cataloguing in Publication Data
A catalogue record for this book is available from the British Library

Library of Congress Cataloging in Publication Data
A catalog record for this book has been requested

ISBN: 978-1-138-65293-4 (hbk)
ISBN: 978-1-138-32750-4 (pbk)

Typeset in Sabon and Futura
by Florence Production Ltd, Stoodleigh, Devon, UK

 Printed in the United Kingdom by Henry Ling Limited

CONTENTS

1 Moving to praxis: reading the readings 1

2 The interrogation of case records as a basis for constructing curriculum perspectives 30

3 Credential bearing enquiry-based courses: paradox or new challenge? 40

4 Putting teacher professional judgement to work 46

5 Painting the educational landscape with tea: rereading *Becoming Critical* 61

6 My professional self: two books, a person and my bedside table 76

7 Professional knowledge formation in the Australian educational market place: changing the perspective 89

8 Questions of quality in practitioner research: universities in the 21st century – the need for safe places for unsafe ideas 99

9 Ethics in practitioner research: an issue of quality 106

10 Student voice: essential testimony for intelligent schools 118

11 Co-operative change management through practitioner inquiry 132

12 Learning outside the classroom: a partnership with a difference 143

13 Living ethical practice in qualitative research 154

14 Concerning equity: the voice of young people 163

15 Weaving a web of professional practice: the coalition of knowledge building schools 177

16 Mentoring teacher inquiry: lessons in lesson study 189

Index 200

CHAPTER 1

MOVING TO PRAXIS
Reading the readings
Susan Groundwater-Smith

The aim of this introductory chapter is to reveal features of my self-understanding as illuminated through the selection of readings that follow. I seek to explain and justify why I have chosen to present these in a linear rather than thematic fashion since I uncover both content and method in my exegesis. It situates my work within my professional life history as well as in relation to extant writings on theory and practice where they connect to an insight of 'praxis', being a term concerned with moral human action in education. It has required both a reflective and reflexive authorial voice as I establish the contents within a complex cultural and theoretical context that lays bare the strengths and weaknesses of my ongoing academic and personal development. It is designed to contribute to the understanding of the readers should they progress through each piece, one after the other. Embedded in the chapter is an ongoing analysis of the distinction between professional practice and praxis and the manner in which the latter is perceived as desirable as it has related to both the form and content of each selection.

As in the writing of any material, a number of choices are available to the author. A major one for me was whether to develop this introduction in a linear fashion, tracing the evolution of my thinking over time, moving from 'practice' to 'praxis', or to adopt a more recursive rendition that would journey across experience thematically. In deciding to adopt the former stance, it seemed to me that effectively both possibilities were being met – the historical route necessarily was also thematic, but rather more 'chaotically' even 'playfully' so. In this struggle for a coherent structure I was reminded that being 'playful' may be to engage with what the romantic poet John Keats (1795–1821) nominated as 'negative capability'.

Keats coined the phrase 'negative capability' in a letter written to his brothers George and Thomas on the 21st December, 1817. In this letter he defined his new concept of writing:

> I mean Negative Capability, that is when man [sic] is capable of being in uncertainties, mysteries, doubts, without any irritable reaching after fact and reason.[1]

What Keats did was strive to accept a willingness to embrace uncertainty, to live with mystery and tolerate ambiguity as a living form. The notion of 'being in uncertainties' is a powerful ontological enjoinment to be in the moment. Readers of this introduction will only share part of the writer's journey that is based, in effect, on her own incomplete knowledge of her professional life. At the commencement of that life of being an educator there was a time that, for this writer, stood as a period 'before practice'.

When Jack Hexter (1972) wrote his book *The History Primer*, he commenced with a 'non-chapter' (that is, a chapter that did little to advance the overall argument of the book but provided a reader with something of the context in which the book was written). I shall discuss more of Hexter's orientation to writing, and not only the writing of history, at a later point in this introduction. For now, I wanted to place the notion of 'before practice' as a precursor in much the same way, to understand the concept of practice itself in terms of being a classroom teacher, a teacher educator and an educational researcher.

Before practice

How can one write of becoming a teacher and not write of practice? When I began to teach in the 1960s, as I went about my daily work in the classroom I did not conceive of it as 'a practice'. Rather I was engaged in a daily struggle with questions: 'Why did this child not seem to enjoy learning?' 'How was it that another was mute in the classroom?' 'What happens when a toddler is abandoned and grows into delinquency?' 'How can it be that children are expected to engage in schooling when the classroom consists of bare boards and fixed desks with a raised platform on which the teacher is to perform?'

These questions arose from my early career, spanning teaching infants through to working with special needs children; continuing on to work in a girls' home; and moving from one Australian state to another to teach in a school identified as 'the neediest school in the state' by a university student group that sought to raise funds to repair its dilapidated conditions. None of these appointments led me to consider teachers' work as a *practice*.

So what contributed to a change in my understanding? My initial teacher education was one of 'training'. Mid-century teachers' colleges in Australia set out to graduate young people who were competent in a range of proficiencies: managing the classroom; devising a work plan; employing teacher-centred 'micro' skills such as questioning, explaining and demonstrating; and assessing and reporting upon student learning. All of this within the policies of the relevant state authorities that determined the teacher-training curriculum. It was after a decade of work in classrooms that I realised that to progress beyond competence towards a position that was better informed and theorised, I needed to participate in a community that would not only enhance my tools for teaching, but enable me to develop critical insights into the profession of which I was a part. It was as a mature-age student that I began my studies of education at university.

The Department of Education at the University of Sydney was then a department in the Faculty of Arts. Education was to be studied as multi-disciplinary, informed *inter alia* by history, philosophy, psychology and sociology. Just as in the UK universities of the day, 'the aim was to produce the well-rounded "scholar" who happened to want to be a teacher' (Furlong, 2013, p. 25, quoting Bell, 1981). As a teacher by day, now in a privileged school working with intellectually gifted children, I was exploring the foundations of my work in the evenings in ways that encouraged me to become not only better informed regarding its antecedents, but also to develop a critique of the ways in which some education provisions were unfair and unsustainable, causing harm and injustice. At the same time, I was enabled to consider recent innovations that shifted attention from how teachers taught to how children learned. It was by now the heady days of the 1970s and progressive education.

Already I was turning to major thinkers of the day to give me purchase upon what was taking place in the classroom and the school, even a little in relation to the system within which I taught. Writers such as Lawrence Stenhouse, Stephen Kemmis and Jurgen Habermas, to whom I shall turn later, were enabling me to frame my own theories of 'practice' – that is, what happens when one actually acts within a set of self-conscious, coherent, professional beliefs. It was no longer a matter of acting as a teacher, but of knowing how and why I was acting in such and such a way.

At the same time, I was developing the confidence to write about my work for my colleagues in the field. One such piece (Groundwater-Smith, 1974) documented a project undertaken with young people in which we sought to investigate the processes of persuasion in advertising by simulating our own campaign. This was during the era of the development of mass media education that sought to uncover the ways in which the media was seen to construct a particular kind of 'reality'. The two-teacher open-space classroom was divided into a series of departments: copy, lay-out, packaging, music, film, still photography, cartoons, budgeting and research, each of which was responsible for some aspect of the campaign. A local radio station was curious about why children were calling asking about costing schedules, while a parent spoke to the group about audience research and the development of new products. At the conclusion to the article published by the Primary English Teachers Association, I wrote:

> If Marshal McLuhan has some of the truth when he asserts that the medium is the message, then perhaps we should apply his insight to today's educational 'medium', the schools. By retaining an authoritarian character they will engender an intellectually passive 'message'. The children will be intellectually becalmed. An altogether different 'message', we believe, is nourished by the open-space classroom, a message composed of initiative, self-reliance, cooperation, creativity and criticism. (p. 48)

Another example of an early venture into the publishing world was the framing of a selection of poetry (Groundwater-Smith, Nelson & Nieminen,[2] 1977) collected into themes and designed for the reader, the school student, showing:

> [T]hat poetry is very much part of day-to-day living. It reflects both ordinary events and those rare, once in a lifetime moments . . . [by which the reader] may share the experiences of a person with an unusual and sensitive vision – the poet. (p. vii)

In addressing the teacher, I wrote:

> We live in a world of multi-dimensional change. In our world, systems are all too often geared to the technical rather than to the human needs of the community. The modern classroom has not only to take cognizance of this environment, but also to struggle for a change for the better – to provide experiences for children which will allow them to cope with the nature of ambiguity with flexibility and self realization. (p. vii)

I was a classroom practitioner on the cusp of advocating for action research. In this endeavour I was increasingly interested in changing my practice on the basis of systematic inquiry followed by designing new ways of going about my work and making my experiences public.

Understanding practice

In the late 1970s I left the school classroom to become a teacher educator at the University of Sydney, preparing tertiary students to become primary school teachers. Although not subject to the great pressures that the academics of today face in relation to key performance indicators in the form of publications and external grants, it was expected in a professional program that one would actively connect with the field through writing that reached beyond an academic audience and had meaning and relevance for teachers. To this end I worked with a colleague exploring ways in which teachers might consider evaluating their practice (Groundwater-Smith & Nicoll, 1980). This venture was in the context of the burgeoning of what became known in Australia as the Disadvantaged Schools Program (DSP). The ill-fated Whitlam government identified education as the cornerstone for equity and as such provided an opportunity to strive for a fair and just society (Reid, 2012). Gough Whitlam argued that society as a whole was diminished when its citizens were denied a decent education.

Schools experiencing severe economic disadvantage were, for the first time, allocated discretionary funding that enabled them to identify those matters that were of specific concern to them and develop curricula and pedagogy to address them. Necessarily, schools were expected to be able to account for the ways in which they developed their projects and the impacts that they had upon learning. Along with Viv Nicoll and encouraged by Stephen Kemmis, a number of guidelines for project evaluation were developed and widely distributed in New South Wales. Thus a career-long interest in action research came to life – that is, a process that enabled practitioners to make their work intelligible to themselves and others, a process that was supported by academic partners who themselves became an integral part of the studies that were undertaken.

John Elliott (1991) defined action research as 'the study of a social situation with a view to improving the quality of the action within it' (p. 69). Brief as they may be, these are not innocent words. How would the social situation be defined? How would it be studied? How might it be improved? What would the 'quality of action' look like? Elliott himself was not entirely happy with the much-quoted definition. In his acceptance speech on the occasion of the awarding of an honorary doctorate at the Universitat Autonoma de Barcelona (Elliott, 2003, quoted in Elliott, 2007), he averred that in the minds of many there was too strict a boundary set between field-based practitioners and their academic counterparts, particularly in relation to the knowledge interests served by each party. He argued:

[A]n assumption [of the existence of such a boundary] implies that the pursuit of practical knowledge through action research is for the sake of practical goals that can be defined independently and in advance of the action research process, whereas research aimed at the construction of theory is the pursuit of knowledge for its own sake. Conceived in such instrumental terms, practical knowledge has no value in itself, and is set against theoretical knowledge regarded by those who pursue it as valuable in itself. My own work was being selectively appropriated to legitimate a conception of action research that privileged practice over theory, *whereas I had seen it as an attempt to redefine the relationship between theory and practice in a way which dissolved the dualism.*[3] (Elliott, 2007, p. 203)

By working alongside field-based practitioners I was coming to a more nuanced understanding of practice that was informed by robust and challenging theories. Early in the 1980s I had the privilege of spending six months at the Centre for Applied Research in Education (CARE) at the University of East Anglia. Here, with the encouragement and support of Jean Rudduck, I was introduced to the work of the late Lawrence Stenhouse who had been such a significant figure in the emergence of teacher research in the UK (Stenhouse, 1975; Stenhouse, 1979/1983). At the same time, I was encouraged in reading widely the work of Jurgen Habermas (1972) as a key figure in understanding the human interests that impel a search for knowledge. Habermas has argued over a number of decades that while the empirical-analytic sciences have an orientation to serve a technical interest (of which there are many in educational practices), the interpretive-hermeneutic sciences inform an interest in developing insights into practice (how they have come to be as they are), whilst the critical-emancipatory sciences underpin a liberatory impulse to change things for the better.

During my time at CARE, Jean Rudduck introduced me to Lawrence Stenhouse's concept of 'the case record', the lightly theorised assemblage of data that will later inform the case study or, as Stenhouse himself put it, 'an edited primary source' (1978, p. 37). It is the gathering together and organisation of the case data by the fieldworker(s) prior to its interpretation and discussion (Rudduck, 1985). The case record is the foundation upon which the case study is built. Like any building enterprise, the foundations will play a significant role in the later act of construction. But that construction will itself be mediated by a range of factors, including the skill and craftsmanship of the architect and builders.

Rudduck also recommended that I think deeply about the relationship between information and knowledge as understood by Stenhouse. 'Information is not knowledge until the factor of error in it is appropriately estimated' (Stenhouse, 1979, quoted in Rudduck *et al.*, 1983, p. 141).

This distinction between information and knowledge and its relation to the development of the case study from the case record took place in the context of working on a British Library Research and Development project that sought to understand the ways in which school library resources were used by students for independent study in the academic sixth form (Rudduck *et al.*, 1983). Along with Jean Rudduck, David Hopkins and Bev Labbett, I examined the accumulated case records consisting mainly of extended interviews with young people from schools in England and Wales. From these a series of curriculum-based case studies emerged, with the individual researchers turning to one another, as a form of membership checking, for a validation of the interpretations and narratives of practice that were being constructed around the learning of particular subjects such as English literature and science.

The power of this experience stayed with me as I returned to Australia to undertake further research into my own practice as a teacher educator that would form the basis for my PhD study of the ways in which tertiary students might come to understand the complexity of curriculum theorising.

This brings me to the first inclusion in this series of articles:

Groundwater-Smith, S. (1988a). The interrogation of case records as a basis for constructing curriculum perspectives. In J. Nias & S. Groundwater-Smith (Eds.), *The enquiring teacher: Supporting and sustaining teacher research*. Lewes: Falmer Press, pp. 93–105.

For me this chapter is seminal in expressing my own emergent understanding of action research as experienced through the eyes of the practitioner, that practitioner being myself as a teacher educator. I had identified among my teacher education students the struggle that they had in understanding the concept of 'curriculum' not as a series of precepts to be followed with rigid and impermeable boundaries but as a complex, dynamic interaction between texts (the media, written, visual and verbal), pretext (the justifications and reasonings underpinning its architecture) and context (the environment within which the text unfolds). Instead of following my original plan to provide the students with *case studies* of curriculum enactment in a variety of settings as a series of protocols that they could analyse and critique, I chose to provide them with a series of *case records* that they should examine. In effect, the students were enabled to become researchers themselves, working collaboratively to craft the case studies from the records, at the same time taking account of their own histories and experiences and the ways in which these might impact upon their analyses.

In this manner I was not *telling* the students about the nature of the curriculum but discovering with them the ways in which it might be characterised and the consequences of taking a particular stance in terms of the immediate and local conditions under which the cases were evolving. The sites contrasted significantly, ranging from a school that had chosen to focus on specific skills in the areas of literacy and numeracy and marginalise what it saw to be the 'frills' normally associated with the expressive and creative arts, through to a site that had fully embraced problem-based learning. Over many weeks it became clear that the experience was an unsettling one for both myself and the students; it was difficult for me not to be directive and signpost the salient features of a given case, or for the students to turn to me for reassurance that the stories that they were weaving were 'correct'. However, as I had espoused the value of tolerating uncertainty and ambiguity, I believed the path taken to have been a worthwhile one.

The chapter is one of 17 in an edited collection that gathered together the experiences of academic practitioners who had sought to design courses or elements of tertiary study that were based upon developing and supporting teacher inquiry. All contributors had attended a conference held at Newnham College, Cambridge, in September 1986. In one way or another each presentation was based upon the supposition that while 'knowing' about a phenomenon (for example, the nature of curriculum) is the result of a personal construction, it is essential that the knowledge is publicly interrogated and subjected to a rigorous critique. To make this argument more explicit, a second chapter from this book is also reproduced here.

Groundwater-Smith, S. (1988b). Credential bearing enquiry-based courses: Paradox or new challenge. In J. Nias & S. Groundwater-Smith (Eds.), *The enquiring teacher: Supporting and sustaining teacher research*. Lewes: Falmer Press, pp. 256–262.
It is in this brief chapter, which formed a part of the conclusion to the book, that I make the arguments regarding the impact of the Frankfurt School of Critical Theorists, most notably Jurgen Habermas, that further gives voice to the ways in which knowledge interests play out in educational practice.

In this chapter I elected to marry a series of theoretical constructs with practical outcomes. The piece is, in effect, a plea to transcend those day-to-day judgements that have an immediate appeal when seeking to draw upon the wisdom of experience. Designing courses that encourage a more speculative stance within the development of professional awards is risky business. Today, this would be even more the case with teacher education courses being subject to the stringencies of state-wide accountabilities.

During the 1990s I continued to advance my interest and commitment to action research,[4] particularly as it was evolving not only within schools and between schools and universities, but also across schools seeking to address similar problems.

Groundwater-Smith, S. (1998). Putting teacher professional judgement to work. *Educational Action Research*, 6 (1), pp. 21–37.
Some ten years had elapsed between the publication of *The Enquiring Teacher* and the article cited here. During this time, I had taken an appointment in one of Australia's new universities with a major responsibility to develop an innovative teacher education program, part of which was to nurture a strong and robust partnership between the university and the field of practice. This article grew out of a consideration of the role of academic partners whose desire was to facilitate the work of school-based practitioners in ways that would contribute to the development of each. It reported upon the work of the Australian National Schools Network (NSN) with which I was closely associated. This was a unique period in Australian industrial history governed by what became known as 'the accord'. In order to bring about industrial peace, the Hawke/Keating government of the day established procedures whereby unions, employers and interested third parties would work out ways in which they could function cooperatively to the mutual benefit of each. The accord, then, brought together teachers' unions, employing authorities and university academics to form a network that would enable not only individual school-based projects but also form the basis for an overall discussion of what it is about the ways in which teachers' work is organised that impedes student learning and how might those impediments be addressed.

At its heart the NSN was a 'grass-roots' reform movement. Until this point in time, school reform in terms of organisation was glacial; now schools could consider how they might vary their timetables, their grading arrangements, their allocation of staff and the like. Any changes were to be negotiated through school-based committees that included teachers, unionists and members of the local community. The Network had state-based offices as well as a central organisation that would manage the various projects. As it is pointed out in the article, in order to foster a research culture, NSN established a competitively selected research register of academics who had contributed to discussions associated with school reform and reculturing and who could assist and work alongside school-based practitioners in their endeavours.

Interesting as the work of the NSN was, the particular reason for its selection in this volume is that it demonstrates the increasing attention being given to evidence and ethical procedures as proposed by myself and Viv White (then the National NSN Coordinator). In a publication that we co-authored, designed to support teacher inquiry, it was argued that the collection of evidence involves us in moral and ethical issues with procedures being required to stand the following tests:

> (1) that the process for collecting and judging evidence does no harm;
> (2) that the purposes for collecting evidence are explicit and known to all participants;
> (3) that evidence is triangulated;
> (4) that conditions are such that alternative, socially just explanations and interpretations may be generated and valued.
> (Groundwater-Smith & White, 1995)

Coming as it did at the end of the twentieth century, the article published in *Educational Action Research* is one that reflects particular developments in my own thinking – developments that lead me to more deeply reflect upon ethical and moral reasoning, contributing to an understanding of praxis. Thus the millennium turn was also a critical turn in my own apprehension of practice as praxis.

The twenty-first century and the world of praxis

Much has been written on the notion of *praxis,* that is the moral disposition to act wisely in the interests of the wellbeing of humanity and the good life and informed by long-standing traditions. While this account of my development towards a notion of *praxis* as a tenet informing my own practical reasoning has grown over a span of almost two decades, it is in a context where it is proposed that '*praxis* in education today is endangered' (Kemmis & Smith, 2008, p. 5). The case made by Kemmis and his colleagues is based upon an observation that educators are being positioned as no more than operatives denied their moral agency. Ax & Ponte (2008) write of the fragmentation and decomposition of professional practice in the context of educational managerialism with teachers expected to become morally detached rather than deeply and emotionally engaged with their students as expressed by Fenstermacher (1990).

> Teaching well requires as broad and deep an understanding of the learner as is possible, a concern for how what is taught relates to the life experiences of the learner, and a willingness to engage the learner in the context of the learner's own intentions, interests, and desires. (p. 137)

This sentiment echoes that of Ted Sizer (1999) when he wrote that we cannot teach students well if we do not know them well. Knowing students well is the moral obligation that has driven the Coalition of Essential Schools (CES) led by Sizer (Coalition of Essential Schools, 1998) in the United States, which had a great influence on the Australian National Schools Network discussed previously. The work of the CES has been and continues to be based upon a set of principles: that young people should learn to use their minds well; that the school's goals should be simple and apply to all students; that teaching and learning should be personalised; that the student should be characterised as 'worker'; that mastery is demonstrated through an exhibition of learning; that there should be high but realistic expectations shared between the school and the community; that teachers should see themselves as generalists rather than specialists; that time should be given for planning; and that the school demonstrate inclusive and democratic policies. It is clear that the CES is informed by a notion of *praxis* at least implicitly.

Throughout this emergent development of my own understanding of *praxis* I recognised in particular the influence of Stephen Kemmis and Petra Ponte, both having an unremitting commitment to education as first and foremost a moral practice.

But my respect and admiration for the former did not mean that I could not develop a critique of his work and that of Wilfred Carr as demonstrated in the next publication in this collection:

Groundwater-Smith, S. (2005). Painting the educational landscape with tea: Rereading Becoming critical. *Educational Action Research***, 13(3), pp. 329–346.**
The article was written following two decades of scholarship and practice based upon the publication of Wilfred Carr's and Stephen Kemmis' influential book *Becoming Critical*. It is argued that while times have changed since the book was published, it is possible to continue to discover new ways of reading it. In the article I draw upon the historian Jack Hexter's notion of the 'second record' (Hexter, 1972). As I earlier observed, during my time at CARE Jean Rudduck brought to my attention the ways in which Lawrence Stenhouse drew upon the work of Hexter to understand that behind action there is a second record:

> [T]hat is, the constellation of subjectivities that are held by the researcher at the time of collecting, analysing and interpreting information, and that cannot fail to influence the work, it is 'indefinite in scope, and much of it personal, individual, ephemeral and not publicly accessible'. (Groundwater-Smith, 2005, p. 330; Hexter, p. 104)

In referring to the first record Stenhouse (1980) claimed that it provided the data or evidence upon which the case is built (bearing also in mind the distinction between the case record and the case study as discussed above); the second record is the 'organised trace of the researcher's experience' (p. 7). By this he suggested that each person brings to the interpretation of data-cum-evidence his or her own life histories.

Clearly for each of us 'the second record' is a dynamic one, subject to changing times and circumstances. In my academic life I suggest that these are: changes to professional decision-making space for practitioners, the impact of marketisation and other business/commerce discourses on educational practices; re-emerging concerns for positivism in educational research; the appropriation and technologising of action research as an implementation tool; and the trivialising of theory itself. This echoes the earlier assertion that *praxis* in education is endangered, a challenge to which I return time and again as I come to understand and incorporate the concept into that which I undertake as an educator. It is also vital to acknowledge that such endangering not only comes from the complex world in which one is enfolded, but also through those deep-seated prejudices and beliefs that can unwittingly govern behaviour, something hinted at in terms of the following inclusion.

Groundwater-Smith, S. (2006a). My professional self: Two books, a person and my bedside table. In P. Aubusson & S. Schuck (Eds.), *Teacher learning and development: The mirror maze.* **The Netherlands: Springer, pp. 179–194.**

In the next work in this publication I first and foremost specifically affirm my intellectual and professional debt to two writers, the aforementioned Hexter (1972) and Turnbull (1973). The former for his influence in developing a more profound understanding of the 'second record', and the latter for his reminder that we cannot avoid being judgmental when faced with studying human subjects for whom we have no liking (Turnbull, 1973). The 'person' with whom the title is concerned is, again, Lawrence Stenhouse.

The purpose of the chapter was to uncover the layers of my professional and personal selves, their genesis and interaction in the context of self-study in relation to facilitating and participating in practitioner enquiry. I suggest that Hexter's argument is 'not *whether* the second record should be drawn upon, but *how* and *how best* it might be utilized' (1972, p. 181). In other words, rather than escaping from the influence of life's experiences, it would be wiser to acknowledge them and their impact upon ruminations and writings and make them available to both the self and the reader. In the chapter I make explicit the notion that the boundaries between facilitation and participation are more blurred and permeable than first understood, with the problems and processes associated with the different roles far more interconnected than hitherto imagined. Clearly this reflects the position taken by John Elliott and discussed earlier in this introductory piece.

A particularly poignant illustration is contained in the chapter in the ways in which my second record, in relation to both supporting and undertaking research with a group of troubled boys in a difficult and challenging context, is played out. While not as despairing as Turnbull, a noted anthropologist, regarding his alienation from the Ik people whom he studied and greatly disliked, I acknowledge my irritation with the boys and what I regarded as the ways in which they conspired to resist attempts to support and enhance their learning such that they were 'consuming' their own futures in the interest of being resistant in the present. I saw my reflections as acknowledging the stone in the shoe acting as an irritant such that I might continue to learn about myself and my practice and recognise my moral obligations and responsibilities.

Another kind of stone that requires a different form of recognition is the set of ever-changing circumstances within which education, in particular school education, is evolving. Under these emergent neo-liberal conditions, I argued a more robust sense of praxis will need to emerge in relation to professional knowledge formation and its impact on practice. This, I sought to make explicit in the article that follows. Of course, the transition from the preceding discussion and the one that follows is not a seamless one; what holds them together is my continuing and emerging awareness of those matters that troubled me, from the ways in which I related to those for whom I had no great affection, to the burgeoning neo-liberal conditions under which I and my colleagues were functioning. Effectively the article promulgates forms of resistance made possible through robust practitioner research.

Groundwater-Smith, S. (2006b). Professional knowledge formation in the Australian educational market place: Changing the perspective. *Scottish Educational Review*, **37 (Special Edition, Teacher Education and Professional Development), pp. 124–131.**

In response to an invitation by Ian Menter, this article was developed as an argument for professional knowledge formation in the face of the commodification of educational ideas by those who would sell superficially technical solutions to schools and systems, meeting a 'one size fits all' set of criteria.

It draws upon a more differentiated market place, the *Agora*, that Nowotny, Scott and Gibbons (2003) so powerfully evoke as a metaphor for knowledge formation in contrast to the disciplined sites of production so characterised by university faculties and government-sponsored research centres, sites that provide little space or opportunity for field-based practitioners' voices to be heard.

The *Agora* is not only pertinent in terms of a place where knowledge as a complex and variable commodity may be traded, but also as a place where knowledge is contested with debates and arguments regarding its validity and utility. The article, in consonance with those discussed earlier, makes the case for professional knowledge formation to be developed within coherent communities of practice – in other words, knowledge-building schools.

Whereas one might wish to eschew the pronouncements of David Hargreaves in relation to his understanding of evidence based practice and its connection to professional knowledge formation (Hargreaves, 1996) where he stated, 'Teaching is not at present a research-based profession. I have no doubt that if it were, teaching would be more effective and satisfying'; his contribution to our thinking regarding schools themselves as professional knowledge-building organisations (Hargreaves, 1999, 2003) is inestimable, even though we may well dispute his characterisation of 'evidence'. He sees such schools, working in partnerships and collectives as dynamic life forms capable of communicating within and across sectors. His advocacy along with the earlier discussion of the Coalition of Essential Schools in this introduction proved to be something of a catalyst for the formation of the Sydney-based Coalition of Knowledge Building Schools (CKBS) that has become so central to my own work and which will be discussed more fully at a later juncture.

Alongside the reference to the formation of the Coalition of Knowledge Building Schools, the article also outlines a major equity project, the Priority Action Schools Program (PASP), whereby a large number of public schools in NSW initiated their own action research projects. Led by myself and Stephen Kemmis, the evaluation brought about a step-change in thinking about relations between school practices and the academy (Groundwater-Smith & Kemmis, 2005). Its inclusion in the article is not in order to celebrate the achievements of PASP, important as they may have been, but to draw attention to a particular process by which schools recorded and documented their development as a form of learning. Each school collected together what became understood as a corporate learning portfolio defined as 'evidence-based documentation of organisational learning regarding a workplace transformation':

> Portfolios contained a contextual framework that traced the history and social geography of the school and the vision that it had for its students and the community. It outlined the plan of operation that would be the focal point of its PASP project. Interventions ranged from: changes in staffing organization with enhanced mentoring and modelling for less experienced teachers; curriculum change with an emphasis upon a more liberatory pedagogy that would allow for genuine debate and interaction between teachers and students, particularly in areas of literacy and information and communication technologies; through to behaviour management. Both qualitative and quantitative evidence was collected as the work progressed. Each school was supported by an academic partner and/or critical friend who also contributed their reflections to the portfolio. (Groundwater-Smith & Kemmis, 2005, p. 37)

The notion of the corporate learning portfolio was designed to deal with the kind of participation gap with which both Hargreaves (2003) and Elliott (2003) *inter alia* were concerned. The process encouraged peer-to-peer learning both within and between schools, between schools and universities and between the academic partners themselves. Importantly, the program led me to reflect more profoundly on the problematics of supporting practitioner research within the university sector itself, raising questions of quality and professional recognition. This brings us to the next inclusion in this volume.

Groundwater-Smith, S. (2007a). Questions of quality in practitioner research: Universities in the 21st century – the need for safe places for unsafe ideas. In P. Ponte and B. Smit (Eds.), *The quality of practitioner research*. Rotterdam: Sense Publishers, pp. 57–64.

As an increasing peripatetic academic, I found myself working closely with Professor Petra Ponte, first at Fontys University in Amsterdam and later HU University of Applied Sciences Utrecht. Part of my brief was to make a contribution to a series of publications that were designed to make the case for practitioner research in the academy.

Functioning in such a different arena, namely European universities, with their own traditions and academic touchstones presented a clear challenge. However, I found a receptive audience to the employment of examples that took myself and my Dutch colleagues to new places for thinking.

Drawing upon the discussion in the museum sector of the representation of the dropping of the first atomic bomb by the *Enola Gay*, the B52 bomber that was perceived to have brought the war in the Pacific to an earlier end than might otherwise have been the case, I touched upon the ways in which the controversy regarding the exhibition raised the notion of museums being 'safe places for unsafe ideas' and suggested that this should also be the case for universities. I argued that dissonance and debate are healthy practices within the academy, where students and academics alike are learners and where merit and quality count in relation to the search for praxis in a context of participative research that is inclusive of practitioners in a given profession.

There has been an ongoing struggle in the academy, whether in Anglophone countries or continental Europe, to give credence to research, undertaken in the professional field, where it not only gives voice to practitioners but also engages them as co-researchers undertaking inquiries into their practice. There is a certain irony in the lack of regard for an authentic conversation between the academy and the field when universities are perceived as places that are open to new and adventurous ideas (or so we would wish). In this chapter I argued that seeking for consensual values may be seen as an inhibiting factor and that debate and dispute should be seen as both healthy and essential to matters of quality in research and scholarship. Thus knowledge generated *with* the field can address matters of practice, particularly in relation to trustworthiness and ethical practice, in ways that knowledge formation *independent* of the field cannot.

There is a certain poignancy to the notion that universities may be hospitable to practitioner research as long as it is conducted on their own grounds. It is, as Derrida (quoted in O'Gorman, 2006) put it, a kind of conditional hospitality:

> 'Make yourself at home', this is a self-limiting invitation.... it means: please feel at home, act as if you were at home, but remember that is not true, this is not your home but mine and you are expected to respect my property. (p. 51)

Nonetheless, it is said that for Derrida, being open and accepting the outsider opens the host to new experiences, perhaps even new ways of conceiving of quality in the research enterprise.

Indeed, this matter of quality in relation to research with the field, importantly in the context of a discussion of ethics, was taken up by myself and Nicole Mockler and later published in the next entry in this book.

Groundwater-Smith, S., & Mockler, N. (2008). Ethics in practitioner research: An issue of quality. In J. Furlong & A. Oancea (Eds.), *Assessing quality in applied and practice-based research*. London: Routledge, pp. 79–92.[5]

In considering praxis as morally informed action, it is inescapable that matters related to ethics must be considered. In their edited collection in which this chapter is included, Furlong and Oancea consider praxis as a form of social action with a strong ethical component, i.e. 'virtuous action in the public space' (2008, p. 8), and thus a domain worthy of consideration of quality. We argued in our chapter that practitioner inquiry 'must be able to stand up to the scrutiny of both the field of practice and the academic community's expectation that it be systematically undertaken and theoretically robust' (p. 81). To this end, and following a carefully constructed series of premises, we argued that it would be salutary for researchers to consider a series of guidelines that link to traditional conceptualisations of research as well as the discourse associated with the ethical professional, dubbed by Judyth Sachs as 'the activist professional' (2003).

We acknowledged that first and foremost any proposed inquiry should observe ethical protocols and processes, importantly those in relation to informed consent. This concern is one that has a singular impact upon notions of praxis as morally informed action. Schools can be represented as coercive institutions where students are required to attend and few opportunities given for them, or indeed their parents, to provide any kind of consent regarding research practices or any other regimes of practice typically provided by them. Following ethics protocols is an essential first step to satisfy criteria for quality. We followed this injunction with a need to build transparent and collaborative procedures that are justifiable and transformative.

This chapter is one of several where I have worked to make explicit my concern for observing ethical procedures – a concern that has grown steadily over the years, particularly as they have related to working with children and young people, as informants, as consultants and as co-researchers as demonstrated in the piece below.

Groundwater-Smith, S. (2007b). Student voice: Essential testimony for intelligent schools. In Anne Campbell and Susan Groundwater-Smith (Eds.), *An ethical approach to practitioner research: Dealing with issues and dilemmas in action research*. **New York: Routledge, pp. 113–128.**

The book in which this piece originally appeared is one of several edited by myself and Anne Campbell. I have been privileged over the years to hold adjunct professorial positions in institutions where Anne was working at the time, namely Liverpool Hope University and Leeds Metropolitan University. We were fortunate in dealing with vice chancellors who recognised the merit of practitioner inquiry within professional practice and provided us with opportunities to invite colleagues from UK, USA and Australia to gather together and consider specific issues with an eye to assembling an edited book. The two universities offered hospitality and accommodation while participants met their own travel expenses. I note this here because it is an indication that work around practitioner inquiry and action research can find a place in the academy as personal, relational and participative.

It is also worth drawing attention to Susanna Gorman's chapter in the book, 'Managing research ethics: a head-on collision?' (2007b). As the then-manager of the human research ethics committee at the University of Technology, Sydney, Susanna held to a particular stance regarding the ways in which universities could best deal with human research ethical questions. Her position, balancing risk, benefit and consent, is a carefully constructed one, with a belief that a significant responsibility for the management of ethics should be such that the benefits flow across the board to the participants, to the institution and to research itself. A well-informed ethics committee will enhance the quality of the research and should not be seen as a negative force.

In the context of Gorman's discussion and in the light of the other contributions to the book, my own position was an emergent one relating to student voice as a means of meeting our responsibilities to young people as the consequential stakeholders within schools. At a later point in the development of my understanding, I have come to a more nuanced understanding regarding honouring the voices of children and young people as a fundamental human right (Groundwater-Smith, Dockett & Bottrell, 2015; Mockler & Groundwater-Smith, 2015). But in this chapter I was most cognisant of providing conditions for young people to be enabled to contribute in a meaningful way to school-based inquiries that relate to their experience of schooling. The chapter provides advice and a number of exemplary case studies from schools as members of the Coalition of Knowledge Building Schools referred to earlier in this introduction. It is also cautious of being overly celebratory or using student voice as a means of covertly disciplining them.

It was my desire, in the chapter, to remind myself and my readers that students are key witnesses to the conditions of their schooling. In understanding school change, the testimony of those who are the consequential stakeholders is paramount. It is, therefore, curious that they are so often provided with few opportunities to be anything but bystanders.

Groundwater-Smith, S. (2009). Co-operative change management through practitioner inquiry. In B. Somekh & S. Noffke (Eds.), *Handbook of educational action research***. London: SAGE Publications, pp. 186–194.**

Before turning to the contents of this chapter in the Somekh and Noffke publication, I wish to acknowledge the enormous contribution to action research made by each of these outstanding scholars as over many years they have continued to expound upon and amplify the work of action researchers, including myself.

In summarising the scholarly work undertaken over three decades by Bridget Somekh in relation to action research, John Elliott (2010) has drawn attention to the ways in which she developed her ideas of 'actionable knowledge' based upon self-knowledge and a deep professional relationship with others in the conduct of research in context. When he cited a particular project that Somekh worked on, namely Pupil Autonomy in Learning with Micro-Computers (Elliott, p. 21), I was reminded that I too was a fellow researcher with Bridget during my sabbatical leave at the Cambridge Institute in 1987, where we evaluated an electronic mail project (Groundwater-Smith, 1993). Since then I have had many opportunities to meet with Bridget and for us to share our ideas regarding the nature of action research. I have had much to learn from her.

Less well known to me, but nevertheless an academic colleague whom I did hold in high regard, was the late Susan Noffke. Following her death, *Educational Action Research* published a number of articles (Issue 4, Volume 22, 2014) by writers such as Marie Brennan, Marilyn Cochran-Smith and Bridget herself. They all noted her passionate commitment to social justice, anti-racism and ethical issues in teaching and learning. The combination of Bridget and Susan in the editing of this collection proved to be a formidable one.

My own contribution was deliberately provocatively titled: 'Cooperative change management through practitioner inquiry'. It could be taken to signal a piece of writing of an instrumental kind, satisfying the most basic of Habermasian knowledge interests, namely the exercise of technical control, thus seemingly outside the norms of action research. Instead the chapter reported upon the Priority Action Schools Program (PASP) that was evaluated by myself and Stephen Kemmis (Groundwater-Smith & Kemmis, 2005) and briefly referred to earlier in this introduction in relation to the development of school learning portfolios.

PASP was created to provide resources, both human and material, to 74 schools facing difficult circumstances in the state of New South Wales. The objectives of the program were *inter alia* to support schools in improving learning outcomes and student behaviour and attendance; facilitating staff development; implementing whole school approaches to change and improvement; and working with communities and community agencies.

The chapter reported on two examples of schools that had 'escaped the old bonds of practice'. One case was drawn from schools in geographically isolated circumstances, the other from an urban region isolated by way of persistent, negative representations. These cases speak for themselves within the chapter. The evidence is considered in the concluding pages in terms of collegiality and the formation of communities of practice within a large-scale action research project. Retrospectively it is saddening to find that the generosity and flexibility of this program is a rarity, so that the learnings from it, so applauded in the final report, would have appeared to have fallen on deaf ears. Although, one is heartened to read of the ways in which the project has impacted more widely as it morphed into other studies conducted in other places. Lori Beckett (2016) cites the project as critical to her development of partnership work in the North of England, concluding that practitioner research within a collegial context can be capable of generating reform rather than being 'merely a transmission or relay station in the service of political forces' (p. 58).

Perhaps another hope is for smaller and more independent studies that may be brought together to form a coherent whole, as in the next example.

Groundwater-Smith, S., & Kelly, L. (2010). Learning outside the classroom: A partnership with a difference. In A. Campbell & S. Groundwater-Smith (Eds.), *Connecting inquiry and professional learning in education*. London: Routledge, pp. 179–191.

Several references have been made in this introduction to the Coalition of Knowledge Building Schools (Mockler & Groundwater-Smith, 2011), an account of which follows at a later point. Suffice to say here that the Coalition is a hybrid collection of New South Wales schools – government and independent, primary and secondary, single sex and co-educational – and cultural institutions that work together to develop and enhance professional knowledge through systematic inquiry. An example of a significant and sustained partnership, that has been developed and nurtured between the school members and the cultural institutions, is the subject of this chapter.

Furthermore, the chapter illustrates the ways in which my own engagement with cultural institutions such as museums and libraries has enabled another kind of intellectual and professional growth in my own understanding of their roles and functions, well beyond the curatorial. I have personally come to perceive collections and accompanying explanations as having significant possibility in engaging visitors through provocations such that they are able to re-shape their knowledge of the complex society of which we are all a part.

The chapter specifically spells out the evolution of this relationship in terms of young people taking a consultative role in designing and evaluating exhibitions that would have an impact upon their learning in the context of programs offered by the Australian Museum in Sydney. As well as reporting on a series of what became known as 'Kids' Colleges', the chapter also affirms the kind of substantive engagement in learning that can result from sustained dialogue between museum and school educators with an eye to better considering matters of design and fostering collegiality and professional growth.

'Designerly learning' does not just happen by chance. Museums offer unique spaces to provide for learning through objects: How are they assembled? Why are they collected? How do we understand them? Can something be appreciated for its aesthetic value alone? Do all exhibits need to be interactive? Is it possible to ask questions for which there can be no ready answers? By consulting young people beyond apprehending their likes and dislikes, but rather probing and provoking them, it is possible that new and fresh insights regarding the nature of learning outside classrooms, or indeed, inside classrooms as well, can be developed.

Critical to the work of the Coalition members, through such consultation, is the desire to respect the insights of young people and see them not merely as users of services but as agents who have an understanding of their own learning. Being 'agentive' carries implications for learning in relation to both cognitive and affective domains. Learners are required to examine, more substantially and fruitfully, how they see and process their worlds.

Groundwater-Smith, S. (2011a). Living ethical practice in qualitative research. In J. Higgs, A. Titchen, D. Horsfall & D. Bridges (Eds.), *Creative spaces for qualitative researching.* **Rotterdam: Sense Publishers, pp. 201–212.**

Indeed, 'agency' is a well worked concept in the literature regarding the participation of children and young people in research and inquiry as well as in relation to their learning as discussed above. It is often raised in the context of structures. It is posited that their capacity to act independently and make their own choices is necessarily constrained by structural factors such as social class, culture, ethnicity, gender and the like, including their quantum of participative capital that crosses these designations and determines, in part, who gets asked in a research context, what, how and why (Groundwater-Smith, Dockett & Bottrell, 2015).

However, while such attention is paid to the 'subjects' of research, how often do we ask ourselves about the agency in different terms; that is, what is experienced by researchers or of the structures that inhibit or even liberate their practice? Clearly there are macrostructural features that reflect various regulatory requirements, not the least being the role played by human research ethics committees that are now part of the university apparatus. But what of situations that are not governed in this way? In this chapter I reflect on the agency of both the academic researchers and school-based practitioners when they are working together within a participatory action research (PAR) environment untrammeled by the rules and regulations of others, particularly through small, modest consultancies. In effect, the responsibility to act ethically rests directly with those concerned with undertaking the enquiry. Thus they have greater agency but also greater responsibility.

Two cases are cited in the chapter that serve to illustrate the very real ethical dilemmas that are experienced in the context of a beneficence argument – that is, minimising harm and maximising good. As with all dilemmas, 'there is no foolproof plan to avoid ethical dilemmas in any research, but there is a necessity [to arrive at] skilled judgments' (Bhatta, 2013, p. 21).

Returning to my central theme for these latter chapters of this book, the yardstick that can best guide such judgment is that of praxis – morally informed action, being sensitive to the needs and rights of all who participate in a particular research enterprise. In many ways this is articulated by Loftus, Higgs and Trede (2011, p. 4), the editors of *Creative Spaces for Qualitative Researching*, when they write, citing Bourdieu:

> [O]ur practice is not exclusively the result of rational decision making but, in large part, an embodied sense of what is to be done that comes from an implicit understanding of our place in the relationships that make up our social world.

In effect, praxis becomes a form of communicative action through which participants seek to reach common understanding and form their actions through reasoned argument, consensus and cooperation as opposed to forms of strategic action that satisfies personal goals and aspirations (Habermas, 1984) Praxis is thus necessarily achieved through public dialogue rather than as an individual and often implicit exercise of power.

Importantly, praxis understands and engages with such tricky matters as equity and social justice. It involves dialogue as a social process with the objective of 'dismantling oppressive structures and mechanisms prevalent both in education and society' (Freire & Macedo, 1995, p. 383). In this next piece I return to the ways in which participatory enquiry with young people provides a means for such disruption.

Groundwater-Smith, S. (2011b). Concerning equity: The voice of young people. *Leading and Managing*, 17(2) Spring/Summer, pp. 52–65.

Prior to the publication of this paper, I had ruminated upon some of the distinguishing features that relate equity to equality.[6] Before turning specifically to equity in education, I wanted, first, to provoke thinking regarding the nexus between equity and equality, drawing upon an example that we face daily, the provision of public toilets – an unexpected illustration. In a recent Australian Radio National broadcast, there was a discussion of the ways in which decisions are made regarding the regulation of the building of toilets in spaces such as theatres, parks, conference centres and the like. Seemingly, regulators veer towards an equality argument rather than an equity argument, having developed building codes that allocate the same amount of space to male and female toilets and washrooms. Harvey Molotch, a New York sociologist, examined public restrooms and the politics of sharing (Molotch & Noren, 2010). He argued that equal access was not equitable because it does not take account of either anatomical differences or social differences in such matters of clothing, hygiene and the accompaniment of children. Thus while there may be equal space, there are unequal opportunities in utilising the space.

Perhaps this is a matter not so far from schooling as was first imagined, in that Darling-Hammond (2010) makes reference to the poor toilet provisions made in many US public schools, not only in their design but also in their accessibility. In her book, she describes schools where the sewer backs up into hallways frequently and toilets may have no doors or have doors that are locked and unusable. Most poignant and disturbing is the extract about one middle school in particular, Luther Burbank Middle School in San Francisco. In this case we have neither equal nor equitable provision.

> Two of the three bathrooms at Luther Burbank are locked all day, every day. ... Students have urinated or defecated on themselves at school because they could not get into an unlocked bathroom.... When the bathrooms are not locked, they often lack toilet paper, soap, and paper towels, and the toilets

frequently are clogged and overflowing. (*Williams et al. v. State of California*, 2000, pp. 22–23, cited by Darling-Hammond, 2010, p. 7)

Turning, then, to schooling in Australia with which this article deals, much of the argument in the supply of resources, whether the curriculum, the staffing or the buildings seems to revolve around a *desire* to allocate them equally, although, of course, this is manifestly not the case. However, in some ways the matter of equity, that means of providing young people of different racial, ethnic, gender and socioeconomic backgrounds with those *necessary* resources to be able to fully take advantage of the opportunity to learn and to be encouraged and motivated to do so, has managed to slip and slide away. As Teese and Lamb (2011) put it in the conclusion to their submission to the Gonski Review of Funding for Schooling in Australia, 'If our aim is to ensure high standards of achievement for all Australian Children, we cannot build castles for some and cottages for others'.

In my paper, I claim that 'equity' is a slippery term. For most practitioners in education it is associated with concepts allied to social justice; that is to say that it is fair and reasonable for members of a given society to have their needs met in relation to those resources and opportunities that will enable them to achieve what Amartya Sen (2009) calls 'well-being'. In particular, citizens may become self-actualised through participation in education and the range of social activities that will enable them to manage their daily lives.

While space did not permit an economic discussion regarding equity and the provision of schooling, it is worth digressing for a moment to consider some features of this argument when it comes to praxis, fairness and social justice. The OECD report *Divided we stand: why inequality keeps rising* (OECD, 2011) indicates that the gap between rich and poor has widened with particular reference to inequality in wages and salaries. It is argued that where there are disparities in educational provisions, access to decent wages and broader social conditions will vary accordingly. This has been shown to be of particular concern in such countries as the United States and the United Kingdom. In these countries, the gap between rich and poor is at its highest level in 30 years. Today in OECD countries, the richest 10 per cent of the population earn 9.6 times the income of the poorest 10 per cent. In the 1980s, this ratio stood at 7:1, rising to 8:1 in the 1990s and 9:1 in the 2000s (OECD, 2015).

Not only that, but with poor or inadequate access to education, the capacity for full participation and inclusion in society becomes limited, with diminished opportunities to have a voice that can influence decision making across a range of enterprises. In a Productivity Commission staff working paper, *Deep and persistent disadvantage in Australia* (McLachlan, Gilfillan & Gordon, 2013), the claim is made:

> There is strong evidence to show that education is the key to improving life chances. Education not only provides skills and the capacity to learn, it improves a person's employment prospects and earning capacity. The evidence also points to a relationship between education and better health and social cohesion and reduced crime. In contrast, poor educational achievement increases the probability of poorer employment prospects, lower lifetime earnings and reduced ability to participate in society. (McLachlan *et al.*, 2013, p. 17)

As Reid (2012, p. 11) reminds us, education *is* a public good, *for* the public good and for the *renewal* of the public. If equity, within the terms of social justice and inclusion, is to have meaning for us as members of the education profession, then its pursuit is a significant and ongoing challenge. It is in this context, then, that the argument was made in the paper to create conditions that would enable young people in schools to have their say in the nature of the schooling to which they were subjected, not only as an attempt to enhance the conditions under which they learned, but also that they might become more confident to express their views and have them heard.

The paper in the main makes the argument that if we are to attend to the voices of young people in our schools, then the equity case becomes critical in that too often it is those who are already legitimated within the political ecology of the school who are consulted and thus enabled to have a voice (Groundwater-Smith, Dockett & Bottrell, 2015, p. 77). This is a recognition of the differentiated experiences of children in their schools. It is argued that students accrue different and unequal 'participatory capital' depending upon their social identities based on such factors as class, race, gender, age and ability (Wood, 2014). Making participation accessible and transparent requires attention to what Shier (2001, p. 110) has modeled within five levels of participation: young people are listened to, they are supported in expressing their views, these are taken into account, they are involved in decision-making processes and they have a share in the resultant power and responsibility. Importantly, as it is pointed out in the article, Shier does not stop there; he intimates that at each level of participation there are three stages of commitment: openings, opportunities and obligations. Two cases are presented to illustrate the ways in which, in the interests of equity, schools can make an attempt to build and consolidate the participative capital of a group of students over time and not merely, as Fielding (2004, p. 302) puts it, 'redescribing and reconfiguring students in ways that bind them more securely into the fabric of the status quo'.

Working in this way takes courage as schools face the 'unwelcome truth' that their students may have perspectives at variance with the policies and practices of the establishment. In the chapter that follows, along with my colleague Nicole Mockler, I portray the way in which schools and cultural institutions have formed a collective to formulate strategies that enable a higher level of participation and engagement.

Mockler, N., & Groundwater-Smith, S. (2011). Weaving a web of professional practice: The Coalition of Knowledge Building Schools. In B. Lingard, P. Thomson & T. Wrigley (Eds.), *Changing schools: Alternative models.* **London: Routledge, pp. 294–322.**

There have been a number of references throughout this introduction to the Coalition of Knowledge Building Schools. This hybrid collection of government and independent schools and a range of cultural institutions from libraries to museums has evolved over a period of many years. In this chapter we liken it to the weaving of a complex web, commencing with the construction of a modest bridge built between a small number of participating schools that had made a commitment to establish sustained links with each other and the academic community. The purpose was to enable ongoing teacher professional learning and to engage in what became known as facilitated practitioner inquiry, whereby nominated academic partners assisted in modest action research projects in schools as discussed in Groundwater-Smith (1998) above.

As well as articulating the principles for participation that were developed between the schools, there has been an emphasis upon the Coalition's voluntary nature. Costs were more in the way of opportunity costs rather than financial ones. Members, including the convener, devoted time and energy to the enterprise, while the hosting Faculty of Education and Social Work at the University of Sydney provided legitimation. Accountability did exist, but more in the form of social accountability whereby members contributed to the growing body of professional knowledge that was developed by the community of practice as understood by Wenger (1998, p. 73), including three key dimensions, namely: joint enterprise, mutual engagement and shared repertoire.

A notable feature of the Coalition has been the engagement of cultural institutions that take the learning of young people seriously and regularly consult with them about the ways in which they provide for learning outside the classroom. In this collection of articles and chapters, I have referred to the ways in which such institutions such as the Australian Museum and the State Library of New South Wales have turned to students in Coalition schools for advice regarding exhibitions and visitor pedagogy. Their inclusion in the Coalition has added a richness to the debates and discussions that have been conducted over a number of years.

But not all narratives have a 'happy ending'. It was noted at the beginning of this section on praxis in the twenty-first century that the instrumental purposes of education are now taking precedence over any that take a liberatory stance. After 16 years the Coalition is coming to a close. Schools find it more and more difficult to devote resources such as teachers' time to investigating the local as opposed to paying attention to policy regimes that grow out of large meta-analyses. In summing up many of these, Hattie (2015), who has had a significant influence on educational policy in Australia and elsewhere, has reminded us that many of what he has called 'the distractions' have been characterised as 'fixes': appease the parents, fix the infrastructure, fix the students; fix the schools and fix the teachers. He argues that too much discussion has been focused on differences between schools when the greatest issue is the differences within schools and the variability in the effectiveness of teachers. However, his arguments continue to rest on large-scale studies with little recognition of the nuances of local conditions. Taking a praxis position *requires* us to better consider the many and varied local conditions and their consequences.

In their latest groundbreaking work, Kemmis, Wilkinson, Edwards-Groves, Hardy, Grootenboer and Bristol (2015, p. 208) have argued for a return to site-based educational development:

> We begin with an idea that seems a truism but turns out not to be. It is that education – life, in fact – always happens *at* and *in* particular sites, and that changing education means changing the things that happen *at* and *in* particular sites.

Their advocacy is based upon understanding the complexities of practice based upon the notion of place in its various geographical, historical and socially discursive configurations. Certainly, the Coalition understood the ways in which its members faced very different challenges. Its members also understood that in sharing and questioning solutions, professional learning could be produced. The uncertainty of its continuation was less to do with the viability of communication and more to do with providing the spaces in which this could happen.

Even so, a strong ethos of mentoring, within and between school-based practitioners and academic partners, has emerged within the Coalition and continues to inform practice beyond it. This rather clumsy segue enables me to turn more specifically to matters in relation to mentoring practitioner inquiry and a particular project that provided me with opportunities to observe practice across a range of different sites. I find myself somewhat saddened that so many of my talented colleagues in the academic sector are now so trammeled by regulatory frameworks, requiring them to comply with one edict after another, that they have fewer degrees of freedom to engage in site-based facilitation such as that portrayed in the following piece.

Groundwater-Smith, S. (2012). Mentoring teacher inquiry: Lessons in lesson study. In S. Fletcher & C. Mullen (Eds.), *The SAGE handbook of mentoring and coaching in education.* **London: SAGE, pp. 494–505.**

As an opening to this chapter, I make the observation that much of the practice of mentoring in education has been individualistic. Mentors and coaches have been increasingly appointed as a part of formal induction programs with typologies ranging from apprenticeship models and competency-based procedures through to the support of reflective practice (Vozzo, Aubusson, Steele & Watson, 2004; Cullingford, 2006). Generally, mentors were not seen as autonomous but would act as mediators and facilitators and even, in some cases, as assessors of teacher quality (Strong, 2009).

More recent work has focused on mentors acting as 'pedagogical advisors'. They are seen to be those who are familiar with the tools that initial teacher education students need to 'fulfill their roles well, and impart them with an expertise' (Flavian & Kass, 2015, p. 49). There is an expectation that they will assist in problem solving through instruction rather than through reciprocal dialogue. This is a position challenged by Lopez (2013, p. 294) when she characterises what she has termed 'collaborative mentoring' as a form of mentoring grounded in critical educational discourses that challenge power and privilege but which, nonetheless, continues to maintain the relationship as individualistic.

Taking a somewhat different stance in this chapter, I parallel the role of mentor with that of the 'knowledgeable other' who may assist practitioners in methods of inquiry particularly in relation to implementing programs of lesson study as a form of teacher professional learning. Rather than following an individualistic relationship, the concern was to establish conditions for the nurturing of a community of practice directed to enable collective professional learning as sustained inquiry and dialogue through a form of participatory action research.

The project reported upon in the chapter, Deeds not Words, involved four schools working in concert with one another; thus, participants were liberated from their individual classrooms and their varying school cultures. Nevertheless, the specific nature of those cultures and the ways in which they had evolved were also taken into consideration. The project was focused upon planning for learning, observing learning and interpreting learning. As a dialogic project it transcended the established norms that have been associated with various enterprises based upon lesson study where seemingly it was possible to develop a template for the 'ideal' lesson that was to be employed to teach difficult and intractable concepts.

Instead, the vehicle that was employed was a lesson study model that was not only flexible but also enabled practitioners to better fit professional learning to their particular circumstances (Fernandez & Yoshida, 2004; Lewis, Perry & Hurd, 2004; Rock & Wilson, 2005). The process was seen to offer to participants, means of constructing and reconstructing their perceptions of practices that could contribute to a supportive learning environment where students would engage in purposeful learning activities. Lesson study was thus seen to create conditions for reflection and collaborative investigation in that it required time to practice, experiment and analyse teaching episodes. My task as the mentor was to facilitate this process by continuing to assist in questioning the responses and precepts of the practitioners.

Importantly, along with the teacher, the most significant resource in the classroom was seen to be located in the students themselves: what had been their experiences, how much did they already know, how could they best share their knowledge, how would they evaluate each other's knowledge and understanding? As a process that would permit a closer examination of learning, as it happened, the focus was less upon the students' work and more upon the students at work. A strategy that was proposed was to closely observe only one learner, using Johann Wolfgang von Goethe's (1982) notion that:

> [M]erely looking at an object cannot be of any use to us. All looking goes over into observing; all observing into reflecting; all reflecting into connecting; and so one can say that with every attentive look we cast into the world we are already theorising.

Thus my role as the mentor recognised that professional practice is a many layered and complex phenomenon; it is both purpose oriented and norm oriented; it encompasses mental, social and physical activity and codes and is governed by both internal and external factors. The teachers in the study were by no means autonomous agents; they were expected to conform to the policies that are laid down within systems and within schools. Nonetheless, we cannot disregard an understanding that they are guided by the key question 'How can I behave in an educated, well-informed moral and ethical manner?' This reminds us that in relation to *praxis*, the process of lesson study and indeed all of the various projects embodied in this volume are shaped and formed by the circumstances that determine how practice will be carried out, these being cultural and discursive preconditions, material and economic preconditions and social and political preconditions.

Conclusion: praxis as dialogic

Throughout the latter part of this introductory essay I have argued for praxis as *morally informed action* and I have asked myself: 'How has this stance developed?' and 'What have been the dialogic conditions that have informed my own understanding?' Further to these questions, 'In what ways has that nascent understanding been enabled through my transactions with others?'

It will be clear to the reader that my authorial, narrative voice is intersected with the voices of others, including not only the voices of those who have participated in the various moments and events outlined in the range of writing published here but also those of my co-authors, thus contributing to a greater multiplicity of perspectives. These pieces, then, are essentially in dialogue with each other as my capturing of the concept of 'praxis' emerges, knowing that such an understanding is neither final nor closed off from future assertions and developments. This dynamic interplay that has been required to produce co-authored pieces has depended upon those Habermasian conditions discussed at an earlier point in this introductory reflection, where I wrote of the value of reasoned argument, consensus and cooperation.

Just as Habermas reminds us of the creation of dialogue as a social practice, with all of the consequences that result thereof, so too does another influential social theorist, Mikhail Bakhtin, who wrote:

> The word in language is half someone else's. It becomes 'one's own' only when the speaker populates it with his [sic] own intentions, his own accent, when he appropriates the word, adapting it to his own semantic and expressive intention. Prior to this moment of appropriation, the word does not exist in a neutral and impersonal language ... but rather exists in other people's mouths, in other people's contexts, serving other people's intentions; it is from there that one must take the word and make it one's own. (Bakhtin, 1981, p. 294)

In his commentary on Bakhtin's approach to language, Eagleton (1996, p. 106) notes that language, as a social practice, is infused with valuations. Thus words may not only refer to objects, thoughts and events but also infer the attitudes that we may have to these.

A marriage between Bakhtin and Habermas would seem, at first glance, to be a strange liaison, but as Nielsen (1995) explains in the context of a discussion of transculturalism:

> If it is possible to conceive of joining Bakhtin's dialogism with Habermas' concept of communicative action we might conclude that whereas a right to reasoned disagreement is the groundwork of the public sphere, dialogism is the cornerstone of everyday existence. (p. 828)

What is being alluded to here is that the many discourses from which this introduction has been drawn, both in terms of publication and collegial interaction, are complex and interwoven. The thoughts are not exclusively my own but have evolved and developed and, indeed, continue to evolve and develop as a social process.

From practice to praxis is an unfinished story beset by the kind of uncertainties and doubts outlined at the beginning of this piece of writing. As my own reflexive turn, it represents a recognition that by looking into the assortment of my various writings and publications I have come to know myself a little better, speaking to my academic and professional past and reimagining my intellectual future.

I commenced this introductory essay with a reference to Keats and the notion of negative capability. I conclude by turning to an extract from *The Little Gidding*, the last of Eliot's four quartets, where he wrote and I have personalised:

> What we call the beginning is often the end
> And to make and end is to make a beginning ...
> I shall not cease from exploration,
> And the end of all my exploring will be to arrive at where I started
> And know the place for the first time.of everyday existence.

It has been my experience that the journey from practice to praxis has not only taken me to my beginning but also cast light upon where I now stand, still seeking for the kind of practical wisdom that can continue to inform my writing and thinking. The task has provided me with a moral compass, but one that will always require re-calibrating as I come to continually re-evaluate the many achievements and challenges experienced along the way.

Notes

1. http://h2g2.com/dna/h2g2/A813962 (accessed 10th November, 2011).
2. Lance Nelson was the photographer with Tanja Nieminen the illustrator. The selection of the poetry and the ways in which the poems might be located at the core of the curriculum was my task.
3. My emphasis.
4. Often referred to in the Australian context as 'practitioner research'.
5. In assembling these pieces, I have observed a chronological order with respect to their publication dates as noted in the introduction. While this chapter would seem somewhat out of order, its genesis was in work undertaken earlier and was being composed at much the same time as 'Questions of quality in practitioner research', the preceding article.
6. It was as a result of presenting my paper, 'Concerning equity the voice of young people', to the Equity in Education, Connecting for Change Conference conducted by the Australian College of Educators in Sydney, 13th–15th July, 2011, that I was invited to submit it under the same title to the journal *Leading and Managing*. Restrictions on word length meant that my discussion regarding equity and equality was not included. However, I believe that the example is a salient one and I have decided to refer to it here.

References

Ax, J., & Ponte, P. (2008). Praxis: Analysis of theory and practice. In J. Ax & P. Ponte (Eds.), *Critiquing praxis: Conceptual and empirical trends in the teaching profession*. Rotterdam: Sense Publishers, pp. 1–20.
Bakhtin, M. (1981). *The dialogic imagination*. M. Holquist (Ed., Trans.). Austin: University of Texas Press.
Beckett, L. (2016). *Teachers and academic partners in urban schools*. London: Routledge.
Bell, A. (1981). Structure, knowledge and relationships in teacher education. *British Journal of Sociology of Education*, 2(1), 3–23.
Bhatta, D. (2013). Moral dimensions of research ethics: Ethical dilemmas and challenges in human participants' research among different settings. *World Journal of Preventive Medicine*, 1(3), pp. 19–21.
Coalition of Essential Schools (1998). *The ten common principles*. http://education.state university.com/pages/1840/Coalition-Essential-Schools-Common-Principles.html accessed 6th January, 2015.

Cullingford, C. (2006). (Ed.) *Mentoring in education: An international perspective*. London: Ashgate.

Darling-Hammond, L. (2010). *The flat world and education: How America's commitment to equity will determine our future*. Columbia, NY: Teachers College Press.

Eagleton, T. (1996). *Literary theory: An introduction*. 2nd edition. Oxford: Blackwell Publishers.

Elliott, J. (1991). *Action research for educational change*. Open University Press: Milton Keynes.

Elliott, J. (2003). The struggle to redefine the relationship between 'knowledge' and 'action' in the academy: Some reflections on action research. Paper presented on the occasion of the awarding of an Honorary Doctorate at the Universitat Autonoma de Barcelona, 5th August, 2003.

Elliott, J. (2007). *Reflecting where the action is*. World Library of Educationalists, London: Routledge, pp. 203–214.

Elliott, J. (2010). Building social capital for educational action research: The contribution of Bridget Somekh. *Educational Action Research*, 18(1), pp. 19–28.

Fenstermacher, G. (1990). Some moral considerations on teaching as a profession. In John I. Goodlad, Roger Soder & Kenneth A. Sirotnik (Eds.), *The moral dimensions of teaching*, (1982) San Francisco: Jossey Bass, pp. 130–154.

Fernandez, C., & Yoshida, M. (2004). *Lesson study: A Japanese approach to improving mathematic teaching and learning*. Mahwah, NJ: Lawrence Erlbaum Associates.

Fielding, M. (2004). Transformative approaches to student voice: Theoretical underpinning, recalcitrant realities. *British Educational Research Journal*, 30(2), pp. 295–311.

Flavian, H., & Kass, E. (2015). Giving students a voice: Perceptions of the pedagogical advisory role in a teacher training program. *Mentoring and Tutoring: Partnership in Learning*, 23(1), pp. 37–53.

Freire, P., & Macedo, D. (1995). A dialogue: Culture, language, and race. *Harvard Educational Review*, 65(3), 377–402.

Furlong, J. (2013). *Education: An anatomy of the discipline*. London: Routledge.

Goethe, W. (1982). Preface to *The theory of colours*. (Translated Charles Lock Eastlake) Cambridge, MA: The MIT Press.

Gorman, S. (2007). Managing research ethics: A head-on collision? In A. Campbell and S. Groundwater-Smith (Eds.), *An ethical approach to practitioner research*. London: Routledge, pp. 24–41.

Groundwater-Smith, S. (1974). Communication at its best. In R. Walshe (Ed.) *The new English in action*. Ashfield: The 1974–5 journal of the Primary English Teachers Association of NSW, pp. 43–49.

Groundwater-Smith, S. (1988a). Credential bearing enquiry-based courses: Paradox or new challenge. In J. Nias & S. Groundwater-Smith (Eds.), *The enquiring teacher: Supporting and sustaining teacher research*. Lewes: Falmer Press, pp. 93–105.

Groundwater-Smith, S. (1988b). The interrogation of case records as a basis for constructing curriculum perspectives. In J. Nias & S. Groundwater-Smith (Eds.), *The enquiring teacher: Supporting and sustaining teacher research*. Lewes: Falmer Press, pp. 93–105.

Groundwater-Smith, S. (1993). Beyond the individual: Collaborative writing and the micro-computer. In M. Monteith (Ed.), *Computers and language*. Bristol: Intellect Books, pp. 9–20.

Groundwater-Smith, S. (1998). Putting teacher professional judgement to work. *Educational Action Research*, 6(1), pp. 21–37.

Groundwater-Smith, S. (2005). Painting the educational landscape with tea: Rereading *Becoming critical*. *Educational Action Research*, 13(3), pp. 329–346.

Groundwater-Smith, S. (2006a). My professional self: Two books, a person and my bedside table. In P. Aubusson & S. Schuck (Eds.), *Teacher learning and development: The mirror maze*. The Netherlands: Springer, pp. 179–194.

Groundwater-Smith, S. (2006b). Professional knowledge formation in the Australian educational market place: Changing the perspective. *Scottish Educational Review*, 37 (Special Edition, Teacher Education and Professional Development), pp. 124–131.

Groundwater-Smith, S. (2007a). Questions of quality in practitioner research: Universities in the 21st century, a safe place for unsafe idea. In P. Ponte and B. Smit (Eds.), *The quality of practitioner research*. Rotterdam: Sense Publishers, pp. 57–64.

Groundwater-Smith, S. (2007b). Student voice: Essential testimony for intelligent schools. In Anne Campbell and Susan Groundwater-Smith (Eds.), *An ethical approach to practitioner research: Dealing with issues and dilemmas in action research*. New York: Routledge, pp. 113–128.

Groundwater-Smith, S. (2009). Co-operative change management through practitioner inquiry. In B. Somekh & S. Noffke (Eds.), *Handbook of educational action research*. London: SAGE Publications, pp. 186–194.

Groundwater-Smith, S. (2011a). Living ethical practice in qualitative research. In J. Higgs, A. Titchen, D. Horsfall & D. Bridges (Eds.), *Creative spaces for qualitative researching*. Rotterdam: Sense Publishers, pp. 201–212.

Groundwater-Smith, S. (2011b). Concerning equity: The voice of young people. *Leading and Managing*, 17(2), pp. 52–65.

Groundwater-Smith, S. (2012). Mentoring teacher inquiry: Lessons in lesson study. In S. Fletcher & C. Mullen (Eds.), *The SAGE handbook of mentoring and coaching in education*. London: SAGE, pp. 494–505.

Groundwater-Smith, S., & Nicoll, V. (1980). *Evaluation in the primary school*. Sydney: Ian Novak.

Groundwater-Smith, S., & White, V. (1995). *Improving our primary schools: Evaluation and assessment through participation*. Sydney: Harcourt Brace.

Groundwater-Smith, S., & Kemmis, S. (2005). *Knowing makes a difference: Learnings from the NSW Priority Action Schools Program*. Report presented to the New South Wales Department of Education and Training, Sydney, NSW. http://lowsesschools.nsw.edu.au/Portals/0/upload/resfile/Knowing_makes_the_difference_Learnings_from_the_NSW_Priority_Action_Schools_Program_2004.pdf accessed 29th January, 2015.

Groundwater-Smith, S., & Mockler, N. (2008). Ethics in practitioner research: An issue of quality. In J. Furlong & A. Oancea (Eds.), *Assessing quality in applied and practice-based research*. London: Routledge, pp. 79–92.

Groundwater-Smith, S., & Kelly, L. (2010). Learning outside the classroom: A partnership with a difference. In A. Campbell & S. Groundwater-Smith (Eds.), *Connecting inquiry and professional learning in education*. London: Routledge, pp. 179–191.

Groundwater-Smith, S., Nelson, L. & Nieminen, T. (1977). *Over my shoulder: An anthology of verse*. Adelaide: Rigby.

Groundwater-Smith, S., Dockett, S., & Bottrell, D. (2015). *Participatory research with children and young people*. London: Sage.

Habermas, J. (1972). *Knowledge and human interests*. Trans. Jeremy J. Shapiro. London: Heinemann.

Habermas, J. (1984). *Reason and the rationalization of society, Volume 1 of The theory of communicative action*. Trans. Thomas McCarthy. Boston: Beacon Press (originally published in German in 1981).

Hargreaves, D. (1996). *Teaching as a research based profession: Possibilities and prospects*. Teacher Training Agency (TTA) Annual Lecture. London.

Hargreaves, D. (1999). The knowledge creating school. *British Journal of Education Studies*, 47, pp. 122–144.

Hargreaves, D. (2003). From improvement to transformation. Keynote address presented to the International Conference of the International Congress for School Effectiveness and Improvement (ICSEI). Sydney: Sydney Convention Centre, Darling Harbour, 5th–8th, February.

Hattie, J. (2015). *What doesn't work in education: The politics of distraction*. London: Pearson.

Hexter, J. (1972). *The history primer*. London: Allen Lane.

Kemmis, S., & Smith, T. (2008). Praxis and praxis development: About this book. In S. Kemmis and T. Smith (Eds.), *Enabling praxis: Challenges for education*. Rotterdam: Sense Publishers, pp. 3–14.

Kemmis, S., Wilkinson, J., Edwards-Groves, C., Hardy, I., Grootenboer, P. & Bristol, L. (2015). *Changing practices, changing education.* Rotterdam: Springer.

Lewis, C., Perry, R. & Hurd, J. (2004). A deeper look at lesson study. *Educational Leadership,* 61(5), pp. 18–22.

Loftus, S., Higgs, J. & Trede, F. (2011). Researching living practices. In J. Higgs, A. Titchen, D. Horsfall & D. Bridges (Eds.), *Creative spaces for qualitative researching.* Rotterdam: Sense Publishers, pp. 3–12.

Lopez, A. (2013). Collaborative mentorship: A mentoring approach to support and sustain teachers for equity and diversity. *Mentoring and Tutoring: Partnership in Learning,* 21(3), pp. 292–311.

McLachlan, R., Gilfillan, G. & Gordon, J. (2013). *Deep and persistent disadvantage in Australia,* Productivity Commission Staff Working Paper, http://www.pc.gov.au/research/supporting/deep-persistent-disadvantage accessed 3rd August, 2014.

Mockler, N., & Groundwater-Smith, S. (2011). Weaving a web of professional practice: The Coalition of Knowledge Building Schools. In B. Lingard, P. Thomson & T. Wrigley (Eds.), *Changing schools: Alternative models.* London: Routledge, pp. 294–322.

Mockler, N., & Groundwater-Smith, S. (2015). *Engaging with student voice in research, education and community: Beyond legitimation and guardianship.* Rotterdam: Springer.

Molotch, H., & Noren, L. (2010). (Eds.) *Toilet: Public restrooms and the politics of sharing.* New York: New York University Press.

Nielsen, G. (1995). Bakhtin and Habermas: Toward a transcultural ethic. *Theory and Society,* 24, pp. 803–835.

Nowotny, H., Scott, P. & Gibbons, H. (2003). Mode 2 revisited: The new production of knowledge. *Minerva,* 41, pp. 179–194.

OECD (2011). *Divided we stand: Why inequality keeps rising.* http://www.oecd.org/els/soc/49170768.pdf accessed 2nd August, 2014.

OECD (2015). *In it together: Why less inequality benefits all.* OECD Publishing. doi: 10.1787/9789264235120-en accessed 2nd May, 2015.

O'Gorman, K. (2006). Jacques Derrida's philosophy of hospitality. *The Hospitality Review,* 50 (October) pp. 50–57. file:///Users/admin/Downloads/Jacques%20Derrida's%20philosophy%20of%20hospitality.pdf accessed 28th January, 2015.

Reid, A. (2012). Federalism, public education and the public good. *Perspectives.* University of Western Sydney: Whitlam Institute.

Rock, T., & Wilson, C. (2005). Improving teaching through lesson study. *Teacher Education Quarterly,* 32(1), pp. 77–92.

Rudduck, J. (1985). A case for case records. In R. Burgess (Ed.), *Strategies for educational research.* Lewes: The Falmer Press, pp. 101–119.

Rudduck, J., Hopkins, D. & Labbett, B. (1983). *Independent study, books and libraries and the academic Sixth Form.* A report to the British Library Research and Development Department.

Sachs, J. (2003). *The activist teaching profession.* Buckingham: Open University Press.

Sen, A. (2009). *The idea of justice.* London: Allen Lane.

Shier, H. (2001). Pathways to participation: Openings, opportunities and obligations. *Children and Society,* 15(2), pp. 107–117.

Sizer, T. (1999). No two are quite alike. *Educational Leadership,* 57(1), pp. 6–11.

Stenhouse, L. (1975). *An introduction to curriculum research and development.* London: Heinemann Educational.

Stenhouse, L. (1978). Case study and case records: Towards a contemporary history of education. *British Educational Research Journal,* 4(2), pp. 21–39.

Stenhouse, L. (1979). Research as the basis for teaching. Inaugural lecture at the University of East Anglia. In L. Stenhouse (1983) *Authority, education and emancipation.* London: Heinemann, pp. 177–195.

Stenhouse, L. (1980). The verification of descriptive case studies. Mimeo, Centre for Applied Research in Education, University of East Anglia.

Strong, M. (2009). *Effective teacher induction and mentoring: Assessing the evidence.* New York: Teachers College Press.

Teese, R., & Lamb, S. (2011) Submission to the Gonski Review of Funding for Schooling http://www.deewr.gov.au/Schooling/ReviewofFunding/SubGen/Documents/Teese_Richard_and_Lamb_Stephen.pdf accessed 8th July, 2011.

Turnbull, C. (1973). *The mountain people.* London: Jonathan Cape.

Vozzo, L., Aubusson, P., Steele, F. & Watson, K. (2004). Mentoring retrained teachers: Extending the web. *Mentoring and Tutoring,* 45(3), pp. 275–286.

Wenger, E. (1998). *Communities of practice: Learning, meaning and identity.* Cambridge: Cambridge University Press.

Williams et al. v. State of California, Superior Court of the State of California, County of San Francisco, 2000.

Wood, B. (2014). Participatory capital: Bourdieu and citizenship education in diverse school communities. *British Journal of Sociology of Education,* 35(4), pp. 578–597. doi:10.1080/01425 692.2013.777209, 1–20.

CHAPTER 2

THE INTERROGATION OF CASE RECORDS AS A BASIS FOR CONSTRUCTING CURRICULUM PERSPECTIVES

Susan Groundwater-Smith

Introduction: examining the curriculum terrain

The unifying theme for this discussion is 'critique', an approach to enquiry which is conducted in ways which have the potential for improved practice based upon enlightened understandings. Critique, in this instance, is evolved as a result of collaboration between enquirers, wherein they investigate in a manner which is predicated upon self-reflective and socioculturally reflexive deliberation. (The construct 'reflexive' refers to the practice of being able to perceive not only that one's personal history is influential in shaping one's world view, but also that this history is located in the midst of a larger sociocultural canvas which too must be deliberated upon.)

Curriculum work spans a great variety of perspectives and practices which may be contrasted in several ways. For some it presents itself as a series of segmented activities bounded by technical guidelines and is largely unproblematic. For others it is perceived as an intricate web of actions, apparently seamless and credible, but paradoxically subject to a plethora of opposing tensions and pressures.

I shall take the view that it is the latter representation which is the more appropriate and explore this map of curriculum work within three intersecting and overlapping categories: text, context and pretext. That is, I shall briefly examine the cultural artefacts of curriculum work as well as the media by which it is expressed; the settings within which it occurs; and the reasonings which underpin its practices. Or, to put it another way, the what, the where and the why of curriculum work will be examined. I will suggest that such a trilateral portrayal will secure and identify curriculum work in ways which will disabuse us of the notion that its endeavours are amenable to simple, allegedly neutral functional analysis, but will enable us rather to see that what is required is a demanding, ongoing interrogation, both reflective and reflexive in nature.

In the first instance, to represent curriculum work as text is to expose the embedded 'geomorphology' of the many competing and varying curriculum theories. The rises and falls of such theories have been sketched in by many including Lundgren (1983) who characterizes them variously as classical, realistic and moral curriculum codes. He reminds us that we need to locate these texts in the demands and pressures of the day. Indeed, such a sociohistorical analysis is well supported by Foucault (1972) who argues that the historical lens is viral to an understanding of contemporary, burgeoning rationalization in all fields of social endeavour. This rationalization has been expressed in curriculum work, Lundgren argues, by the hegemonic insistence upon the equation of curriculum theory with learning theory to the exclusion of social theory.

Today's curriculum texts (this term 'texts' is inclusive here of writings embracing prescriptions for practice) or discourses have grown out of reasoning following World War II and the advent of the space race marked initially by the launching of the first Russian satellite in 1957, and continued into the eighties in the US 'Star Wars' project. Curriculum, that interface between teaching and learning, has been seen as that which most efficiently realizes goals which are set in behaviouristic and mechanistic ways; as Popkewitz (1985) says:

> Knowledge is presumed neutral and fixed, or at best, unattached to any social group or cultural interest. (p. 6)

Indeed, Tyler (1969) defended his scientific and mechanistic means of assembling curriculum knowledge, via the generation of behavioural objectives, with some impatience:

> Any of the objections given by teachers to instructional objectives seem to be predicated upon inadequate conception of education, curriculum and instruction. (quoted in McDonald Ross, 1975, p. 355)

Certainly there has been, in recent years, a much greater recognition of cognitive diversity, but nonetheless, the significant drive has been to find more effective means of specifying curriculum objectives rather than problematizing their whole *raison d'être*.

Although there was some flirtation during the seventies with 'open' procedures which allowed learners more actively to construct their own knowledge (this counter-ideology has been well documented by Abbs, 1982), the general regression to this rationalistic stance has been noteworthy in most English-speaking countries.

If the study of curriculum work as text is the study of the meaning of the artefacts of curriculum, then the study of curriculum work as context is the study of that total environment wherein the meaning is embedded. As Halliday and Hasan (1983) put it:

> There is text and there is other text that accompanies it: text that is 'with', namely the context. This notion of what is 'with the text', however, goes beyond what is said and written: it includes other non-verbal goings on – the total environment in which a text unfolds.

The environment itself generates a complex, interactive dynamic which affects bilaterally the selection of text (both in the commonsense meaning of published materials and in the sense of policies) and the modes of delivery. The context in which schooling occurs shapes the curriculum itself. An example which is illustrative of the context of curriculum work as a major problematic is Keddie's now classical study of teachers' perceptions of their students and how these affected their pedagogical practices. Keddie revealed how the typifications and categories used by teachers, regarding their students, influenced their curriculum choices. Moreover, these belief systems revealed themselves in an extensive study in Australian schools conducted by Connell, Ashenden, Kessler and Dowsett (1982) in which it was indicated that teachers' assessments and assumptions regarding a child's social origins distorted the curriculum itself in significant ways, so that the experiences designed for middle-class students were consonant (or organic) to their general life experiences whereas those designed for working-class students were diminished and depleted.

It is useful, therefore, to examine the interplay between text and context as an interplay between intentions and operations set against a sociohistorical backdrop. Certainly a number of curriculum researchers have explored the nexus between planning and implementation (cf. Cohen and Harrison, 1982). However, they have not concerned themselves with the grounding of the case in the articulations between the state, the economy and the schools themselves. Given our current social arrangements for schooling and the role played by government (and indirectly, business and industry) in resourcing and providing directions in policy-making it seems to me to be cavalier indeed to leave this territory uncovered.

Apple (1979) has argued both by an analysis of cases and by reasoning that the relationships between planning and practice can only be explored fruitfully if it is recognized that curriculum work is undergirded by social and economic ideologies and their institutional affiliations. It is to these underpinnings that I now turn.

Public pretexts for curriculum work are generally voiced in liberal and humanistic ways:

> The central aim of education which, with home and community groups the school pursues, is to guide individual development in the context of society through recognizable stages of development, towards perceptive understanding, mature judgement, responsible self-direction and moral autonomy. (Aims of Primary Education in New South Wales, 1977, p. 14)

The rhetoric of liberal democracies is to guarantee free, secular, universal state schooling which will confer upon its participants equality of opportunity, if not equality of outcomes. Some curriculum theorisers have been at pains to point out that such rhetoric acts only to elucidate the surface features of curriculum work and that there is an additional and more insidious agenda (Bowles and Gintis, 1976). It is contended that schools are social sites wherein two forms of knowledge are transacted; the one being overt and publicly stated, the other covert and transmitted as values and beliefs via social relations, artefacts, organizational structures and routines, i.e. the 'hidden curriculum'. The school plays contradictory roles at one and the same time by teaching about democratic values but demanding, in its own environment, social control.

The difficulty with many of these analyses of curriculum work as pretext is that they lead to a significant apportioning of 'the blame' to teachers within the school without seeking to locate them in their own historical and cultural spaces. It is important to make the distinction set down by Giroux (1983a) which separates ideologies about school and ideologies in school. Giroux makes a plea for a climate of questioning which will lay bare the normative assumptions underlying our modes of representing curriculum work:

> Furthermore, if the notion of the hidden curriculum is to become meaningful it will have to be used to analyse not only the social relation of classroom and school but also the structural 'silences' and ideological messages that shape the form and content of school knowledge. (p. 61)

What is singular about Giroux's approach is that he sees such an identification of the pretext for curriculum work as the beginnings of a move from the practical to the emancipatory. Thus the gaining of authentic insights into curriculum work, in all of its manifestations, text, context and pretext, requires a reappraisal of the ways that we come, over time, to know about and understand curriculum practices. It is to 'ways of knowing' that I would like now to turn.

Coming to know

An important observation to make at the outset is that there is a distinction between information and knowledge. This is not just a quibble about shades of difference since the one may be seen as a significant variant of the other. Stenhouse (1979) put it most succinctly:

> Information is not knowledge until the factor of error in it is appropriately estimated. (quoted in Rudduck *et al.*, 1983, p. 141)

Essentially, what Stenhouse is saying to us is that we are the inventors of our own knowledge and the quality of the invention is dependent upon our ability to evaluate the information which is available to us, be it sensory, first hand information or vicarious, received information. This involves us in a never-ending stream of judgments, of broad and fine discriminations, so that the gaining of knowledge is a transforming process. As such it is personal, dynamic and never complete. This representation of the knowledge-gaining process applies to both knowledge about things and knowledge about ideas, it embraces the physical and the imaginative worlds.

While it is not yet entirely clear what the relationship is between language and thought, it is generally agreed that language and the construction of knowledge are closely linked. The influential Bullock Report (DES, 1975) put it in this way:

> It is a confusion of everyday thought that we tend to regard 'knowledge' as something that exists independently of someone who knows. What we know must in fact be brought to life afresh within every knower by his (sic) own efforts. In order to appreciate what is offered when we are told something, we have to have somewhere to put it.... Something approximating to 'finding out for ourselves' needs therefore to take place if we are to be successfully 'told'. ... The development of this individual context for a new piece of information, the forging of the links that gave it meaning, is a task we continually tackle by talking to other people.

That this knowledge is personal does not mean that it is diminished in any way, that one dismisses the position as 'merely subjective'. Rather, from this perspective we can rigorously account for the place of judgment and critical reflection. The problematic is not one of subjectivity but of the conditions under which judgments are arrived at. Carr and Kemmis (1986) point out that educational practices are *always* conducted in the light of judgments made by practitioners, but that too often these judgments are based largely upon habit, precedent and tradition rather than by way of informed critical reflection. Knowledge which, in a sense, is 'right knowledge' (Kemmis, 1982, p. 3) is knowledge which is truly emancipatory in its nature; which will enable the knower not only to know, but to act; not only to act, but to act correctly ... wisely ... justly. This, of course, is not to say that there is one single way of acting, but rather that the action must be undergirded by prudence brought about by careful deliberation.

The interplay between knowing and acting is central to the arguments of Carr and Kemmis. Knowing is not of itself an end, but is a propellant moving the knower forward to improved and more productive actions. This view is taken up by Giroux (1983a) who argues that a socially critical view provides us with the theoretical tools for reform and change. The knower, in this way, is released from potentially oppressive and culturally reproductive practices and is motivated towards a commitment to a struggle for a better and more equitable world.

A strong source of influence for Carr and Kemmis (1986) and Giroux (1983b) has been the collection of writers/philosophers related to the 'Frankfurt School' of critical theorists. Most noteworthy of these has been Jurgen Habermas. The scope of this writing does not allow for a full analysis of his influence and a brief gloss would not do credit to the complexity of his position. Rather, I would prefer to acknowledge his considerable and continuing impact upon the evolution of critical theory, particularly as it applies to gaining understandings of curriculum work.

This brings me to the implications of all that I have said thus far for practical work.

Providing the means to craft curriculum knowledge

I want to couch this portrayal in personal ways for it has been my own practice as a lecturer in curriculum studies in both pre-service and in-service teacher education which I have sought better to understand and improve. Two contiguous events led to the evolution of the Curriculum Issues Project. One was reading in the area of critical theory and reflecting upon its implications for my own practice. The other was working, all too briefly, with Jean Rudduck on the British Library Project. The elements of the story to be told were all there in the form of the case records collected, under the guidance of Lawrence Stenhouse, from a large number of schools in England and Wales. The challenge was to craft a portrayal from the many different and often contradictory perspectives in the case records. The experience of: challenging and defending analyses; taking account of Jean Rudduck's constant evocation to 'attend to the voices of the case records'; and sharing and shaping incomplete ideas in a collegial way was emancipatory for me in that it led me to re-examine many taken-for-granted features of my practices. And the final experience was to develop insights with Bev Labbett, then working at the Centre for Applied Research in Education (CARE) at the University of East

Anglia upon aspects of the Microelectronics Education Program (MEP) regarding the means by which one could construct a curriculum wherein 'correctness' was not an overarching consideration and where the 'problem' itself remained the responsibility of the learner rather than being taken over by the teacher too precipitously.

Whereas I had planned co contextualize students' learning experiences in relation to curriculum issues by providing them with case studies as protocol materials, I now came to see that the process of constructing the studies was itself the essentially empowering feature. The role of the students would change from investigating materials which had already been transformed several times to working, where possible, with materials which were closer to the primary sources. I sought to create conditions under which learners could become active enquirers within the framework proposed by Nias (1984). This framework assumes *inter alia* that learners will know (or learn) how to undertake such enquiries; that the issues will be substantive; that educational theory can be derived from the enquiry; that the knowledge will be personal; and that, furthermore in a cumulative and formative sense, the enquiries will assist the individual's professional development.

Consequently, the project was designed to provide resources and conditions whereby participative, collaborative enquiry could be undertaken and the participants could both evolve a personal critique as well as contribute to collective understanding. Particularly, by including policy statements, accounts of teachers' planning and 'snapshots' of practice, it was hoped that the connections between intentions and operations might be perceived. The course held the following aspirations:

(a) To set up through the case records a resource which allows the learner to become a skilful researcher/interpreter of curriculum actions;
(b) To create an environment wherein it may be seen that there are alternative explanations, i.e. that there is no one correct answer, but that each explanation in itself must be judiciously defended; and
(c) To empower the students to see themselves as creators of theory.

Fundamental propositions were also set down:

(a) It will not be possible to pre-define with precision what the outcomes will be;
(b) The principal issues must emerge from the data and the learners' interactions with them;
(c) Although all learners will have the same information there will be a diversity of interpretations;
(d) The thrust is to create sufficient intellectual space for the learners to experience problems rather than invading their space by telling them what they need to know;
(e) There will be uncertainty but this should not descend into chaos;
(f) At times, learners will explore unproductive avenues and this is part of the enquiring process;
(g) The roles of listening, questioning and speculating will be more appropriate for the teacher than those of criticizing and/or explaining.

36 *The interrogation of case records*

The course was prepared to cover the equivalent of one semester and was broken down in the following manner:

Week 1

(a) Meeting each other in curricular terms. The intention here was to open up talk about curricular issues by basing them upon personal experience. This would acknowledge the personal lens through which we all experience the world. Members were instructed to break into groups thus: 'each time you join a group meet and talk with each other in terms of the criterion for the group's formation and its relationship to curriculum decision making.'

    Division (i) Most schooling in streamed classes/most schooling in mixed ability classes;
            (ii) Secondary schooling in a co-educational/single sex school;
            (iii) Being a teacher as well as/never having been a parent;
            (iv) Having a preference for arts/science subjects.

(b) Writing about personal experiences of schooling following the readings of extracts from:

    Portrait of the Artist as a Young Man
    David Copperfield
    My Brilliant Career
    Where the Whistle Blows

Weeks 2, 3, and 4

Identifying issues within one school. In small groups students select a school and collaboratively draw together a portrayal of that school's curriculum concerns and actions.

Week 5

Presenting the findings in a plenary session.

                mid-semester break

Weeks 6 and 7

Identifying issues across schools. Working in small groups students again collaborate to locate issues by making comparisons and contrasts and seek further perspectives by examining the relevant literature.

Week 8

Presenting the findings in a plenary session.

Week 9

What would I do? Taking a fragment from the case records the student projects himself or herself into the situation and proposes his or her actions.

Weeks 10 and 11

Directions and strategies for change. Additional resource people were invited to these sessions.

Individual essays identifying and debating curriculum issues were to be handed in four weeks later.

The records themselves were materials collected from four different primary schools in the Sydney Metropolitan area in Australia. Each school was regarded as distinctive in that it was drawn from a particular community with all of the attendant sociological, economic and ethnic implications, but also the schools could be regarded as part of a larger whole in that they were all schools of the NSW State Department of Education and thus governed by that Department's policies and practices. Each record contains negotiated transcripts of interviews with teachers which probed their professional histories and personal philosophies, as well as lesson observations. School curriculum policy documents were included as were community profiles and census materials from the Australian Bureau of Statistics.

The records are not regarded as ever 'complete'. Recently a video tape was made at one school 'Try Seeing It Through Our Eyes' which represented an attempt to capture something of the children's views of schooling. As Walker and Wiedel (1985) have already demonstrated, photographs can be a powerful means of generating critical talk about the lived life of the classroom. In this instance a small group of children were given simple cameras, film and flash cubes. They were invited to take photographs throughout the school day of experiences and events which moved them. They were then interviewed in pairs regarding the meanings behind their photographs. The process allowed for the emergence of a multiplicity of perspectives of the same events. A videorecording crew was present throughout the sequence.

In terms of their interactions with the materials the orientation of the learners' social discourse was necessarily towards 'problem-setting' rather than 'problem-solving' (cf. Smyth, 1985, p. 2). The concerns were to raise issues, grounded in practice, in such a way that vigorous debate would follow, and through this a clarification of the position taken up by any one protagonist. Learners were required to confront and tease out both the inconsistencies in their own positions and the genesis of their own ideologies. The engagement with the project, then, was clearly a reflective one, remembering that:

> Reflection is a practice which expresses our power and reconstitutes social life by the way we participate in communication, decision making and social action. (Kemmis, 1985, p. 140)

While not generous in its time allotment, there was sufficient room in the project for reflection to occur. Ingvarson (1985) has suggested that activities and courses in teacher education, particularly in-service education, need to be planned over longer periods of time, with intervals between sessions. While he was arguing to support action-oriented courses, the same holds true for those for whom the action is the raising rather than the solving of problems. The strategy is necessarily a powerful, but preliminary one. For as Mezirow (1981) says:

> A self-directed learner has access to alternative perspectives for understanding his or her situation and for giving meaning and direction to his or her life, has

acquired sensitivity and competence in social interaction and has the skills and competencies required to master the productive tasks associated with controlling and manipulating the environment. (p. 21)

By adopting, albeit on a modest scale, strategies to facilitate such a reconstructive process, it is my hope that not only will the students become more prudent and reflective in their practice, but that I too, as a teacher-learner, will continue as an enquirer who seeks to improve her practice.

References

Abbs, P. (1982) *English within the Arts*, Sevenoaks, Hodder and Stoughton
Apple, M.W. (1979) *Ideology and Curriculum*, London, Routledge and Kegan Paul.
Apple, M.W. and Weis, L. (1983) 'Ideology and practice in schooling: A political and conceptual introduction', in Apple, M. (Ed) *Ideology and Practice in Schooling*, Philadelphia, PA, Temple University Press, pp. 3–34.
Bowles, S. and Gintis, H. (1976) *Schooling in Capitalist America*, New York, Basic Books.
Carr, W. and Kemmis S. (1986) *Becoming Critical*, Lewes, Falmer Press.
Cohen, D. and Harrison, N. (1982) *Curriculum Action Project*, Sydney, Macquarie University.
Connell, R., Ashenden, D., Kessler, S. and Dowsett, G. (1982) *Making the Difference*, Sydney, George Allen and Unwin.
Department of Education and Science (1975) *A Language for Life* (The Bullock Report), London, HMSO.
Foucault, M. (1972) *The Archeology of Knowledge,* translated by A.M. Sheridan Smith, New York, Harper Colophon.
Giroux, H.A. (1983a) *Theory and Resistance in Education,* London, Heinemann Educational.
Giroux, H.A. (1983b) *Critical Theory and Educational Practice*, Geelong, Deakin University Press.
Halliday, M.A.K and Hasan, R. (1983) *Language Context and Text: Aspects of Language in a Social Semiotic Perspective*, Geelong, Deakin University Press.
Ingvarson, L. (1985) 'Policy related issues in school based professional development', paper presented at the annual conference of the Australian Association for Research in Education, Hobart, November.
Keddie, N. (1971) 'Classroom knowledge', in Young, M.F.D. (Ed) *Knowledge and Control*, London, Collier Macmillan.
Kemmis, S. (1982) *Three Orientations to Curriculum*, Geelong, School of Education, Deakin University, mimeo.
Kemmis, S. (1985) 'Action research and the politics of reflection', in Boud, D., Keogh, R. and Walker, D. (Eds) *Reflection: Turning Experience into Learning*, London, Kogan Page.
Lundgren, U.P. (1983) *Between Hope and Happening: Text and Context in Curriculum*, Geelong, Deakin University Press.
Macdonald, R. (1975) 'Behavioural objectives: A critical review', in Golby, M. Greenwald, J. and West, R. (eds) *Curriculum Design*, London, Croom Helm.
Mezirow, J. (1981) 'A critical theory of adult learning and education', *Adult Education*, 32, 1, Fall, pp. 3–24.
Nias, J. (1984) 'Teaching enquiry-based courses: Implications for the providing institution', opening lecture, Downing College Conference, Cambridge, 16–18 July.
Popkewitz, T. (1985) 'History and social science: Considering an historical sociology of schooling', Geelong, School of Education, Deakin University, Mimeo.
Prosch, H. (1971) *Cooling the Modern Mind* Skidmore College Faculty Research Lecture.

Smyth, J.W. (1985) 'Teachers as clinical inquirers into their own practice', paper presented at annual conference of the Australian Association for Research in Education, Hobart, November.

Stenhouse, L. (1979) quoted in Ruddock, J., Hopkins, D., Groundwater-Smith, S. and Labbett, B. (1983) *Independent Study, Books and Libraries and the Academic Sixth Form*, a report to the British Library Research and Development Department.

Walker, R. and Wiedel, J. (1985) 'Using photographs in a discipline of words', in Burgess, R. (Ed.) *Field Methods in the Study of Education*, Lewes, Falmer Press, pp. 191–216.

CHAPTER 3

CREDENTIAL BEARING ENQUIRY-BASED COURSES
Paradox or new challenge?

Susan Groundwater-Smith

Enquiry-based courses, as they have been described in this book, are predicated upon a fundamental assumption about the nature of knowledge – that knowledge is a personal invention. The argument is that for knowledge to be truly authentic it requires the knower more than merely to assimilate the information which is available to him or her. A positive act of construction is required whereby the knower tests the information against the yardstick of personal experience. The quality of the emerging understanding is dependent upon the ability of the knower to evaluate the information in a prudent and exhaustive fashion. Each person's knowledge is the next person's information. In transmitting information we should not be persuaded that we are fabricating identical forms of knowledge.

This view permits us to see that we are involved in a never ending stream of judgments which themselves are transformed as we are challenged by new and contradictory information. Thus knowledge is personal, dynamic and never complete. To use Polanyi's (1958) view of knowledge we 'dwell' personally in a world of clues and sense impressions which we create and recreate in meaningful wholes (Prosch, 1971). The lived experience of becoming knowledgeable is cognitive, social and sensory. It is not catalogued in our minds in neat, verbal formulations but is organized as a series of complex maps, pictures and semantic tokens.

I have already indicated that there is a qualitative question attached to knowledge. Formulations based upon hasty and unreflective judgment will be less authentic than those which are predicated upon careful, systematic and rigorously interrogated evaluations. There is little doubt that educational practices are conducted as a consequence of judgements made by practitioners; the problem is that these judgments are too often based upon habit, precedent and tradition and are organized into what might be described as 'ersatz' knowledge structures. Contributors to this book have argued for the provision of conditions which will allow the process to remain fluid and be based upon continuous critical reflection.

There is, threaded through the preceding chapters, a second fundamental assumption regarding enquiry-based courses and their relation to the formulation of knowledge. That is that there is an inextricable link between 'knowing' and 'acting'. Professional knowledge is not seen as an end in itself, but as the propellant which moves the knower forward to consolidate, improve and possibly radically change practice.

Thus far, there is agreement among those who have seen themselves as advocates for enquiry-based courses regarding three issues:

(i) that the knower is engaged in his or her world in ways that are inseparably sensory, cognitive and affective;
(ii) that the knowledge which is personally crafted via such involvement is never complete;
(iii) that action is predicated upon the individual's personal knowledge, so constructed.

But from hereon a thread of dissent begins to emerge. For there is a third assumption, both in this book and the wider field, which is explicit in the work of some and not of others. This assumption is that action, to be worthwhile, must carry within it the seeds of emancipation. That is to say, there should be a continuous, relentless interrogation of sedimented social practices with the intention of changing those which result in inequality and injustice. Emancipation is seen as a moral imperative.

Stenhouse (1983) reminds us that while the appeal to personal judgment is fundamental, its effect must be expressed in emancipatory terms:

> The essence of emancipation, as I conceive it is the intellectual, moral and spiritual autonomy which we recognize when we eschew paternalism and the rule of authority and hold ourselves obliged to appeal to judgement. (p. 162)

Stenhouse's work has been greatly influential in the generation of enquiry-based courses. It rejects the view that practitioners should be dependent upon the work of academic researchers who aspire to a position of detached objectivity. He argues that it is not possible to separate facts from values, for if we should attempt to do so we shall also separate the possibility of examining the normative structures which 'produced' those facts. The teacher enquiring into his or her practice should recognize, first of all, and above all else, that he or she operates within a number of institutional norms, and that these norms have their own sociohistorical antecedents.

Knowledge, in this emancipatory sense, functions to free the knower from taken-for-granted constraints. Knowledge is not only intensely personal but also morally purposeful. Knowledge, then, in these terms, is not some sort of portable self-contained thing which may be transmitted by technically controlled conduits, or by reference to the wisdom of self-declared authorities, but is personally constructed and itself located in sociohistorical space, and is the basis for prudent and constructive action.

A number of writers who have contributed chapters in this book have indicated the influence of those identified with the Frankfurt School of Critical Theorists, most notably Jurgen Habermas. This influential contemporary thinker has argued that knowledge about social reality carries with it certain ideological, political and evaluative convictions. All social knowledge, for Habermas, is infused with 'politically relevant values' (Farganis, 1975, p. 483). More explicitly, Habermas makes connections between logical-methodological rules, i.e. ways in which knowledge is derived, and knowledge constitutive interests. He proposes that there are three levels of knowledge interests, with each level transcending the one which came before. These interests are expressed as technical-cognitive interests, practical interests and emancipatory-cognitive interests (Habermas, 1978, p. 308).

Habermas argues that the technical-cognitive knowledge interest is dominated by an unquestioning acceptance of the tenets of enquiry in certain branches of the physical sciences, although perhaps less so in the study of physics itself. An attempt is made, in much conservative science, to create behavioural laws. Habermas sees this, when applied to the social sciences, as not only illusory but also as the basis for manipulation of sociopolitical practices which assume specialized competencies, thus allowing one group to manage and control another. It is this set of knowledge interests which Popkewitz et al. (1987) have argued has been served by conventional teacher education courses at both the pre-service and in-service levels.

Practical knowledge interests, on the other hand, provide for understanding to be derived by seeking for meaning rather than by being dependent upon surface level observation. The knower is a reasoning interpreter of the action. However, those social norms which lie in the very bedrock remain unexamined, unchallenged and unaltered. It may well be argued that a number of the descriptions of practices offered in this book fall into this category.

The third, and final knowledge-forming interest, that which is described by Habermas as emancipatory-cognitive, addresses closely the matter of intersubjectivity, self-reflection and reflexivity. The impetus is towards the empowerment of the knower to perceive the genesis and evolution of ideas in sociohistorical space, and having thus identified them to understand their consequences upon individuals and groups, students, teachers, parents....

> It (emancipation) is based on reflection and self-recognition by reasoned beings of the historical and social location of their own reasoning and results in the practice of emancipation from dogma. (Young, 1983, p. 9)

Arguably, several chapters in this book may be seen as attempts, albeit imperfect, to realize this ideal. However, a severe constraint exists and one which is highly problematic in the face of all this rhetoric. That is the matter of facilitating emancipatory action-oriented enquiry within award-bearing courses. In order to meet institutional demands, there is a considerable pressure for work to be presented for assessment purposes which is of an individualistic, rather than a collaborative, kind. Even the York Outstation Program for teams of teachers, which was outlined by Ian Lewis, rewards individual effort at the end of it all. As Holly (1986) points out, 'this approach extends the "cult of the individual" the acquisitive, self-centred competitive strain of autonomous professionals' (p. 1).

Herein lies the conflict. On the one hand, the argument favouring emancipatory-cognitive knowledge interests insists upon conditions which will allow for open communication within collaborative communities of interest, on the other, award-granting institutions require evidence of individual academic effort resulting in assessable products. Alongside this difficulty lies another to do with the asymmetry of power relations within enquiry-based courses. Even given a situation in which group work might be judged as such, what of relative status within group membership? If enquiry-based courses aspire to take a truly emancipatory form then the provision of a collaborative critical community whose members hold equal status and rights is essential.

Why do I assert this so strongly? To answer this question in part we need to return to Habermas and his notions of communicative competence which lie at the heart of critical social theory as he sees it. Habermas' central endeavour is directed to developing the ideals of freedom, equality, companionability and rational public discourse. Through his various writings he has evolved the notion of the Ideal Speech Situation (ISS) which proposes that each time we speak, the claim is made that what we have to say is intelligible, true, correct and sincere. Furthermore that claim rests upon a background consensus about what these terms mean and a mutual recognition that they actually prevail. This means, necessarily, a set of ideal conditions. There is to be no domination or coercion and all speakers are to have equal rights to assert, to question and to discuss. The extent to which the ISS varies from the actual speech situation is the extent to which communication, and from it emancipatory knowledge, are smoothly shaped or distorted.

Habermas sees the ISS as counterfactual, i.e. that it is a formulation which stands in contradistinction to reality. The plea is for a commitment *towards* its realization. In all of our exchanges and discourses wherein we are creating policies and practices which will affect the lives of others we need to be continually alert to the extent to which the ISS does *not* exist. The most systematically distorting feature for Habermas (1984) is the desire of participants, in such discourses, to succeed in socially competitive situations as opposed to an authentic desire to reach understanding. Award-bearing courses, by their nature, have embedded within them elements of competitiveness. Habermas says: 'Such communication pathologies can be conceived of as the result of a confusion between actions oriented to reaching understanding and actions oriented to success' (p. 332). It may well be that individual teacher-initiated research will gain short-term benefits for that teacher and his/her class, but militate against more enduring long-term benefits for that community.

Certainly this view of enquiry-based courses, kindled by emancipatory knowledge interests and requiring collaborative reasoning and collegiality (an almost impossible condition to meet), is not without its critics. The most colourful and trenchant of these is to be found in Gibson's (1985) critique of *Becoming Critical* (Carr and Kemmis, 1986), a work which has been cited by a number of writers in this book. Gibson's criticisms rest very much upon the concern he has that action research, as a particular form of teacher enquiry, has moved beyond the interpersonal and institutional and into the structural. It is this very aspiration to influence the structural which impedes, perhaps even prohibits, its realization. And yet it is this very aspiration which is also truly emancipatory. Without question the provision of award-bearing courses is itself deeply embedded in structural practices; are those who offer such courses both willing and able significantly to question and challenge the institutional mores of which they are themselves a part?

How then does a critical community form? Does it exist only in the imagination of the academic theorist? And, if so, does it then become the ultimate paradox? One thing which is clear to me is that enquiry-based courses of the ideal, emancipatory kind, free of coercion, with participants holding symmetrical relationships, one with the other, are not possible within the confines of award-bearing courses.

Indeed, it might be argued that the conduct of teacher enquiry within award-bearing courses may have contributed to the reification of certain practices in complete contradiction to the intentions of those offering such courses. It may well be that some enquiry-based teacher research has become a strategy for reproducing technical behaviour more expertly.

For example, the Action Research Planner (McTaggart and Kemmis, 1981) was designed to assist those undertaking enquiry-based reaching, often within Deakin University's own award-bearing courses offered to off-campus students. It was intended as a means of facilitating teacher research, but became seen as a set of technical rules for the conduct of the action research game complete with a snakes and ladders spiral which would allow movement around the board, leading ultimately to the granting of a credential. (Indeed, Bell, in an earlier chapter in this book, refers to the spiral having gained iconic properties.) The credential game exists in time and space, it has well-defined boundaries, a start, a finish, winners and losers. It has its umpires and referees, both on and off the field. No matter how congenially the game is run, no matter how democratic its management, the award-bearing course cannot provide the truly symmetrical conditions which would lead to collective emancipation.

All of which leads me to wonder whether teacher research, serving emancipatory-cognitive knowledge interests, is a chimera, mythological rather than possible. In Greek mythology the chimera is characterized as a fire-breathing monster with a lion's head, a goat's body and a serpent's tail. Figuratively it is used to characterize a mere wild fancy, an unfounded conception. Is the assembly of an award-bearing course based upon teacher enquiry such a beast, an attempt to bring together such disparate and contradictory ideas that it becomes an impossibility?

I think not. I believe that emancipatory teacher research is possible and that award-bearing courses can create conditions which, while not *directly* resulting in such emancipation within the course itself, can set in motion small disturbances, awkward unanswered questions, unsettled conditions, irritations and scratchiness. These might lead to both the participants themselves and those around them beginning to question profoundly their own certitude. What must remain unanswered is how enduring such changes in the individual psyche will be and the extent to which transformed individuals can themselves enable others to re-examine their knowledge and actions. Perhaps then, at the end of the day, enquiry-based courses can be a powerful means of bringing us to the very threshold of emancipation. That part of the journey, alone, is a difficult and challenging struggle. To step over, however, goes beyond the bounds of that which any course can promise.

References

Carr, W. and Kemmis, S. (1986) *Becoming Critical*, Lewes, Falmer Press.
Farganis, J. (1975) 'A Preface to critical theory', *Theory and Society*, 2, pp. 483–508.
Gibson, R. (1985) 'Critical time for action research', *Cambridge Journal of Education*, 15, 1, pp. 56–64.
Habermas, J. (1978) 'Appendix "Knowledge and human interests: A general perspective"', *Knowledge and Human Interests*, 2nd edn, translated by J.J. Shapiro, London, Heinemann Educational Books.
Habermas, J. (1984) *The Theory of Communicative Action. Vol. One: Reason and Rationalization of Society*, London, Heinemann Educational Books.

Holly, P. (1986) 'Action research: Teacher based, teachers based, or staff based?', paper presented at the International Symposium Concerning Theoretical Models and Strategies for Educational Innovation, University of Murcia, Spain.

McTaggart, R. and Kemmis, S. (1981) *The Action Research Planner*, Geelong, Deakin University Press.

Polanyi, M. (1958) *Personal Knowledge*, Chicago, University of Chicago Press.

Popkewitz, T. (1987) *Critical Studies in Teacher Education: Its Folklore, Theory and Practice*, Lewes, Falmer Press.

Stenhouse, L. (1983) *Authority, Education· and Emancipation*, London, Heinemann Educational.

Young, R.E. (1983) 'Towards a critical theory of education', University of Sydney, mimeo.

CHAPTER 4

PUTTING TEACHER PROFESSIONAL JUDGEMENT TO WORK

Susan Groundwater-Smith

Introduction

Each year, in Australia, a prominent citizen is given the opportunity to develop a sustained commentary upon our society through a series of public broadcasts known as the Boyer Lectures. Eva Cox, feminist and economist entitled her series "A Truly Civil Society".

In the first of her Boyer lectures, Cox suggested that processes of change which are made up of an accretion of small, local changes, but with common purpose, are more likely to be successful than processes which are driven by some kind of pronouncement from above. The common purpose, for Eva Cox, is the desire to create a society which is more equitable, just and caring, but will also encourage debate and dissent.

The Cox agenda sounds very much like that of the National Schools Network (NSN). The common purpose is to improve learning outcomes for all students in schools by rethinking teachers' work practices (Ladwig et al, 1994). The changes are brought about by working consensus at the local level.

The essential question that the NSN asks schools to investigate is What is it about the way in which our work is organised that impedes student learning? Having identified impediments schools then go about the business of changing and testing these barriers in order to improve student learning outcomes.

The studies which I report here are ones which examine change in teachers' work organisation in relation to, in one case, changes to the schools' curriculum and assessment practices in the context of reculturing; in the other, the impact upon participating schools of generic key competencies[1] in a curriculum framework based upon designated learning areas. Each site has resolved its challenges in different ways and with different consequences; but each has also contributed to a larger discourse on the nature of change in schools.[2]

The studies were undertaken not only to inform and improve local school practices, but most importantly to inform the profession itself. As a reform movement the NSN is concerned to both support teachers in their own schools, and to provide its own professional research base to support its work across schools.

The National Schools Network and reform

In its own background information to researchers the NSN describes itself in the following manner:

> All members of the Network, including the member schools (200 in the NSN Schools Register in 1995), are bound together by a common set of principles, ideas and ideals which are based on the fundamental belief that we can improve what we do in schools and that we can make a difference to the learning and working lives of students and teachers who work in them. The focus is to improve schools from within, with external support from the partners in the Network, the unions and employing authorities.

The Network recognises that schools are complex communities which breed complex problems. NSN does not have technical solutions which are to be applied to those problems; rather it creates the conditions for schools to enquire into their own problems, identify the challenges and generate their own resolutions.

As a reform movement, the NSN has some unique characteristics. It was born of a national project which was established to examine the quality of teaching and learning in Australia (National Project on the Quality of Teaching & Learning, NPQTL, 1993). From its inception it has been founded on a partnership between employing authorities (both government and non-government) and teachers' unions in each Australian State and Territory. Ordinarily, these relationships can be said to be somewhat uneasy, and at times difficult and competitive. States and Territories guard their education portfolios carefully, and are suspicious of federalism. Similarly, relationships between employing authorities and unions are often problematic. So the partnership is unusual in a number of respects.[3]

The partnership is a recognition that industrial and professional concerns impact one upon the other; if the conditions under which teachers work are the conditions under which students learn, then it is important to recognise that those conditions carry industrial and professional connotations.

In these ways the NSN, while drawing upon experience from overseas, particularly in the USA, is not replicating the agenda of those reform movements, which have been driven by economic rationalist arguments rather than educational ones. Shea et al (1989) have collected a series of essays into an anthology which represents a trenchant critique of reform based upon dominant economic interest groups' determination to rebuild labour productivity and American economic power at the expense of comprehensive liberal education for all.

> The real intent of the reform reports is, in reality, the selecting and sorting of a small corps, of technocratic elite for the new high tech workplace. (Martin, 1989, p. 54)

While the Network has as a basic premise that schools must meet the learning needs of students in a rapidly changing world it does not see itself as instrumental in selecting and nurturing only those students who may be the designers and planners of that world. This is an essential difference between the American and Australian reform movement.[4]

The NSN focus for action is best summed up in the concluding comments of the review of the National Schools Program from which it arose. Such areas of action could include:

> Collaborative working relationships among and between teachers, non teaching staff and students.
>
> Changes to school culture and climate to make schools a better workplace for teaching and learning.
>
> Structural/Organisational change (such as changes to timetabling etc.). This includes cooperative arrangements with external bodies able to contribute to the work of the school.
>
> Applications of technologies to increase the effectiveness and efficiency of teaching, learning, assessment etc. (NPQTL, 1993, p. 35)

Finally, in this brief discussion of the work of the National Schools Network it is important to recognise that it sees for itself a responsibility to systematically enquire into the reforms themselves. The Network has a research office whose task it is to "build a culture of research in member schools as an integral part of their rethinking processes" (Harradine, 1996, p. 1). To foster the development of such a research culture the Network has established a competitively selected Researcher Register of academics in the field of school reform. As well as supporting research at the local level the office also commissions cross site enquiries focused upon issues of strategic significance as they are identified by the NSN's Steering Committee. It is expected that such enquiries will be participative and liberatory for those who are involved, school practitioners and university academics alike. This brings us to the methodology adopted for the studies reported here.

Methodology

In the research proposals to the NSN Research Steering Committee we argued that the data would be organised and collected in ways which would allow for systematic cross site comparisons to be made and for the development of generalisable principles. Importantly, the methodology would allow for insider and outsider accounts.

> In effect the case studies will be based upon facilitated practitioner research. The researchers will work with key practitioners in each school enabling them to gather and interpret local data. As well, the researchers will undertake to investigate local socio-economic and historical conditions. Each portrayal will be co-written with practitioners, with the researchers taking responsibility for synthesising the data across the sites. (p. 3 Proposal)

Research workshops were conducted with participating teacher researchers from each school. The workshops focused both upon research methods and the research questions.

Case study number 1

In the case of the Study of Curriculum and Assessment Reform in the Context of Reculturing focus questions and means of collecting data were negotiated in an initial research training workshop. It was agreed that in order to synthesise the studies across the sites a common methodology would be required. The teachers, as associate researchers, and myself as facilitator produced the following set:

- In what ways have we organised our curriculum and assessment work that is a change from past practice?
- How do we justify the changes we have made?
    - Researcher interviews with Principal and executive.
    - Analysis of school documentation – Researcher
    - Research Associate interview with three staff members taking account of gender and teaching experience.
- In what ways have the changes impacted upon classroom practices and student learning outcomes: from the school's perspective, from teachers' perspectives, from students' perspectives, and from parents and caregivers' perspectives?
    - Research Associate jointly developed portrayal with two others.
    - Student questionnaire and focus group discussions conducted by Research Associate.
    - Parent focus group discussion – Researcher
- What have been the impediments and constraints?
- What have been the enabling conditions?
    - Brainstorm and prioritise with whole staff Research Associate
- What would we change and why? Where to now?
    - Anonymous questionnaire – Researcher.

Case study number 2

In the case of the Key Competencies Project the focus was upon the development of Talking Circles to be conducted at the local, regional and national levels.

This was not an implementation study, although clearly some of the schools which took part were well advanced in working with key competencies in their curriculum and assessment practices. In research, such as that conducted in this case, the imperative was not to control variability, but to recognise and document it. We were concerned to 'act educatively' that is to "create, select, transmit, transform and evaluate knowledge" (Schratz & Walker, 1995) in ways which would enhance practitioners' own insights.

Our objective was to develop a research methodology which was integral to the workplace and which maximised opportunities for discussion and debate. We wished to capture and render problematic the emergent discourses and practices related to key competencies in the curriculum. We wanted to gain insights into practitioner thinking, stakeholder beliefs and the social organisation of schooling in ways which would not mystify, but would enable all of us concerned with the improvement of schooling to gain a better purchase upon a particular aspect of it.

The strategic device at the heart of the methodology was what we have chosen to call *Talking Circles*.[5] Below are set out the conditions for *Talking Circles* followed by the means we used to articulate them into a coherent and developmental pattern.

The purpose of *Talking Circles* is to allow for multiple perspectives and interpretations to emerge. Its theoretical basis lies with the Habermasian notion of the speech act which ideally allows social participants to speak and act for themselves in a context which is untrammelled by hierarchical and institutional constraints (see Beilharz, 1995). Also this purpose is underpinned by notions of constructivism which recognise that ways of knowing are necessarily subjective:

> Knowledge is not passively received either through the senses or by way of communication; knowledge is actively built up by the cognizing subject. (von Glasersfeld, 1995, p. 51)

All the same, it should not be taken that we were looking for highly idiosyncratic views to emerge, but rather the *Talking Circle* was managed so that the range and variety of views could be openly tabled and discussed in order that participants could critically evaluate them and accommodate them to their own knowledge bases. Furthermore, we wanted to emerge a kind of consensual understanding, not as something which is exactly matched, but rather something which fits together relatively coherently.

For this to happen *Talking Circles* need to be constructed so that:

- Participants are valued.
- Participants feel safe.
- The management is democratic.
- Views are openly and honestly expressed.
- Views can be contested.

In the project, *Talking Circles* became the moments where the group came together, with whatever evidence had been collected, to make sense of it. They were convened at the local, regional and national levels.

The initial *Talking Circle* was convened as a national one. Two teacher participants from nine schools located variously in Western Australia, South Australia, Victoria, New South Wales and Queensland attended alongside National Schools Network (NSN) State Coordinators, the National Coordinator and Research Coordinator of the Network, and the external researchers, including a video recording team. Observers from the then Department of Employment, Education and Training, a Victorian Youth Project and the South Australian Key Competencies Project were also present.

Local, school-based *Talking Circles* were convened by the participating teachers and designed' to focus upon questions of concern to each school in its context. Depending upon the question at hand, membership varied. On some occasions students attended, on others the whole school staff participated. External researchers met with local *Talking Circles* on at least two occasions.

Regional *Talking Circles*[6] were convened midway through (1 day) and at the conclusion to the project (2 days). These *Talking Circles* were linked nationally via video conference for at least one session on each occasion.

Evidence and validation

Schools have been encouraged, during these projects to collect a range and variety of evidence which will assist the enquiries in their focus and direction. At all times participants have been concerned to collect evidence in socially responsible ways.

It has been argued that the collection of evidence involves us in moral and ethical issues. Procedures need to stand the following tests:

(1) that the process for collecting and judging evidence does no harm;
(2) that the purposes for collecting evidence are explicit and known to all participants;
(3) that evidence is triangulated;
(4) that conditions are such that alternative, socially just explanations and interpretations may be generated and valued. (Groundwater-Smith & White, 1995)

It is worth noting that in both projects data were not collected by way of observation of teachers' classroom practices. This was a deliberate policy and followed from Goodson's (1993) injunction:

> I wish to argue that to place the teachers' classroom practice at the centre of the action for action-researchers is to put the most exposed and problematic part of the teachers' world at the centre of scrutiny and negotiation. In terms of strategy, both personally and politically, I think it is a mistake to do this. I say it is a mistake to do this – and this may seem a paradox – particularly if the wish is to ultimately seek reflection about and change in the teachers' practice. (p. 9)

In the fiercely busy world of teaching, taking small samples of classroom practice; (and in practical terms they would only be small) would not only be threatening and impose considerable strains on the schools. They would also be difficult to validate as reasonable samples. Good classroom ethnographies take enormous resources. It is unfortunate that what pass for ethnographies are often only composed from a series of fleeting visits, rather than a sustained immersion in the classroom. Of course, this does not discount where teachers themselves may have chosen to have sampled their own classroom behaviours. However, they did not choose to do so in either of these projects.

Cochran-Smith & Lytle (1993) have characterised teacher research as a "way of knowing" (p. 41). They argue for the practitioner to have greater control of the research agenda and to be encouraged to have greater confidence in their own professional knowledge. Furthermore, Altrichter et al (1993) argue that it is essential to make teachers' knowledge public. By creating a collaborative relationship between the school researchers and academics I contend that we have been able to develop a research culture which not only recognises and publishes teacher professional knowledge and researcher 'expert' knowledge (about research), but also makes that knowledge problematic. All those involved in the research have been enabled to challenge each other's analyses and interpretations.

Throughout the research there have been possibilities for participants to check each other's perspectives, in effect to check what Somekh (1994) calls "The trustworthiness of [the] research knowledge" (p. 371). For example, in the first study, when the researcher interviewed the school Principals an initial account was written and then returned to the Principal for confirmation or amendment. When research associates interviewed colleagues regarding changes to past practice a statement was prepared and then discussed with those participating in the interviews. Following focus group discussions with students, the research associate worked with a colleague to generate a jointly authored analysis of the student questionnaires and audiotaped discussion. When case studies were drafted they were returned to schools for discussion with the whole staff prior to clearance. In the second study, the design and interactions of the Talking Circles acted to validate the multiple perspectives and interpretations.

These processes not only allowed a high degree of participation; they could also be said to satisfy a number of validity requirements. In an earlier study for the National Schools Network (Groundwater-Smith, 1996) I suggested that validating qualitative research presents us with a number of challenges. Maxwell (1992) considers the following to be essential considerations:

- *Descriptive validity*: is the account accurate?
- *Interpretative validity*: do the principal actors find the account recognisable?
- *Theoretical validity*: is the portrayal theoretically coherent?[7]
- *Generalisable validity*: to what extent can one extend the account beyond the cases studied?
- *Evaluative validity*: if evaluations are made are they consistent and justifiable?

By using the procedures outlined above it was possible for a range of validity checks to be made.

It is important to understand that these case studies are not being offered as models for practice. Each is the result of continuous problem-solving within the context of the given schools. The solutions are themselves tentative and open to reconceptualisation. However, behind the specifics of each case there lie dilemmas which are recognisable to educators working in the field of reform. For example: "How fast should we proceed?" Move too quickly and some will feel unsure, even alienated; move too slowly and others will become frustrated and thwarted.

Generalisability is without doubt a great problem in educational research; whether it be quasi-experimental, quantitative or qualitative. Eisner (1995) emphasises that artistically crafted research helps us to recognise what teachers do in highly complex and interactive environments:

> I think the question regarding what counts as research is a question of critical importance ... As I see it the primary tactical aim of research is to advance understanding ... A capacity to generate an awareness of particularity. What artistically crafted work does is to create a paradox of revealing what is universal by examining what is particular. (pp. 2–4)

"Generalisation is always based on extrapolation" (Firestone, 1993, p. 22). Firestone makes the case that with qualitative research studies, particularly case studies, the extrapolation from one case to another, is not made exclusively by the researcher but by the reader. In traditional research this extrapolation is made possible by sophisticated, and often opaque, statistical manipulations; these are driven by the researcher. However, when the research is developed as a narrative, as is the case in this research, then readers have greater access and opportunity to create their own interpretations and to make judgements about those interpretations in terms of their educational practices. The readers' reason and imagination come into play. Cherryholmes (1993) suggests:

> Research findings tell stories. Often they are about putative causes and effects. Sometimes they are descriptive, sometimes explanatory. Research findings tell stories that are, more or less, insightful and useful in shaping what we think and do... They are more or less useful in helping us to understand our social world as we navigate our way through it. (p. 2)

Cherryholmes goes on to remind his readers that it is possible to read poorly, to be so weighed down by prejudices and unspoken beliefs that only an impoverished understanding is achieved.

Robinson (1992) has claimed that educational research contributes little to the resolution of educational problems. Her argument rests on the tradition of research being conducted in a manner which effectively quarantines the researcher from the school based practitioner. Traditionally, researchers do not take sufficient account of the theories of action of the participants. This is not the case in these projects. The teachers' theories of action lie at the heart of the studies and the research has been constructed in such a way as to allow a critical dialogue between the academics as the outsiders, and the research associates, as the insiders. They, in turn, have engaged in similar dialogue with their peers. Furthermore, it has not been our role to instigate solutions to problems, but to be a co-learner, working with socially recognisable evidence (see Ladwig, 1994) about the nature of change in the nominated schools. First and foremost, these research projects are learning projects in which the participating schools, the National Schools Network and the academics are all active learners about the nature of change.

Some findings

While the purpose of this paper is to focus upon facilitated practitioner research in the context of school reform, it is of interest to examine a range of the findings arising from the projects. The title of the paper is "Putting Teacher Professional Judgement to Work". By examining some of the findings it is possible to see that the judgements of the participating teachers have indeed been put to work.

The change process

The change process of which we see evidence in the case studies is one based upon continuous problem-solving. Continuous problem-solving requires developing solutions which are, in effect, custom built. This is not to say that there may not be strategies which others have tried which become useful, but rather to adopt such strategies only to the extent that they have relevance to the problem in hand. Much of the innovations work of the 1970s foundered because solutions were applied inappropriately to local problems. Altrichter et al (1993) see the situation in this way:

> No advice from experienced colleagues, and no book can replace your own analysis of the situation, an understanding of its complexities, and a clear view of what you are aiming for. But both sources may yield valuable ideas if they fall on fertile ground; if you have already developed an understanding of the situation and possible action strategies which can be broadened and modified by external suggestions. This is because such suggestions, instead of remaining discrete and separate, are integrated with your own conception of the situation. (p. 160)

Clearly, a view shared by the Principal of one Primary School, who eschews the solution driven approach:

> One of the things that I have observed over time is the sort of reform which is a kind of bandaid that never lets you get to the big issues, you just skirt around the outside. If you look at teachers' work and that's the National School's view you can't just look at one part or another, they all impact on each other. We had the opportunity in a new school to really think things through. I didn't want to hear 'this is the way we do things around here' (coming from other schools) it was our chance to build something on the question 'what do we believe is best for the children?' After all if you improve what is happening in the classroom, you will improve teachers' conditions of work. It's the big issues which are important. (Principal)

Continuous problem solving also requires patience and tolerance. Again the process is beset by dilemmas. People are at different points in the change process; some are highly committed and anxious to proceed, others concerned to be well grounded before commencing. Many believe that there should be considerable preliminary professional development. For example teachers at St P's Primary School, in their 'advice to others' make reference to 'in-servicing' teachers. I have reproduced the whole set here because it is illustrative of the very dilemmas referred to above.

- To go slowly – to inform parents at the outset and make sure they understand the steps and reasons behind the changes; then take parents along with them (not leave them behind). To in-service staff so they are all clear on what is happening.
- Make sure staff understand what is happening – allow them to actually see it in process. Make sure parents are informed so they can go with you and accept change.
- Take your time; experiment and evaluate and invite all staff to be part of the process of change! If possible in-service staff as a whole rather than just a few at a time.

- In-service teachers and prepare them for reform, if possible allow them to observe similar situations and speak with experienced teachers. In-service and prepare parents. Develop guidelines within the school as to where it is heading and how to achieve the reform. Change in stages, not dramatically. Prepare children for the change.
- Whole staff induction over a period of say, at least 6 months to a year. With people who have studied the theory as well as put it into practice. Thence, perhaps, a monitoring process with experienced staff.

The kind of professional development required in a context of reform which is driven by practitioners is highly problematic. I have already indicated that merely taking the solutions which others have generated and believing them to be some kind of recipe for successful implementation is an unhelpful strategy. I would also argue that it is an unprofessional strategy. If good teaching is to be recognised for the complex and difficult task that it is, then the professional education of the teachers should also be acknowledged to be complex and difficult.

Giroux (1988) believes that teachers have it in them to be intellectuals, capable of transforming the conditions of schooling. However, they are not going to achieve that kind of intellectual power by being the subjects of traditional teacher in-service professional development. Indeed, he argues that teachers should resist the technical, top down forms of in-service teacher education which educational employing authorities use to ensure fidelity to their policies. Instead, they need to feel more confident about their capacity to analyse and critique policies and engage in a kind of critical discourse.[8]

It is clear from the case studies that in each school a considerable part of teacher professional development has been the process of enquiry and reflection within the school itself. Teachers have been putting their professional judgement to work.

Curriculum and assessment reform

There is not a State or Territory in Australia which has not seen massive curriculum and assessment reform as a direct intervention of governments. Whereas in the 1970s and early 1980s there was a trend to school based curriculum development, we find today that departments of school education are specifying to a much greater extent the structure and content of the curriculum and the ways in which its effectiveness might be assessed in terms of student learning outcomes:

> Schools in the 1990s have been subject to pressure to adopt business like approaches to accountability and management. Knowledge is often spoken of as an industry. It is no longer acceptable for teachers to speak of the 'unknowable consequences of teaching and learning'. The output is to be measurable in quantifiable terms, hence the demand for precise level-related outcomes. (Eltis, 1995, p. 11)

This is true across the Western World (c.f. Carlson, 1995). The spaces for curriculum reform, then, lie in the interactions between teachers and learners and learners and learning. Much of the remainder is already settled. Effectively it could be said to be the pedagogical dimension of curriculum. As Van Manen (1994) puts it:

> In ever-changing practical situations it is constantly required of teachers that they distinguish instantly, yet thoughtfully, what is appropriate from what is less appropriate, what is good from what is not good in their interactions with children. This pedagogical dimension is involved in everything teachers do or do not do in classrooms; yet this dimension is often little understood, undervalued and marginalised. (p. 140)

In effect, it might be said, that curriculum reform has been pedagogical reform. I suggested in an earlier NSN study that these are two sides of the one coin (Groundwater-Smith, 1996).

Assessment and reporting has been a matter of concern to all of the schools in the studies. It would seem that although some considerable advances had been made with forms and timing of reporting, all schools believed that alternative forms of authentic assessment still had some way to go. Nancy Mohr, in her address to the ATC/NSN Spring School (1995) provoked some Australian teachers into thinking by suggesting that assessment should lead curriculum and not the other way round. She proposed that if we first thought out our goals "What do we want for our students when they have completed their schooling with us?" and then considered how they might be validated "How do we know if we have succeeded?" then we might be more likely to make assessment the heart of the curriculum. This does not mean testing and teaching to the test; but engaging in authentic, substantial tasks which demonstrate learning. If we are interested in continuous learning improvement then an assessment led curriculum makes sense. However, it is hard work to reorientate our thinking in this way.

Impediments to change and reform

In both of these projects it has been important for practitioners to find means for identifying the impediments which exist, not only in locally based work practices, but at a structural level as well. The key competencies project was particularly powerful in identifying such impediments and noting the range and variety of responses which the participating teacher researchers and their colleagues had available to them.

Teachers' work was seen to have significantly intensified in a context of political volatility. This had different consequences:

- For some change was seen to be coming from above; the view was 'wait and see, it may be supplanted by something else'.
- Many were suffering change fatigue, which led to resistance, particularly because it was seen that schools were being driven by the employers' agenda.
- Others asked themselves, 'why change – we are already doing this'.
- For most teachers directly involved in the project the view was that further change must be warranted – 'Is the change commensurable with the core values business of the school?' This seemed the most positive and promising direction.

Other impediments were attitudinal. Participants engaged in a significant debate with respect to the extent to which teaching practices should be explicit. Some thought teachers' work is not necessarily explicit and neither should it be – "we are here to teach subject matter, not educational theories about learning". Being practical was highly valued. It was seen that the underpinning ideas behind key competencies, for example, were too theoretical and too consuming of scarce time. There was no time to rethink before reforming.

Issues for practitioner research

So what has been learnt here? I would argue that the processes of facilitated practitioner research have been productive and enlightening. There has been mutual recognition and regard for both the school based professionals and the university-based participants.[9]

Both have had the time and space to listen and learn from each other. All research has its surprises. One of the great surprises of these studies was the capacity of students to reflect on their own learning and the ways in which their teachers helped them to learn either in a broad sense, or in relation to key competencies. In the subsequent discussion with the teacher researchers this was clearly an important contribution to the whole schools' capacities to reflect upon their practices. It has also given me much food for thought regarding research methods, which often give the learners little opportunity to respond in open ways to complex questions.

Most importantly, professional judgement has been accorded a high regard in both projects. The National Schools Network has used the teachers' professional judgement to enable it to reformulate its policies and practices. In a fashion, it could be suggested that these case studies themselves are curriculum and assessment artefacts for the National Schools Network, for the Network itself is a learning organisation and its business is the business of school reform.

Feedback from teachers has been positive. Participants at the final Northern Talking Circle in the Key Competencies Project were requested to write either discursively, or in point form, about perceived strengths, weaknesses and changes in relation to the research process which was adopted. All responses were anonymous. In such a context it was possible for participants to express freely any concerns they might have maintained. However the reflections indicated strong affirmation for the processes and outcomes of the project.

> It seems that at all stages of this project the valuing of participants as professionals and individuals has been paramount. The processes utilised to focus on the expected tasks and outcomes of the project were thoughtful and supportive. They also showed respect for the intellectual reasoning and discussion that can come from a group of teachers with a common purpose, regardless of the diversity of schools that they come from.
>
> This is a marvellous discourse to use at the beginning in bringing KCs into school based curriculum. I would like for it to happen on a regional basis, or dare I say it State wide. Working at the 'front line' however, on a smaller scale is more exciting and perhaps more manageable.
>
> The greatest strength of the talking circle was the time allowed for reflection and discussion of a wide range of issues relevant to key competencies and quality learning. The diversity of different circles, teachers/parents/students opened up new perspectives.

> The talking circle process has been extremely successful and an enjoyable method of seeking out information. This can be verified by the sorts of issues brought up! One of the strengths of the project would have to be the wide ranging group of participants. Being an Australia-wide project I feel we all learnt from each other. A second strength was the inclusion of both primary and secondary schools to explore the issues. There were many aspects of education that I found I was taking for granted.

While the participating teachers greatly valued the time that they had available to them they also regretted that it was inadequate for them to continue to explore the many significant issues which arose:

> The time we had from the beginning to the end of the project. It sometimes seemed that the next part was there before satisfactorily dealing with the last. We seemed to end just when we were ready to start!
>
> The major weakness or problem was the lack of time. I found I was pushed for time to do all that I wanted to do in my own school research. The video conference was interesting, however; at this stage of the technological development, I felt we did not gain a heck of a lot from it.

As one who worked closely with these teachers I affirm and resonate to their voices as they are expressed here.

Conclusions

Popkewitz (1991) has concluded that we need to "understand (educational) reform as an object of social relations rather than accept reform as truth producing and progressive" (p. 244). He is concerned to broaden the opportunities for debate about reforms, so that many voices may be heard. The methodology for these projects, facilitated practitioner research, was designed to do precisely that.

In an educational world where the activists in education are more likely to be governments than educators it is essential that the professional voice is strengthened.

Alford & O'Neil (1995), in their discussion of Victorian state government policy, argue that contractualism is becoming the dominant form of social organisation. Contractualism allows little space for dialogue and debate. Agreements are built upon the individual making and fulfilling of promises. The kind of collegiality embodied in the National Schools Network is currently being significantly threatened. Writing this article has been an opportunity to celebrate and affirm its corporate contribution to the education profession and to argue that it is through such agencies that we can build, in Eva Cox's words "A Truly Civil Society".

Acknowledgements

I wish to acknowledge the work of the participating teachers in the studies reported here. Most importantly, I wish to thank Vivienne White, National Coordinator of the National Schools Network, for her vision and belief in the professionalism of teachers, and their capacity to make a positive difference to students' life chances.

Correspondence

Professor Susan Groundwater-Smith, Centre for Applied Education, Griffith University, Gold Coast, PMB 50, Queensland 9726, Australia.

Notes

1. Known in England as 'foundation skills' or 'workplace competencies', or in Scotland as 'core skills'.
2. This paper draws extensively upon two reports made to the National Schools Network: (i) Groundwater-Smith (1996) *Let's Not Live Yesterday Tomorrow*. Ryde: National Schools Network; (ii) Carbines, R. & Groundwater-Smith, S. (1996) *Key Competencies & Teachers' Work*, Ryde: National Schools Network. The second of these studies contained, in addition, video materials prepared by Summer Hill Films. The package was edited by Avrll Keeley and submitted as a report to the Australian Department of Employment, Education, Training and Youth Affairs. It is anticipated that the package will eventually be published as a professional development resource.
3. It should be noted that the NPQTL itself grew from a reform climate based upon an evolving accord between employers and unions more generally. With a change in federal government this accord is no longer operative. Some uncertainty now surrounds the NSN and its future.
4. An exception to this is the work of the Coalition of Essential Schools in the USA. The coalition, like NSN, has a concern for equity and social justice.
5. The actual phrase *Talking Circles* is one used by indigenous groups to illustrate the ways in which they favour communication. The term signifies that there can be authentic group knowledge and that no one individual has a monopoly over wisdom. The process is one which avoids being adversarial and combative, but respects and builds upon views and insights which are expressed. We thank Bob Morgan, Director of Jumbunna Aboriginal Education Centre at the University of Technology, Sydney, for this information.
6. Southern *Talking Circle* comprised schools from WA, SA and Victoria. The Northern *Talking Circle* comprised schools from NSW and Queensland. Each was also attended by respective NSN coordinators. In the case of the midterm Northern *Talking Circle* two secondary school students also attended.
7. The theoretical coherence, in this case could be seen to refer to the body of knowledge which deals with the progressive school reform agenda.
8. It might be argued that the joint NSN and Australian Teaching Council Professional Development Schools, conducted during school vacations attempt to do just this – they engage the participants in dialogue about practice, rather than instruct the participants in implementation strategies.
9. It is probably important to point out that my own position is a somewhat unusual one. While I am attached to a University as an adjunct professor I am also an independent educational researcher and professional development consultant. This privileges me, in that I have to devote less of my time to administrative work and have greater flexibility in my opportunities to engage with the profession.

References

Alford, J. & O'Neil, D. (1995), *The Contract State; Public Management and the Kennett Government*. Geelong: Centre for Applied Social Research, Deakin University.

Altrichter, H., Posch, P. & Somekh, B. (1993). *Teachers Investigate their Work*. London: Routledge.

Beilharz, P. (1995) Critical theory – Jurgen Habermas, in D. Roberts (Ed.) *Reconstructing Theory*. Melbourne: Melbourne University Press.

Carbines, R. & Groundwater-Smith, S. (1996) *Key Competencies & Teachers' Work*. Ryde: National Schools Network.

Carlson, D. (1995) Making progress: progressive education in the postmodern, *Educational Theory*, 45, pp. 337–357.

Cherryholmes, C. H. (1993) Reading research, *Journal of Curriculum Studies*, 25, pp. 1–32.

Cochran-Smith, M. & Lytle, S. (1993) *Inside/Outside: teacher research and knowledge*. New York: Teachers College Press.

Cox, E. (1995) *A Truly Civil Society; 1995 Boyer Lectures*. Sydney: Australian Broadcasting Corporation.

Eltis, K. (1995) *Focusing on Learning; report of the review of outcomes and profiles in New South Wales schooling*. Sydney: NSW Department of Training and Education Coordination.

Eisner, E. (1995) What artistically crafted research can help us understand about schools, *Educational Theory*, 45, pp.1–6.

Firestone, W. A. (1993) Alternative arguments for generalising from data as applied to qualitative research, *Educational Researcher*, 32(4), pp. 16–23.

Giroux, H. (1988) *Teachers as Intellectuals*. Massachusetts: Bergin & Garvey.

Goodson, I. F. (1993) The Devil's bargain: education research and the teacher, *Education Policy Analysis Archives*, 1(3), pp. 1–14.

Groundwater-Smith, S. & White, V. (1995) *Improving Our Primary Schools: evaluation and assessment through participation*. Sydney: Harcourt Brace.

Groundwater-Smith, S. (1996) *Learning is When: teachers help teachers; kids help kids; teachers help kids: kids help teachers*. Ryde: National Schools Network.

Harradine, J. (1996) *The Role of Research in the Work of the National Schools Network*. Ryde: National Schools Network.

Ladwig, J. G. (1994) Science, rhetoric and the construction of socially recognisable evidence in educational research, *The Australian Educational Researcher*, 21(3), pp. 77–96.

Ladwig, J., Currie, J. & Chadbourne, R. (1994) *Towards Rethinking Australian Schools*. Ryde: National Schools Network.

Martin, D. (1989) A critique of the concept of work and education in the school reform reports, in C. Shea, E. Kahane & P. Sola (Eds) *The New Servants of Power: a critique of the 1980s school reform movement*. New York: Greenwood Press.

Maxwell, J. A. (1992). Understanding and validity in qualitative research, *Harvard Educational Review*, 62, pp. 279–300.

Moore-Johnson, S. (1991) *Teachers, Working, Contexts and Educational Productivity*. Working Paper 14, School of Education, Center for Research in Education Finance. Los Angeles: University of Southern California.

National Project on the Quality of Teaching and Learning (1993) *National Schools Project – a report of the national external review panel*. Canberra: Australian Government Publishing Service.

Popkewitz, T. (1991) *A Political Sociology of Educational Reform: power/knowledge in teaching, teacher education and research*. New York: Teachers College Press.

Robinson, V. (1992) Why doesn't educational research solve educational problems? *Educational Philosophy and Theory*, 24, pp. 8–28.

Schratz, M. & Walker, R. (1995). *Research as Social Change: new opportunities for qualitative Research*. London: Routledge.

Shea, C., Kahane, E. & Sola, P. (Eds) (1989) *The New Servants of Power: a critique of the 1980s' School Reform Movement*. New York: Greenwood Press.

Somekh, B (1994) Inhabiting each other's castles, *Educational Action Research*, 2, pp. 357–381.

Van Manen, M. (1994). Pedagogy, virtue and narrative identity in teaching, *Curriculum Inquiry*, 24, pp. 135–170.

von Glasersfeld, E. (1995) *Radical Constructivism: a way of knowing and learning*. London: Falmer Press.

CHAPTER 5

PAINTING THE EDUCATIONAL LANDSCAPE WITH TEA
Rereading Becoming Critical

Susan Groundwater-Smith

In her short, but erudite discussion of Milorad Pavic's *Landscape Painted with Tea* the late Angela Carter (1993) reminded us that we need new ways of reading, new ways of grasping the subtext of what lies beneath a 'rich palimpsest of stories and counter stories that provide the material for Pavic's crossword clues' (p. 18). Such is the case with *Becoming Critical* (Carr & Kemmis, 1986); each reading becomes a new reading as we, the readers, change and the times themselves alter. Just as there are many subtleties in the shades of colour offered by teas – fruit teas, tisanes, caravan tea, green tea, Lapsang Suchong – so too there are subtle intricacies in the rich and varied brew offered up to us by Carr & Kemmis.

In this brief article, it is my intention to revisit *Becoming Critical* some 20 years from my first reading, which was a rather troubled one. But more of that later. My reading both then and now has to be contextualised in terms of being an Australian one and the ways in which Australian educationists, in both the school and academic sectors, have taken up the ideas, philosophy and beliefs of the work. The reading is also mediated by my own 'second record', that is, the experience of having worked on several projects, spaced some years apart, with Stephen Kemmis.

For the historian Hexter (1972) who first defined the 'second record', that is, the constellation of subjectivities that are held by the researcher at the time of collecting, analysing and interpreting information, and that cannot fail to influence the work, it is 'indefinite in scope, and much of it personal, individual, ephemeral and not publicly accessible' (p. 104). The second record is that which the historian or for that matter any practitioner such as myself, brings to the practice that comes from his or her life experience. It is omnipresent. Thus, Hexter's various attempts to render the past intelligible come not only from his scholarship and enquiries, but also from those things that he has encountered on his life's journey:

> Once one recognises that a very, very large part of each man's (*sic*) second
> record consists of the knowledge of himself and of others that he uses to steer

himself through the daily dilemmas and difficulties of living. To question whether in his struggle with the record of the past a historian should use knowledge so relevant to understanding human conduct and so regularly tried in the crucible of experience becomes almost impertinent (Hexter, 1972, p. 125).

Hexter's argument is not *whether* the second record should be drawn upon, but *how* and *how best* it might be utilised. Thus, my reading of Carr & Kemmis cannot but be influenced by my working relationship with one of the authors – a relationship that for me has been profoundly enriching.

To argue that *Becoming Critical* has had an impact upon educational thinking in Australia can be readily substantiated. University courses related to teacher inquiry, both in initial teacher education and in relation to continuing teacher professional learning inevitably cite the work as seminal. Although Kemmis (2004) himself downplays the effects of its publication thus:

The truth is that most of the people it aimed to challenge and persuade simply continued to do the kinds of positivistic and interpretive social and educational science that they had always done. And they still do. (p. 2).

The fact of the matter is that much depends upon whom it was intended for in the first place. If 'most of the people it aimed to challenge and persuade' are those already wedded to traditional forms of data used to inform bureaucratic decision making then he is probably right, but for many who seek to improve and understand their own educational practices and the contexts in which they occur the effect has been profound. However, it is also clear that while much has stayed the same in educational reasoning as at the time the book was written, a great deal of the morphology of the educational landscape has changed. Although the contours are still recognisable and the substrata remain, many ideas have been eroded, even bulldozed, while others have been transformed into features unimaginable 20 years ago.

So what has changed?

Among the many changes that could be discussed I want to concentrate particularly upon those matters that most closely relate to Carr & Kemmis's notion of an emancipatory project for education; one in which practitioners engage with action research as a form of critical educational science in order to contribute to communities of practice governed by principles of honour, trust and social justice. Hence, I shall examine:

- the changes to professional decision-making space for practitioners and, more briefly, the impact of marketisation and other business/commerce discourses on educational practices;
- re-emerging concerns for positivism in educational research;
- the appropriation and technologising of action research as an implementation tool;
- the trivialising of theory itself.

Changes to the professional decision-making space

A major change for educationists in Australia, and the United Kingdom and a number of other nations, has been the narrowing of the decision making space for practitioners (Sachs, 2003). When *Becoming Critical* was written, school-based decision making regarding the curriculum was the norm in Australia. Indeed, this was the case in the country's universities and colleges where the regulatory frameworks were more to do with the admission of students than with what they were to study. While Carr & Kemmis recognise that educators work in institutions that are hierarchically arranged and that they are governed by overall policy to which they are rarely asked to contribute, nonetheless, it was their expectation at the time of writing that there were significant degrees of professional freedom regarding both what was to be taught and how it was to be taught. Today, each Australian State and Territory has developed highly specified outcomes-driven curriculum frameworks. At the same time standards are being developed for teacher education programs at both State and National levels. Similarly over the past two decades national curriculum frameworks have dominated the discourses regarding educational practices in the United Kingdom (UK), England in particular.

Some would argue that rational curriculum planning was already a matter for some concern in the UK when *Becoming Critical* was first published and that it was seen as a timely antidote. Thirty years ago Lawrence Stenhouse advocated teacher professional autonomy and suggested it could be achieved by: 'autonomous professional development through systematic self study ... and through questioning and testing of ideas by classroom research procedures' (Stenhouse, 1975, p. 144).

Autonomy should not be taken to mean teachers exercising professional judgement in isolation from their peers, but rather that they develop their professional learning through systematic investigation, rather than by fiat.

The increasing international trend to curriculum specification does not necessarily lead to an argument that there are now few opportunities for the exercise of professional decision making, but rather that those opportunities have shifted. In Australia, the movement has been from the curriculum field to the pedagogical arena. The struggle now is for *how* things may be taught. Of course, curriculum and pedagogy are inextricably linked. In my own work, I have argued for a definition of curriculum that proposes a complex interaction between text, context and pretext. Text embodies that which is written, spoken and exchanged in classrooms and in policies; it includes both that which is intended and explicit, and that which is enacted in more diffuse ways. The context alludes to the local, spiralling out to ever larger settings within which the text is enacted; while pretext refers to the reasonings that lie behind the choices and selections that are made (Groundwater-Smith, 1988). All in all, it is the what, where and why of curriculum work.

Returning, then, to pedagogy – the *how* of what takes place and why this has become the new arena for contestation. In Australia it has been the State of Queensland that has led the way in reviving an interest in pedagogy. The Queensland initiatives that bind together what have become known as productive pedagogies, new basics, rich tasks and authentic assessment have acted to stimulate a renewed professional regard for both means and ends in the classroom. Growing out of the research of Fred Newmann and Associates at the Centre for Organisational

Restructuring and Schools (CORS) Wisconsin, a set of empirically constructed standards of 'authentic instruction' were developed for schools in that region of the United States. These were subsequently used to inform the Queensland School Reform Longitudinal Study (SRLS) conducted 1998–2000 (Hayes et al, 2000) and resulted in a policy of the development of rich tasks for learning and a framework of pedagogies that would enhance student engagement in their learning. This policy is particularly important in that it is research based and founded upon clear learning principles, themselves of a constructivist kind (Hayes, 2003). While the work has been admirable it is also problematic as employing authorities set out to codify pedagogical practices, thus denying teachers even further their opportunities for professional decision making. In New South Wales, the country's most populous state, a discussion paper *The NSW Quality Teaching Paper* (New South Wales Department of Education and Training, 2003) resulted in teachers being 'trained' in observing and coding teaching practices based upon a set of video materials that have themselves been de-contextualised from the day-to-day operation of the schools in which they were made. The debates swirl around the accuracy of the teachers' coding, rather than any questioning of the framework itself.

In writing of the English context Elliott (2004) suggests that:

> If one views *educational* change in terms of an intelligent response to the pedagogical problems and challenges that confront teachers in handling the complexity of life in their classrooms, then one might describe it as *pedagogically driven education reform*. This view of educational reform stands in marked contrast to the *standards driven reform* movement that has tended to shape pedagogy in educational institutions according to a change agenda which ignores this complexity and views the ideal learning environment as a simple, stable, linear system that behaves in quite predictable ways. (p. 285; original emphases)

Elliott goes on to argue that pedagogically driven reform requires practitioners to develop a deep situational understanding of the context in which they work, an understanding that is best obtained by engagement in sustained and focussed inquiry. He goes further and suggests that such inquiry should not only be systematic and rational, but also aesthetic, even artistic, encompassing the educational imagination. One would imagine that Carr & Kemmis would find little to argue with in this stance.

It may appear that this discussion of the changing decision making space in Australia is overly pessimistic. Of course, there are those courageous and imaginative teachers who will find the opportunities to investigate and improve practice within their schools as genuine knowledge-building organisations (Groundwater-Smith & Mockler, 2003). However, every State and Territory Government Schools employing authority has set about increasingly regulating the initial teacher education curriculum by coupling it with the employability of graduates. A not dissimilar situation pertains in England with university programs themselves subject to Office for Standards in Education (Ofsted) inspections. Thus, education authorities exercise a degree of control over teacher professional decision making from the beginning to the completion of a teaching career.

Marketisation and managerialism

The narrowing and changing nature of professional decision-making space is not the result of some capricious set of circumstances, but directly relates to the development of a globally held view that market-driven economies are winning economies and the sooner they are supported by competitive education systems the better. Clearly, the burgeoning dominance of the discourse of markets has been the result of carefully and strategically thought out corporate and managerial policies (Clarke & Newman, 1997; Marginson, 1997). Just as markets are subject to tight quality control, so too is education provision in all sectors to be standardised, managed and controlled leaving little space for the exercise of individual decision making and judgement.

While Carr & Kemmis have well understood the professional limitations placed upon educators they could not have anticipated the rapidity and intensity of the shift to marketisation and managerialism. Quality assurance, league tables, the closure of failing enterprises leave less space for the emancipatory possibilities that were imagined 20 years ago.

Positivism and evidence-based practice

One could argue, in the light of Carr & Kemmis's text, that nothing has changed in relation to the dominance of positivism as a form of social research. Indeed, a great deal of their book is devoted to a careful and trenchant critique of positivism in the ways in which means and ends are separated one from the other. The positivist researcher may find evidence as to how and what ends can be achieved, but does not make claims about what those ends *ought* to be. Philosophy is put aside. As they say:

> Clearly, if educational decision-making were to be based on an application of scientific knowledge, the whole character of educational arguments and disagreements would change. For these would be no longer regarded as expressions of incompatible values, but as 'technical' problems which could be resolved objectively through the rational assessment of evidence. (Carr & Kemmis, 1986, p. 67)

Elsewhere they point out that the absence of debate regarding values and means leads to positivist social science:

> making a shibboleth of 'truth', as if it stood above social life, could be objectively ascertained and could prescribe wise practice without understanding the human, social, economic, political, historical and practical constraints within which real practice occurs. (p. 145)

In espousing a critical educational science, Carr & Kemmis believed that the future promised much. However, this was before the days of the Bush policy in the United States of America, articulated through the *Education Sciences Reform Act of 2002* (http://www.ed.gov/offices/IES) – a policy that is having ramifications across the English speaking world.

The view of science written into law by the Bush administration is clearly a positivist one with its exclusive emphasis upon the employment of randomised controlled clinical trials precisely designed to solve those 'technical problems' to which Carr and Kemmis refer.

Slavin (2002) in his support of the policy argued:

> The experiment is the design of choice for studies that seek to make causal conclusions and particularly for evaluations of educational innovations. Educators and policy makers legitimately ask, 'If we implement Program X instead of Program Y, or instead of our current program, what will be the likely outcomes for children?' For questions posed in this way, there are few alternatives to well-designed experiments. (p. 18)

It is clear that Slavin has utmost faith in one particular form of scientifically-based research, although US scientists themselves have a far more catholic view of how systematic inquiry can take place. As Yates (2004) in her powerful account of these and similar developments indicated, a report by scientific experts from the National Academies in the United States was less wedded to one particular form of investigation, setting out instead the following norms of principles that all science should follow, and which can be applied across the range of social services, not only education:

- Pose significant questions that can be investigated empirically,
- Link research to relevant theory,
- Use methods that permit direct investigations of the questions,
- Provide a coherent and explicit chain of reasoning,
- Yield findings that replicate and generalize across studies,
- Disclose research data and methods to enable and encourage professional scrutiny and critique. (Feuer et al, 2002, quoted in Yates, 2004, p. 25)

Other than the matter of replicability, well argued by Berliner (2002) in his rejoinder to Slavin:

> Doing science and implementing scientific findings are so difficult in education because humans in schools are embedded in complex changing networks of social interaction. . .Compared to designing bridges and circuits, or splitting atoms or genes, the science to help change schools and classrooms is harder to do because context cannot be controlled. (p. 19)

These principles sit well with Carr & Kemmis's search for a critical educational science. One suspects that had Carr & Kemmis written *Becoming Critical* today, they would have joined with the current positivist argument with great vigour.

Appropriation and technologising of action research

Curiously, the very attractiveness of Carr and Kemmis's work lies at the seat of that which is problematic about it. Action research has been popularised and appropriated as an implementation tool instead of as a social change method with far-reaching implications.

As advocates for action research, albeit of a particularly liberating kind, Carr & Kemmis brought its principles and features very much to the fore. Drawing upon the work of the National Invitational Seminar on Action Research held at Deakin University, Geelong, Victoria, in May 1981, they defined action research in this way:

> Educational action research is a term used to describe a family of activities in curriculum development, professional development, school improvement programs, and systems planning and policy development. These activities have in common the identification of strategies of planned action which are *implemented*, and then systematically submitted to *observation, reflection and change*. Participants in the action being considered are integrally involved in all of these activities. (pp. 164–165; original emphasis)

Along with the work of Elliott and others in the Ford Teaching Project (Elliott, 1991) and Stenhouse[1] and his team (Stenhouse, 1975) in relation to the Humanities Curriculum Project, the book has clearly been a powerful influence upon practitioner inquiry. Governments, looking to reinforce education policies have seen in action research an opportunity to bring those policies into practice through action learning projects. As Pring (2004) indicates:

> There is a danger that such research (action research) might be supported and funded with a view to knowing the most effective ways of attaining particular goals – goals or targets set by government or others external to the transaction which takes place between the teacher and learner. The teacher researches the most efficient means of reaching a particular educational objective . . . (p. 134)

In Australia, this is most recently evident in relation to the *Quality Teaching Program* (http://www.qualityteaching.dest.gov.au) a National Government Program that aims to extend teacher professional learning in the key areas of literacy, numeracy, mathematics, science, information technology and vocational education and training. Mediated through state-based agencies, in both the government and non-government sectors, the conditions for grantees are highly specific, with little room to vary from what is required. Thus, the iterative cycle of problem identification, reflection, action, problem reconceptualisation is effectively denied as there is no provision for a critique of any features of the policy itself. The problem is the government's problem, not that of the practitioner. As Carr & Kemmis put it, 'Action research not only attempts to identify contradictions between educational and institutional practices, it actually creates a sense of these contradictions for the self-critical community of action researchers. It does so by asserting an alternative set of values to the bureaucratic values of institutions' (p. 197). Imposed action research, as a form of bureaucratic, hierarchically directed activity as we see it enacted today, is effectively an educational oxymoron.

Action research has not only been appropriated in this way, but has also been technologised through numerous 'how to' books and methodological collections. For example, Cooke & Wolfram Cox (2005), working from a management base, have assembled a four-volume collection covering:

- a history of action research;
- varieties and workplace applications of action research;
- social change applications, practitioner and action research knowledge;
- reviews, critiques and new directions.

The trivialisation of theory

While it would be foolhardy to suggest that education is a theory-free environment, there is no question that recent times have seen academic theory trivialised – reduced to 'what works'. The many references to Habermas, Marx, Gadamer and others, as well as to movements such as the enlightenment, and to methods such as hermeneutics, are central to Carr & Kemmis's work. However, they would be unlikely to be found in more recent writing supporting teacher inquiry.

In his powerful diagnosis of the demise of cultural theory Eagleton (2003) attacks the trend to trivialisation. He craves for a re-establishment of discourses, incorporating major intellectual developments of the past, that will discuss truth, virtue and the good life within carefully constructed and defended moral frameworks. 'When all is permitted, nothing is valuable' (p. 219) lies at the heart of his timely analysis. He recalls a time when the cultural debates, of which of course education is a part, were strong and vigorous, when 'there was a quarrel between those who wanted to turn knowledge into military and technological hardware, or into techniques of administrative control, and those who saw in it a chance for political emancipation' (p. 25). Indeed, he believed that for a brief time universities returned to the tradition of being sites that nurtured and encouraged dissent.

Today, it would appear that there is something unseemly about appealing to 'grand theory' in order to locate and understand practice, let alone critique practice; but that is precisely what *Becoming Critical* is about– it provides us with a rationale for understanding why both positivist and interpretive methods are not enough in and of themselves. In their opening to Chapter 5, 'A Critical Approach to Theory and Practice', they argue that 'the recognition that educational theory must be grounded in the interpretation of teachers is (however) not in itself sufficient' (p. 129). The project is one that requires a capacity for practitioners to liberate themselves from ideologically distorted self-understanding. This requires not only a capacity to be reflective, but also to engage in reflexivity whereby the genesis of one's ideas and beliefs are themselves subject to examination and critique. It is not only a matter of 'now my ideas about so and so are clearer to me', but 'now I can see from whence these ideas came'. This is not possible for the practitioner working alone, but requires a context where clarification is possible through discussion and debate.

As Kemmis (2004) citing Habermas has recently put it:

> I could continue along these lines to describe Jurgen Habermas' theory of communicative action – the kind of action in which people stop what they are doing to explore their shared understandings of things. When they engage in communicative action, they strive to reach intersubjective agreement about the categories they use to understand things, mutual understanding of another's point of view and consensus about what to do in the practical circumstances in which they find themselves. (p. 9)

The trivialising of theory, especially theory of the emancipatory kind, is best found in the discourse of empowerment wherein power is seemingly a gift that can be readily bestowed upon individuals or communities with little or no struggle. This view of empowerment found its most ludicrous voice in a recent sunglass advertisement in a Sydney week-end magazine that enjoined its readers to 'empower your vision'.[2] How ironic that this is precisely, metaphorically, what Carr & Kemmis would have hoped for.

And what remains the same?

It was suggested at the beginning of this piece that while much changes on the surface, other features of the educational landscape persist. While the ways in which theory is understood is problematic it is also the case that the difficult relationship between theory and practice endures. It is a relationship that lies at the very core of practice. It is one that has exercised the educational imagination over eons of time. Carr & Kemmis's section on theory and practice: 'Redefining the problem' (pp. 112–118) is a wonderfully clear exposition on the inseparability of the inter-action between these two elements. For those engaged in forms of practitioner inquiry it assists in an understanding that the perceived gap between theory and practice is a gap between discipline-based theories, for example, educational psychology, sociology of education, even (dare I say) philosophy of education and practice in the field. When one understands that there is a theory of practice in the field, held by those working in that domain, then the relationship between the two becomes much clearer:

> When 'theory' and 'practice' are looked at in this way, it becomes increasingly obvious that the kinds of gap between them that usually cause concern in educational research are not those occurring between a practice and the theory guiding that practice, but rather those that arise because it is assumed that 'educational theory' refers to theories *other than those* that already guide educational pursuits. The 'communication gap', for example, only arises when the language of educational theory is not the language of educational practice. (p. 114)

There remains a need for a critical social science as espoused by Carr & Kemmis. We need a continuing discussion and analysis of what we understand professional knowledge and professional knowledge formation to be. Practitioners and those who assist them in studying their work need not only to be reflective, but to also understand from whence their ideas came. Schon's *The Reflective Practitioner* (1983) had barely arrived on the educational horizon at the time of publication of *Becoming Critical*, but Carr & Kemmis were deeply aware of and committed to self-understanding and the need for what Alvesson & Skoldberg (2000) refer to as a reflexive methodology.

The Habermasian influence, in spite of post-modernism's rejection of 'grand theory' remains and has continued to grow. At the time of writing Jurgen Habermas is Professor Emeritus at Johann Wolfang Goethe University, Frankfurt. He continues to be an active commentator on current matters such as America's war on Iraq (Mendieta, 2004) or the deaths of such luminaries as Jacques Derrida and

Pierre Bourdieu. While he does not write directly to educators his work has ongoing implications for educational policy and practice in a global environment, e.g. Habermas (2000).

What also remains and cannot be changed unless the book were to be revisited by its authors and, in part, rewritten is the alienating effect of some of its language, a reading to which I briefly referred at the beginning of this article as a 'troubled one'. Not long after *Becoming Critical* was issued in its original form by Deakin University Press (Carr & Kemmis, 1983)[3] I reviewed it for the Australian Journal of Education (Groundwater-Smith, 1984). At the time I lamented: 'The problem with the text lies not with its message, but with the medium in which it is expressed. Difficult ideas are represented in particularly opaque ways...' (p. 328). I continued, that given Wilf Carr's position espousing the academic researchers' need to take the language of teachers more seriously (Carr, 1982), it was indeed ironic to:

> come across prose that is so singularly dense, even obfuscating. The authors might defend their style by suggesting that it is a close-knit text requiring careful reading, and that words are used with great precision and, where appropriate, carefully delineated. But it is more than a matter of vocabulary. The hand/head distinction is analysed and rejected in the rhetoric of the text but is epitomized by its structures which to say the least are cerebral. (p. 328)

Of course, not all of the book has these characteristics. Surely it would not have survived had it only been one more dense and difficult tome. As I wrote earlier, the section on the relationship between theory and practice is one noteworthy for its clarity and insightfulness.

Finally, and sadly, what remains is the idea that an emancipatory critical social science is an impossible goal. In the course of writing, this piece a reviewer recommended that I spend more time addressing the matter of *why* the teaching profession has not been liberated from the burgeoning trend to technical rationality. It was suggested that part of the answer might lie in Gadamer's critique of Habermas so thoroughly analysed among others by Bernstein (1982) and discussed by McGee (2005). At the heart of the debate lies the ways in which practical reasoning, knowledge and wisdom can be attained, in particular through the application of the 'ideal speech situation' (Habermas, 1979, pp. 1–68).

The concept of the ideal speech situation (ISS) revolves around the notions that, *ideally*:

- all participants must have an equal opportunity to participate; they must have the right to assert, defend or raise questions regarding factual or normative claims that are made;
- the communication should not be constrained by status differences;
- the motivation should be to reach a consensus about the truth of the statements and the validity of the norms.

The ISS is just that – an *ideal*. It is a powerful tool with which we can think about how distorted communication is, whether it is taking place in a school, a policy environment or the public sphere itself (Wyatt et al, 2000). Gadamer's attack on Habermas's position lies in the effects and influences of culture and tradition that themselves act to distort individual understanding. It is not my intention to more fully discuss this complex and dense debate in the context of this article. However, I do assert that it is as important today as when *Becoming Critical* was first written that we continue to subscribe to a knowledge interest that is emancipatory, difficult as it may be to obtain. Teachers can and should be able to hear each other out; bureaucrats can and should be able to engage with the profession in more liberatory ways; governments can and should seek more consensual routes. It is not that the very idea of an emancipatory critical social science is misconceived as my reviewer suggested, but that we are not yet ready to reach for the radical resocialisation that would be required to realise that ideal goal.

Is there a 'third' way?

If, in the immediate term, an emancipatory critical social science is not possible and that technical rationality is limiting and unsatisfactory, is there then a 'third' way? Very recently, I worked with Stephen Kemmis on a project that shows some promise (Groundwater-Smith & Kemmis, 2004). As meta-evaluators of the Priority Actions Schools Program (PASP), we were able to advise upon strategies for schools to investigate, document and analyse their learning as a result of the program's intervention.

PASP was a New South Wales Department of Education and Training (NSW DET) program, which allocated funds to over 70 schools across the State, resources that would allow them to address significant challenges brought about by difficult social and economic circumstances. What was remarkable about the program was the professional autonomy granted to schools to develop local solutions to local problems. This was a significant departure in policy for a Department that had a general orientation to 'one size fits all', or as a colleague once observed 'one size fits few'. The program recognised that schools struggling to address the needs of alienated young indigenous people in remote communities faced very different challenges to ones located in troubled housing estates on Sydney's fringe.

A particularly noteworthy feature of the work in many of the participating schools was the extent to which students, teachers, school communities, principals – and the Department – changed 'the rules'. They found ways of doing things differently in the interests of the learning outcomes of their students and the professional learning of the teaching and ancillary staff. Schools, and the bureaucratic team who supported them, together bent existing rules, reframed them, reordered their priorities. Habitual and existing practices were challenged and changed, be they staffing priorities, school community relations, or deep-seated beliefs about how children in difficult circumstances can and will learn.

Within a highly centralised, bureaucratic structure, schools, for example, were able to change their staffing profiles to more readily meet their students' needs. Normally, and allegedly in the interests of equity, New South Wales schools are staffed to a formula noted for its inflexibility. PASP schools stepped outside these confines and determined new ways for organising and appointing their teachers. Of course, many 'rules' are not necessarily codified or visible to outsiders. Teachers in NSW are generally not accustomed to watching each other at work, so that when it became possible to observe and be observed by one's peers, it necessarily provided an interruption to normal processes and procedures.

While it is not possible, here, to report upon all of the extensive findings of the study[4], several observations can be made: schools were encouraged to work with an academic partner as they developed their strategies and the evidence that they would collect regarding their efficacy; schools were provided with professional learning opportunities directed towards ways of collecting, analysing and interpreting evidence; schools were provided with a platform, in the form of a whole school learning portfolio, upon which to build their professional knowledge. It was the collection of these learning portfolios that provided a significant basis for the meta-evaluation.

In our report, we argued that one of the reasons so many of the PASP schools did so well in making change was that, while they had some additional resources, they also had permission, encouragement and support to explore how they might do things differently, to try new ideas in practice, to learn from carefully-observed experience, to reflect and change direction in the light of what they learned. In effect, their collective professional decision making space had been greatly enhanced.

The schools saw themselves as *agents* of change, not as *objects* of change (objects, that is, of someone else's ideas about what they could or should be). From the beginning, PASP was structured as 'a knowledge-building program' and it insisted that the participating schools should be 'knowledge-building schools'. It assumed, first, that the schools were committed to building the knowledge and capacities of their students through education and improving learning outcomes for students, and, secondly, that they were committed to building their own corporate or collective knowledge of and capacities to respond educatively to the educational and social needs of students in communities with deep needs, their families and their communities. Furthermore, it was conceived that the bureaucracy and the teachers' union (a partner in the project) would also be enabled to build knowledge about how such programs could be judiciously managed and led.

Optimistic as this account is, it is also the case that the schools were constrained, particularly in relation to curriculum decision making. New South Wales schools are required to abide by the syllabus requirements set down by a statutory body, The NSW Board of Studies. The overcrowded and highly-specified curriculum bears down particularly on senior students and certainly limited what might be achieved in the senior years of Priority Action Schools. However, in recognising these constraints, we would argue that a working consensus was reached in the majority of schools regarding what and how the varying challenges might be addressed.

So perhaps the 'third' way is one that is an ethical route *towards* a critical social science. There is a clear distinction here, between ethics and rules. Relationships among and between staff and their students are governed, in part, by sets of rules in recognition of state legislation. Thus, for example, a teacher may not harass a new and beginning teacher on the basis of his or her race, religion or sexual preference. As well, there are rules about how schools may be staffed and who may do what, although, as we claimed, some of these rules were broken. However, it is the case that behaving ethically goes beyond meeting such requirements, important as they may be. It involves matters of moral deliberation. Pring (2004) makes a distinction between *moral* virtues such as courage, kindness, generosity of spirit, honesty and a concern for justice, and *intellectual* virtues, comprised of a concern to seek out the truth (as it is understood) openness to criticism and an interest in clear communication based upon evidence (p. 145). Such virtues cannot be eschewed on the way to the goal of a critical social science.

Conclusion

Taking the book as a whole, its impact is undeniable. Practitioners and academic researchers are in danger of becoming even more estranged. It is timely that we visit *Becoming Critical* once again. In his contribution to Sikes et al (2003), Carr recognises that research in education is an unfinished story; successive waves of varying paradigms underpinned by varying philosophies contribute to the education debates in an evolving, rather than culminating fashion. Indeed, writers such as Hammersley (2004) are questioning the very foundations of action research. He proposes that research and action are potentially contradictory in a number of different ways, especially in relation to opportunity costs where the very intensity of what is required from practitioner research means that they (the practitioners) cannot be engaged in other, more meaningful forms of professional activity.

Whichever way it is done, theory building is hard work. Whether theory in practice or theory about practice, working theoretically is difficult, challenging and demanding. To quote Griffiths (1974):

> Theory isn't abstract; it isn't words on a page; it . . . it isn't . . . aesthetically pleasing patterns of ideas and evidence. Theory is concrete. It's distilled practice. Above all, theory is felt, in the veins, in the muscles, in the sweat on your forehead. In that sense, it's moral and binding. It's the essential connective imperative between past and future. (Griffiths, 1974, quoted in Gibson, 1985, p. 64)

Rereading *Becoming Critical* has also been hard work. It is not a text to skim and mine for helpful tips and recipes. In my initial reference to a landscape painted with tea, I suggested that *Becoming Critical* was a rich and varied brew. It is also one that has been prepared with consummate skill. My grandmother's ritual for making tea was not one to be transgressed – the kettle must be on the boil; the pot warmed and taken to the stove, a caddy spoonful of Darjeeling for each person and 'one for the pot'; it must stand for 3 minutes and the strainer be of sterling silver. The result was a clear and dark tannin like the work of Carr & Kemmis, a heady brew indeed.

Correspondence

Susan Groundwater-Smith, School of Policy and Practice, Faculty of Education and Social Work, University of Sydney, NSW 2006, Australia (susangs@iinet.net.au).

Notes

1. To whom the book is dedicated.
2. Good Weekend – a supplement to the *Sydney Morning Herald*, December 18, 2004, p. 45
3. Some revision did occur following the first edition; however I believe that this criticism still holds.
4. Which may be read at: https:www.det.nsw.edu.au/reviews/pasp

References

Alvesson, M. & Skoldberg, K. (2000) *Reflexive Methodology: new vistas for qualitative research*. Thousand Oaks: Sage.
Berliner, D. (2002) Educational Research: the hardest science of all, *Educational Researcher*, 31(8), pp. 18–20.
Bernstein, R. (1982) From Hermeneutics to Praxis, *Review of Metaphysics*, 35, pp. 823–845.
Carr, W. (1982) Review of *What is Educational Research?* by G.K. Verna & R.M. Beard, *Journal of Curriculum Studies*, 14, pp. 206–208.
Carr, W. & Kemmis, S. (1983) *Becoming Critical: knowing through action research*. Geelong: Deakin University Press.
Carr, W. & Kemmis, S. (1986) *Becoming Critical: knowing through action research*. Lewes: Falmer Press.
Carter, A. (1993) *Expletives Deleted*. London: Vintage.
Clarke, J. & Newman, J. (1997) *The Managerial State*. London: Sage
Cooke, W. & Wolfram Cox, J. (Eds) 2005 *Fundamentals of Action Research* (4 volumes). Thousand Oaks: Sage.
Eagleton, T. (2003) *After Theory*. London: Allen Lane.
Elliott, J. (1991) *Action Research for Educational Change*. Buckingham: Open University Press.
Elliott, J. (2004) Using Research to Improve Practice, in C. Day & J. Sachs (Eds) *International Handbook on the Continuing Professional Development of Teachers*. Maidenhead: Open University Press.
Gibson, R. (1985) Critical Times for Action Research, *Cambridge Journal of Education*, 15, pp. 59–64.
Groundwater-Smith, S. (1984) *Review of Becoming Critical: knowing through action research*, *Australian Journal of Education*, 28, pp. 327–329.
Groundwater-Smith, S. (1988) The Interrogation of Case Records as a Basis for Constructing Curriculum Perspectives, in J. Nias & S. Groundwater-Smith (Eds) *The Enquiring Teacher: supporting and sustaining teacher research*, pp. 93–105. Lewes: Falmer Press.
Groundwater-Smith, S. & Kemmis, S. (2004) *Knowing Makes the Difference: learning from the NSW Priority Action Schools Program*. Sydney: New South Wales Department of Education and Training.
Groundwater-Smith, S. & Mockler, N. (2003) *Learning to Listen: listening to learn*. Sydney: Faculty of Education, University of Sydney & MLC School.
Habermas, J. (1979) *Communication and the Evolution of Society*, trans. T. McCarthy. Boston: Beacon Press.
Habermas, J. (2000) Crossing Globalisation's Valley of Tears, *New Perspectives Quarterly*, 17(4), pp. 51–56.
Hammersley, M. (2004) Action Research: a contradiction in terms, *Oxford Review of Education*, 30, pp. 165–182.
Hayes, D. (2003) Making Learning an Effect of Schooling: aligning curriculum, assessment and pedagogy, *Discourse*, 24, pp. 225–245.
Hayes, D., Lingard, B. & Mills, M. (2000) Productive Pedagogies, *Education Links*, 60, Winter, pp. 10–13.
Hexter, J. (1972) *The History Primer*. London: Allen Lane.
Kemmis, S. (2004) Against Methodolatry, paper prepared for a symposium on 'Methodolatry' for the Queensland University of Technology, Provocations seminar series, 24 November.
Marginson, S. (1997) *Markets in Education*. St Leonards: Allen & Unwin.
McGee, M. (2005) Phronesis in the Habermas vs. Gadamer Debate. Available at: http://www.mcgees.net/fragments/essay/archives/Phronesis.in.the.Habermas.vs.Gadamer.Debate.htm
Mendieta, E. (2004) America and the World: a conversation with Jurgen Habermas. Available at: http://www.logos.journal.com/habermas_america.htm

New South Wales Department of Education and Training (2003) *The Quality Teaching Paper*. Sydney: NSW DET.

Pring, R. (2004) *Philosophy of Educational Research*, 2nd edn. London: Continuum.

Sachs, J. (2003) *The Activist Teaching Profession*. Buckingham: Open University Press.

Schon, D. (1983) *The Reflective Practitioner: how professionals think in action*. London: Temple Smith.

Sikes, P., Nixon, J. & Carr, W. (Eds) (2003) *The Moral Foundations of Educational Research: knowledge, inquiry and values*. Maidenhead: McGraw Hill.

Slavin, R. (2002) Evidence-based Education Policies, *Educational Researcher*, 31(7), pp. 15–21.

Stenhouse, L. (1975) *An Introduction to Curriculum Research and Development*. London: Heinemann.

Wyatt, R., Katz, E. & Kim, J. (2000) Bridging the Spheres: political and personal conversation in public and private spheres, *Journal of Communication*, 50, pp. 71–92.

Yates, L. (2004) *What does Good Education Research Look Like?* Maidenhead: Open University Press.

CHAPTER 6

MY PROFESSIONAL SELF
Two books, a person and my bedside table
Susan Groundwater-Smith

Introduction

In this chapter I examine how my life-world, which is composed of my professional and personal selves, is historically constructed, ever-changing, interactive, and dynamic. I explore the ways in which I have understood my roles as facilitator and participant in practitioner enquiry in the context of engagement with professional communities of practice and also consider some of the issues and dilemmas that have arisen. I illuminate and reflexively examine a specific issue in relation to the problematics of being judgemental through a case study of student voice in school improvement in a particularly challenging and troubling context.

Turning to myself, in particular, I propose that at one and the same time, my professional self and my personal self are both distinguishable and indistinguishable. I can describe these selves separately, succinctly, and with reasonable accuracy, but I know each one infuses the other. A self-study of my work as a practitioner-research facilitator and participant demands that I acknowledge how each self influences and informs the other. In making explicit the interaction between my professional and personal selves, it is my desire that I uncover, in some small way, the formation of a teacher educator who, towards the end of an academic career, is continuing to reflect on matters of identity and practice.

How then do I see myself as an academic practitioner engaged in facilitating and participating in critical enquiry that avoids being celebratory, cathartic, and confessional (Pillow, 2003). I begin to answer this question by drawing upon an ingenious device used by a radio programme to commence a conversation with its guests – a conversation intended to reveal insights into their ways of understanding themselves.

Two books and a person

A local radio station, in its late night broadcast, regularly interviews a range of participants regarding two books and a person that have influenced them in becoming who they are. You, the reader may say, "surely self understanding rests upon more than such flimsy props?" and of course this is so. However, the very act of selection requires the making of the tacit more explicit, more tangible, and more contestable. So what books and which person, out of the many, would I select?

While on study leave at the Centre for Applied Research in Education (CARE) at the University of East Anglia in the early 1980s, I had the privilege of working alongside Professor Jean Rudduck who was organizing the archives of the late Lawrence Stenhouse. Among his memoranda were several references to *The History Primer* (Hexter, 1972). Stenhouse found this work a powerful critique of what he saw to be a spurious claim on the part of social scientists to a form of detached rationality. On finding the book I was unable to stop reading it and I return to it to this day. I was captured from the outset by the book's structure. It commenced with a "non-chapter". More than a prologue, this section of the book is a reader's organizer that explains how and why the book is titled as it is. The non-chapter acts to seduce the reader by its seemingly accessible and transparent language. You want to read on, because you think you understand, only later to be stopped in your tracks time and again by the complexity of the argument. For me, the engagement with a rich and multilayered text, one that challenges and confronts one's beliefs and practices, is a text to which one wishes to return. In Hexter's own phrasing, it is what makes writing about practice, in this case doing history, so easy and so hard.

But textual seduction is not a sufficient reason to include this book as being one that is both powerful and influential on my development as an academic practitioner. Most importantly, it was Hexter's idea of "the second record" (pp. 104–144) that I found so intriguing, just as it had captured the imagination of Stenhouse. For Hexter the second record is "indefinite in scope, and much of it personal, individual, ephemeral and not publicly accessible" (p. 104). The second record is that which the historian, or for that matter any practitioner, brings to the practice that comes from his or her life experience. It is omnipresent. Thus, Hexter's various attempts to render the past intelligible come not only from his scholarship and enquiries but also from those things that he has encountered on his life's journey.

> Once one recognises that a very, very large part of each man's [sic] second record consists of the knowledge of himself and of others that he uses to steer himself through the daily dilemmas and difficulties of living, to question whether in his struggle with the record of the past a historian should use knowledge so relevant to understanding human conduct and so regularly tried in the crucible of experience becomes almost impertinent. (Hester, 1972, p. 125)

Hexter's argument is not *whether* the second record should be drawn upon, but *how*, and *how best* it might be utilized. Thirty years on, these remain questions for the social practitioner; although today there may be a greater willingness to admit the second record, take, for example, Thomson's (2004) words:

> Some say that all research is autobiographical. The person of the researcher saturates enquiry; from the formulation of the problem, the designation and

production of the data, the analysis of the words, numbers and/or images, to the crafting of the final text. (p. 44)

I want here to pause in order to provide a practical example of a second record that will serve to demonstrate one of the many ways in which it affects and influences my own professional practice. I have chosen to list the books (both fiction and non-fiction) that currently are on my bedside table and provide beneath each one the ways in which it is impacting upon my thinking and deliberations:

- Terry Eagleton's *After Theory*

This was a Christmas gift from my son. Its language is bold and provocative. It proposes that we have already gone beyond the frivolities and hedonism of postmodernism and that we must now more seriously engage with love, evil, death, morality, metaphysics, religion, and revolution. It is particularly apposite in today's troubled world and asks us to "burrow through complex swathes of self-deception" (p. 137). It has assisted me in reconnecting with my modernist roots.

- David Marr & Marian Wilkinson's *Dark Victory*

At the time of writing this chapter Australia has just completed a federal election. *Dark Victory*, a most troubling work, traces the campaign against boat people fleeing such places as Afghanistan and Iraq in leaky and unseaworthy vessels. It commences with the saga of the *Tampa* and concludes with the sinking of the SIEV X and the since discredited tales of throwing children overboard. I borrowed this book from our local library because I wanted to understand better how it is that "evidence" can be so distorted and why we need to treat the term with such caution. I am puzzled by its lack of impact upon the political discussions that swirled around the election. In terms of my professional self, it confirmed my concerns about the unproblematized treatment of the phrase "evidence-based practice" by so many government authorities when looking to make decisions about what counts as good practice. All too often there seems to be an inclination to search for "best practice" on the grounds of irrefutable evidence – a chimera if ever there was one.

- Robert Dessaix's *Night Letters* (1997)

When reading this book I hear the mellifluous voice of the author. A frequent contributor to Australian broadcasting, Robert Dessaix has a distinctive voice and a gift for rendering the most prosaic, poetic. It acts as constant reminder that the text, the writer, and the reader are indivisible. It brings to the fore the ongoing understanding that when engaged in educational enquiry, my own history and value system are inextricably linked into the what, how, and why of my investigations.

- Ian Rankin's *A Question of Blood* (2003)

Yes, I like crime fiction. I like to lose myself in circumstances I am never likely to find myself in. At the same time, I particularly choose writers such as Rankin because they write of places that I know, places that I can return to in my head and have my "safe" adventures.

Each of these books, then, is currently informing my second record, which is a mix of many things including elements of my domestic life such as my daughter's struggle with concepts of history and reconciliation in writing her master's thesis, or my husband's concerns as a community activist forever engaging with government in relation to local environmental problems such as airport noise, waste transfer facilities, and traffic emissions. As I read drafts of my daughter's thesis or newsletters prepared by my partner, or engage in dinner conversation with them, I am meeting new ideas and concepts that cannot fail to influence and affect me.

I return to a second influential book from the past. The other book that I cite as having profoundly influenced me is Colin Turnbull's *The Mountain People* (1973). I was introduced to this text by my brother. He too wanted to interrupt my previously held beliefs about scientific rationality. Turnbull 's study of the Ik, unlike any other of its kind, is brutal, harrowing, and pessimistic. He finds that he cannot escape being judgemental. As the careful recorder of Ik life, Turnbull follows the anthropological code but in the end confesses to a loathing of the people and their way of life. It is not a pleasant book to read; indeed many would wish to dismiss it as some dreadful form of outmoded imperialism. What is significant, for me, is that it is an example of the inescapability of the emotions of the researcher. Turnbull's account is more an account of his own despair than of the desperate conditions of the people he was studying.

Finally, to the person. So many from whom to choose, but as I examine my own public voice, I find the person to whom I most regularly return is the late Lawrence Stenhouse. In a recent chapter on critical practitioner enquiry (Groundwater-Smith & Dadds, 2004, pp. 240–241), I wrote that Stenhouse's minimal definition of research is that it is systematic self-critical enquiry, based upon a stable and deep curiosity (1981). He has also written of research as systematic enquiry made public (Stenhouse, 1979). Stenhouse argues that curiosity is wonderfully dangerous because it leads to social change. It proposes heresy and threatens faith. It gives a better-informed context for action than blind faith would lead us to. In contemporary terms, such research is evidence-based enquiry.

Stenhouse believes the researcher is never free of his or her values; he places a greater emphasis upon *interests* and the ways in which researcher interests can be made transparent. The researcher is interested in the phenomenon being examined, not only in terms of the curiosity but also in terms of perceived advantages and disadvantages that may arise from the work. For Stenhouse, research work is moral work. No one can claim theoretical innocence.

Transparency lies behind Stenhouse's concern with publication. Research that remains private cannot be scrutinized and critiqued. Unfortunately, much that is made public is not made available. Stenhouse (1981) suggests that "perhaps too much research is published to the world, too little to the village" (p. 17). For him the local collegiate group, dedicated to action, is the first audience for practitioner research.

As an academic practitioner who both facilitates and participates in practitioner enquiry, this brief exercise of deciding upon two books and a person has revealed to me some fundamental concerns about my practice, as indeed have those other revelations about bedside reading and family interests. How then is my practice influenced by my second record? How do I deal with matters of judgement? How can I argue that evidence-based practice is moral work beyond mere technical-rational decision-making? Before addressing these questions more directly I think it would be helpful to outline the context in which I currently operate.

Facilitating and participating in practitioner enquiry

Since leaving a full time academic appointment I have had the great pleasure and privilege to work as a consultant researcher and facilitator of practitioner enquiry with individual schools, employing authorities, and teacher education programmes in a number of Australian states and territories. A consistent thread weaving through the various consultancies and honorary appointments has been a concern to enhance understandings of what constitutes practitioner enquiry and how we might engage young people in schools more directly in investigating their lives within them. For young people do not merely "attend" school, they live out a considerable part of their lives within them, including not only their academic lives but their social lives also. Schools and their practices are agents in shaping how young people see and understand themselves.

Where does one draw the line between facilitating and participating in practitioner enquiry? In reflecting upon my academic work I find that the boundaries between the two are not always readily identifiable. In considering a large national Australian programme, Innovative Links Between Schools and Universities for Teacher Professional Development (Groundwater-Smith, 1998), I wrote about the project as an action research – based professional development project initiated as a key component of the National Professional Development Program. Teachers involved in the project worked in partnership with academic associates from 14 universities to use collaborative action research to implement programmes of school reform aimed at improving teaching competencies and learning outcomes for all students. Specifically they were expected to:

- use action research to implement programmes of school reform;
- engage in professional discourse and critical reflection;
- engage in professional reading and writing;
- engage in reciprocal learning about teaching, learning, and educational reform; and
- translate learning into improved teaching and learning outcomes for students.

I argued that the role of facilitator was to assist the practitioners in surfacing issues through the collection, analysis, and interpretation of evidence. The intimation was that the facilitator did not actively engage in these actions himself or herself, but maintained a more removed stance providing advice and resources. In effect, such neutrality is not possible. As McTaggart (2002) maintains, this position would reduce the role to one of "process consultant" acting as technical adviser denying the social responsibility to participate in the change itself. In more recent years, I have found myself more substantially and less ambiguously engaged. In effect, my professional self is undergoing a transformation, partly, I suspect, as a result of being less bound and constrained by the regularities of university life. (While engaged in the Innovative Links Project, I was still a full-time member of an academic staff). As I have indicated, since then I have held a number of honorary positions, including directing the Centre for Practitioner Research at the University of Sydney. At the same time I have developed a consultancy based upon educational research and teacher professional learning. While mindful of engaging in ethical professional practice, I have not found myself constrained by the regulatory frameworks of the University or the specific expectations of what "counts" as educational research (see Yates, 2004).) This change is best represented in my work with the Coalition of Knowledge Building Schools (Groundwater-Smith & Mockler, 2002a, b).

Early in 2001, in New South Wales, Sydney, teachers from a small number of schools three from the government sector and three from independent schools sat together and discussed the possible formation of a Coalition of Knowledge Building Schools. They saw themselves contributing to the ongoing improvement of the work of their schools through the systematic and public collection and discussion of evidence regarding teaching and learning within the lived life of the school. They shared a view that evidence was best considered in the forensic rather than adversarial environment (see Groundwater-Smith & Dadds, 2004 for a further discussion of this distinction); i.e., that it should be constructed and examined in ways that illuminate understanding rather than as a means of proving a particular case.

The Coalition believes that by embedding enquiry practices into the daily work of the schools it is possible to evolve an authentic workplace learning culture. The members recognize that professional learning is not an exclusively individualistic enterprise, but that learning and growth can take place at the organizational or corporate level. In effect, the Coalition is a community of practice (Wenger, 1998). The notable feature regarding this work is not only the detail of what was done and the ways in which it was accomplished but also the ways in which it enables the teachers to reflect together. Much of the previous work on teacher thinking has focused upon reflection as an individual act, rather than a collegial communicative exercise.

The formation of the Coalition has been a dialogic exercise, which has engaged the school-based practitioners with each other and with critical friends in the academic community, including myself. Kemmis (2000) speaks of connecting the life-worlds of educational research. Academic researchers, albeit in an honorary capacity in my case, and practitioner researchers working in the school environment operate in different realms with different mores and rewards; some have characterized these as parallel universes. Nonetheless, as I am coming to see more clearly, the problems and processes on one side are interconnected with problems and processes on the other. Real dialogue between each of us can contribute to a more inclusive critique of educational practices as well as informed, well-judged actions.

Ebbutt (2002) makes a distinction between schools engaged in: (1) no culture of research; (2) emergent research culture; (3) established research culture; and (4) established-embedded research culture. Of the nine schools now in the Coalition, four would be in the second category, three in the third, and two in the fourth. This mix makes for very generative interaction between the schools as they share and discuss their various enquiries.

What is of particular note is that the Coalition did not form in response to external initiatives such as a funded programme or university partnership, but because the schools themselves had an expressed desire to work in a particular way. Indeed, they now look outward to support professional learning further afield. Five of the member schools worked with me and the audience research unit of the Australian Museum to investigate what assists and impedes learning in that museum (Groundwater-Smith & Kelly, 2003).

This, then, is a very different context than that outlined in relation to the Innovative Links Project. It is now the case that I work alongside my school-based colleagues as, together, we design studies, gather data, and make sense of the evidence. Indeed, in a number of situations school students themselves are involved not only as informants but also as active participants in the enquiry processes (Needham & Groundwater-Smith, 2003). It is one such study, where student voice has been paramount, that has served to highlight for me some of the difficulties that are faced when the need to know and understand is confronted by the need to protect, perhaps even self-censor (Tickle, 2001).

On being unsettled

As a result of a large funded study (not cited here in an effort to protect the anonymity of the school), I was invited back to work with a school who could see clear benefits in involving their students in an investigation of what might be done in order to assist them in "learning to do school". The school has also recently become a member of the Coalition.

Schools exist to educate their students, but it is a curious thing that as the "consequential stakeholders" (a phrase that has long been used by the Queensland Board of Teacher Registration) with respect to the many decisions that go into the organization of schools, curriculum, and assessment practices, students are rarely consulted about what happens in their classrooms, in the playground, and more generally in the ways in which the purposes of schooling are discussed. As Crane (2001) indicates in her portrayal of the Students as Researchers project at Shambrook Upper School and Community College, UK:

> Not only can the students come to school to learn; but they can and indeed must be an integral part of the school's own learning. Schools cannot learn how to become better places for learning without asking the students. (p. 54)

The case study upon which I draw demonstrates that students can both participate in enquiry processes and be reflective about their own lives and the place of school in them. This study not only illustrates the power of student voice but also gives insight into the social attitudes and practices that are part of the lives of young boys in a predominantly Arabic community that was and remains under great stress. The study had two components: the first of these was where young students assisted in developing key questions, trained as conductors of focus group investigations, and assisted in analysis and interpretation of the data; the second component, on which I will more fully report, rested upon individual interviews with senior students regarding the ways in which they understood their families and their community contributed to their learning and their judgements and concerns about the conditions for learning within their school.

The second phase of the study followed my observations of the Grade 11 Studies Skills Programme. I was particularly unsettled by the angry and disruptive behaviour of a number of boys. I found it difficult not to judge them as "ingrates" who failed to appreciate the work that had gone into preparing a programme designed to assist them in being ready for the tests and examinations required by the State. In some ways I was experiencing that sense of anger and alienation about which Colin Turnbull wrote. A number of issues were raised with the school principal, the deputy principal, and the head of English. In this sense, I was acting not only as a facilitator of the enquiry but also as an interested, indeed judgemental participant, for the disruptive behaviour of a number of boys greatly concerned me, as it did the teachers. Among the agreed issues were:

(1) The need to connect learning to students' experiences in and out of school and to their goals and aspirations.
(2) The challenges faced by senior students undertaking high stakes assessment when they often do not have the vocabulary for deep engagement with their learning.
(3) The pedagogic requirement for teachers and students to be explicit in teaching and learning strategies.
(4) The necessity to motivate students by drawing attention to the practical implications of the skills of paying attention and dealing positively with distractions.

In discussing these issues I expressed that students had difficulty in fully appreciating what it is to "do school" in the context of a statewide curriculum framework where their achievements and outcomes would be compared to those of other young people of their age and stage in learning. I believed that there was a lack of congruence between experiences in the home and community and those in the school. This was not taken to be a negative judgement of home and community, but rather that the fit was problematic.

As a result of the discussion with the senior management of the school it was thought fruitful to take the concept of "student voice" and extend it to the senior end of the school, in particular grade 11. It was agreed that individual interviews would be conducted with a random sample of one-third of the grade 11 student cohort as they began their grade 12. Some time was spent with key members of staff considering how best to shape the interview in ways that would be engaging for the students.

Prior to the interviews taking place, each student was given the opportunity to sign an informed consent form, which had been explained to him or her. One student decided to withdraw from the interview without sanction or penalty. He returned later requesting an opportunity to undertake the interview. Each interview commenced with an orientation to its purpose, which was to gain students' perceptions of how school works for them against the background of living in their families and in the community. As a method of discussing the home context, students were asked: "If you were to take five photographs of your family, what would you photograph and why?"

This chapter does not have the scope to present the results of this study. Its design has been detailed to illustrate that my role went beyond facilitation as I became involved in the study as a participant in the discourse regarding the educational needs and provisions for boys in a volatile and troubling context. I was certainly not a disinterested participant. On the one hand, I understood the constraints placed upon the school and the boys by State policies developed around a competitive academic curriculum that seemed quite unsuited to a number of the boys' needs. On the other hand, I was concerned that students themselves placed impediments in the way of those of their peers who did wish to engage with that curriculum.

As an outcome of the study and at the request of the school principal, I prepared a discussion paper, and it is to some particular features of that paper that I now wish to turn, in that I became aware of how unsettling the discussion would be in the context of a school environment that acts to test the patience and goodwill of all of the stakeholders: students, teachers, and parents alike. I was mindful of the teachers, who would be the principal audience to the paper, having to deal with many of its matters on a day-to-day practical basis, and that its contents should aim to stimulate some new discussion on old and enduring issues.

In the paper I argued that there is a need for the students and their teachers to understand not only their multiple ethnic cultures but also their youth culture and how and why their daily interactions are affected by their differing cultural practices. As Hickey & Fitzclarence (2000), in their study of adolescent male culture, and Keddie (2003), in her study of younger boys' friendship groups, have indicated, peer culture is a potent force in shaping boys' understandings of themselves and of others. They point to boys' powerful desire for self-legitimation and belonging as central to their construction of their masculine identity.

Importantly, I argued in the paper that it must be acknowledged that students' identity formation is not identical; it should not be imagined that they are an undifferentiated group (Moya, 2002, pp. 136–174). Some play sport, or music; others like art or to tinker. Each has their own biographical history.

Hechter and Okamoto (2001) see that urbanization and the increased crowding of cities is bringing groups into closer and closer contact. They argue that this makes ethnic coexistence, particularly between adolescents, a paramount concern. Therefore, it is essential that connecting learning to students' experiences must first of all recognize not only the diversity of those experiences but also that they are, in the main, positive and valuable ones. As Thomson (2002) has pointed out in her powerful and extended study of schools operating in difficult circumstances, students from varying backgrounds carry (metaphorically) very different things in their school bags and this impacts upon their success within the school system:

> The children who are most often successful are those who already possess, by virtue of who they are and where they come from, some of the cultural capital that counts for school success. Through the game of schooling they acquire more. They are able to do this because they are "at home" with both the ways in which schools operate and with the kinds of knowledge the cultural capital involved. They are at ease in the place called school – it is their place. (p.5)

I indicated, in the discussion paper, that it is important and realistic to recognize that while the students have considerable cultural currency, it is not necessarily in the coinage that is validated by the school curriculum or the high stakes assessment at the conclusion to the senior years. A significant purpose for schools such as the one covered in this case study has been to provide its students with the proper rates of exchange in order that they can participate fully in the mainstream culture.

This brings me to return to what I have found to be so unsettling. In the paper I concluded that nearly 30 years ago Paul Willis, in his study of working class "lads" in England, wrote:

> The difficult thing to explain about how middle class kids get middle class jobs is why others let them. The difficult thing to explain about how working class kids get working class jobs is why they let themselves. (Willis, 1977, p. 1)

Since then he has noticed that

> [a]lthough the social and political landscape has changed there continues to be very hard and persistent elements of resistant culture in schools. Despite their sometimes anti-social nature and the undoubted difficulties they produce for classroom teachers, these cultures continue to pose in living form, crucial and collective questions from the point of view of the working class: What is "progress" for? What can I/we expect from the sacrifice of hard work and obedience in school? (Willis, 2003, p. 396.)

I pointed out that the boys, whose voices have been central to the case study, face a fundamental dilemma; they simultaneously resist and seek for conditions that will allow them to engage more effectively with their learning. School for many of them and their families is akin to "a new land". In his reflections, through the disciplinary lens of ecology, Flannery has written:

> The issue of cultural maladaption is a critical one for these people (inhabitants of new lands). In many instances their maladapted cultures are dramatically incompatible with the environment they find themselves in, and it may take a very long time for them to adjust. (Flannery, 1994, p. 389)

Flannery goes on to propose that one survival strategy has been to survive in the present at the expense of the future. An argument could be made on the basis of observations of classroom confrontation that the students in this challenging school are effectively consuming their futures. This claim is clearly judgemental. Have I stepped beyond the boundaries that are reasonable to expect of my professional self? Has my personal self, which wishes to see schools as calm, creative havens where young people can substantially engage in productive learning (McFadden & Munns, 2002), been so affronted that I would prefer to judge the students rather than the circumstances that have created such residualized schools and such apparently irrelevant curricula in the first place? Has my own second record that is based upon a biography of academic success too readily influenced a belief that such success should be the aspiration of all students? As McNamee (2001) has observed:

> There are ranges of everyday circumstances in which we come to know things we surely wish we did not. The phrase "when wisdom wakens woe" is felicitous

> in precisely these circumstances. One thing is certain, though: our researcher cannot "un-know" matters. There is a sense in which our researcher must wish she had not come to hold such knowledge. It weighs her down. But how to characterise the accompanying emotional state: that is a philosophical and not merely psychological challenge. (p. 433)

Neither I nor the teachers with whom I worked can "unknow" either our own experiences or the values that have infused them and resulted from them. But what we can do is make those values more explicit and transparent, such that they too can be challenged. We need to explore those values in light of our professional and personal histories as Hexter did in his evocation of the second record. We need to understand why it is that we feel hostile to those very young people whose lives we seek to improve. These things we can best do when we follow Stenhouse's direction to make public our reflections.

Conclusion

In this chapter I have raised what I see to be some critical issues regarding the ways in which practitioner enquiry interacts with professional identity for all who participate, but most particularly in relation to my own formation. I have argued that there is an ongoing imperative that, as a professional community, we constantly interrogate our beliefs and values if we are to engage in careerlong professional learning. Each of us needs to develop ways to make our second record explicit by revealing something of our life histories, scrutinizing the ways in which they influence our professional lives, and doing so in a public, rather than private, form.

As I reflect upon my experiences I have come to appreciate that our professional identities are more fragile than I had imagined. During a professional career we need from time to time to stop and reflect upon some large and troubling questions – questions that will certainly lead us to return to some fundamental social issues associated with the very purposes of schooling. Facilitating practitioner enquiry, in general, and the case study that I have cited, in particular, serve to surface some of those questions. Among them are:

- Why do we, as teachers and teacher educators, unintentionally conspire with government policies that valorize the competitive academic curriculum; compel reluctant learners to attend schools that do not meet their needs; assess learning achievement within normative and normalizing frameworks; and, create marketplaces for schools that inevitably lead to residualization?
- Are we consciously aware of our own values and beliefs and the ways in which these infuse our ideological stance with respect to schools and their purposes?
- Do we question the distribution of power in the schools, in which and with which we work, and the consequences that this distribution has upon the ways in which we might act, grow, and develop?
- Can we permit ourselves a right to be angry about the circumstances that we face from time to time, and, if so, can we channel that anger into productive practices and policies?

When I began to write this chapter, I was not entirely comfortable with revealing so much of myself and wondered of what consequence it would be to those who read it with an interest in teacher professional learning and development. Even now, many drafts later, I do not know the nature of its impact, but I do know that I have learned something about myself and the way in which my professional identity is constructed.

For me, facilitating and participating in practitioner enquiry certainly has the effect of being the stone in the shoe. It is often more than a little uncomfortable, but in the end immensely liberating. For all of us, as those who are engaged in professional learning, acknowledging and understanding our second record and its impact upon what and how we engage in our practice is a matter with which we need to be deeply and vitally concerned.

Izaak Walton (1653) wrote in *The Compleat Angler or The Contemplative Man's Recreation*: "Angling may be said to be so like mathematics that it can never be fully learnt." Just as one can always learn more about fishing, or indeed mathematics, so too one continually learns about oneself.

References

Crane, B. (2001). Revolutionalising school-based research. *In Forum*, 43(2), 54–57.
Dessaix, R. (1997). *Night letters*. Sydney: Picador.
Eagleton, T. (2003). *After theory*. London: Allen Lane.
Ebbutt, D. (2002). Developing a research culture. *Educational Action Research*, 10(1), 123–140.
Flannery. T. (1994), *The future eaters*. Kew, Victoria: Reed Books.
Groundwater-Smith, S. (1998). Putting teacher professional judgement to work. *Educational Action Research*, 6(1), 21–37.
Groundwater-Smith, S. & Dadds, M. (2004). Critical practitioner inquiry. In C. Day & J. Sachs (Eds.), *International handbook on the continuing professional development of teachers* (pp. 238–263). Maidenhead, Berkshire: Open University Press.
Groundwater-Smith, S. & Kelly, L. (2003). *As we see it: Improving learning in the museum*. Paper presented to the British Educational Research Annual Conference, Edinburgh, September 2003.
Groundwater-Smith, S. & Mockler, N, (2002a). *Building knowledge, building professionalism: The coalition of knowledge building schools and teacher professionalism*. Paper presented to the Australian Association for Educational Research Annual Conference, University of Queensland, December 1–5, 2002.
Groundwater-Smith, S. & Mockler, N. (2002b). The knowledge-building school: From the inside out, from the outside in. *Change: Transformations in Education*, 5(2), 15–24.
Hechter, M. & Okamoto, D. (2001). Political consequences of Minority Group Formation. *Annual Review of Political Science*, 4, 189–215.
Hexter, J. (1972). *The history primer*. London: Allen Lane.
Hickey, C. & Fitzclarence, L. (2000). Peers peering at the individual: Problems with trying to teach young males not to be like their peers. *Australian Educational Researcher*, 27(1), 71–92.
Keddie, A. (2003). Little boys: Tomorrow's macho lads. *Discourse*, 24(3), 289–306.
Kemmis, S. (2000). Educational research and evaluation: Opening communicative space. The 2000 Radford Memorial Lecture presented at the Annual Conference of the Australian Association for Research in Education, Sydney, December.
Marr, D. & Wilkinson, M. (2003). *Dark victory*. Sydney: Allen & Unwin.
McFadden, M. & Munns, G. (2002). Student engagement and the social relations of pedagogy. *British Journal of Sociology of Education*, 23(3), 357–366.

McNamee, M. (2001). The guilt of whistle blowing: Conflicts in action research and educational ethnography. *Journal of Philosophy of Education, 35*(3), 423–442.

McTaggart, R. (2002). The mission of the Scholar in Action Research. In M. Wolfe & C. Pryor (Eds,), *The mission of the scholar: Research and practice* (pp. 1–16). London: Peter Lang. Moya, P. (2002). *Learning from experience.* Berkeley, CA: University of California Press. Needham, K. & Groundwater-Smith, S. (2003). *Using student voice to inform school improvement.* Paper presented to International Congress for School Effectiveness and Improvement, Sydney, January 2003.

Pillow, W. (2003). Confession, catharsis or cure? Rethinking the uses of reflexivity as methodological power in qualitative research. *Qualitative Studies in Education, 16*(2), 175–196.

Rankin, I. (2003). *A question of blood*, London: Orion Books.

Stenhouse, L. (1979). Research as a basis for teaching. Inaugural lecture, University of East Anglia. In L. Stenhouse (Ed.) (1983), *Authority, education and emancipation.* London: Heinemann Educational Books.

Stenhouse, L. (1981) What counts as research? *British Journal of Educational Studies, 29*(2). Reprinted in J. Rudduck & D. Hopkins (Eds.) (1985), *Research as a basis for teaching* (pp. 8–24). London: Heinemann Educational Books.

Thomson, P. (2002). Schooling the Rustbelt kids. Sydney: Allen & Unwin.

Thomson, P. (2004). Severed heads and compliant bodies? A speculation about principal identities. *In Discourse, 25*(1), 43–59.

Tickle, L. (2001). Opening windows, closing doors: Ethical dilemmas in educational action research. *Journal of Philosophy of Education, 35*(3), 345–360.

Turnbull, C. (1973). *The mountain people.* London: Jonathon Cape.

Walton, I. (1653). *The compleat angler.* Rich Marriot, St. Dunstan's Churchyard, Fleetstreet.

Wenger, E. (1998). *Communities of practice: Learning, meaning and identity.* Cambridge: Cambridge University Press.

Willis, P. (1977). *Learning to labour: How working class kids get working class jobs.* Farnborough Hants, Hampshire: Saxon House.

Willis, P. (2003). Foot soldiers of modernity: The dialectics of cultural consumption and the twenty-first century school. *In Harvard Education Review, 73*(3), 39–15.

Yates, L. (2004). *What does good education research look like?* Maidenhead, Berkshire: Open University Press.

CHAPTER 7

PROFESSIONAL KNOWLEDGE FORMATION IN THE AUSTRALIAN EDUCATIONAL MARKET PLACE
Changing the perspective

Susan Groundwater-Smith

Knowledge creation and the educational market place

On the first Saturday of every month, down by the wharves of Sydney Harbour, there is a Growers' Market. Fresh produce, cheeses, olives, oils, fine fruit and vegetables, organic meats, flowers, tiny cakes and tarts are all set out for those who eschew the banality of the supermarket shelves to sample and buy. People meet, dogs investigate, coffee is drunk in Sydney's balmy weather. Regulars not only buy, they discuss, argue and debate. Points of view are exchanged as much as goods and services; some conversations commence where they left off the month before. This is the market place, the *Agora*, that Nowotny, Scott and Gibbons (2003) so powerfully evoke as a metaphor for knowledge formation in contrast to the disciplined sites of production so characterised by university faculties and government sponsored research centres. The *Agora,* that ancient market place was such a place, where it was not only goods that were traded but was also a site where political, commercial, administrative and social activity occurred. Ideas were as central and vital to the *Agora* as the commodities that were there to be bought and sold. Education, and its emblematic heart, the school, is similarly a site where ideas are developed and traded and where professional knowledge is developed.

For too long the association of Education with the market place has been related to the trading of schooling itself in an environment in which education is treated as a commodity that can be marketed like any other. The current national coalition government in Australia, that has held federal power since 1996 has been a strong advocate of choice in education. It is difficult to argue with Marginson's allegation that the coalition government has been seeking to deregulate the education market (Marginson, 1997: 15). Australian parents are being encouraged to make their choices about secondary schooling. They are led to believe that there is a great distinctiveness between schools. But the implicit message is that the distinctiveness is not between schools in general, but between government and non-government schools in particular. As a case in point, the drift to non-government schooling in New South Wales (one of the six states and two territories of which Australia is composed) can be seen reflected in a continuing trend that showed 65% of secondary school age students enrolled in government schools in 2000, compared to 66.9% in 1998, and 67.5% in 1997.

Market theories of education, within this discourse, see the consumer as the beneficiary. But, of course, matters are not so simple. Certainly, individuals can and do benefit from a market orientation. It has already been widely argued, for example, that elite, prestigious schools can act to support the individual's access to power and status. This can be said to be more to do with cultural capital than cognitive attainment. The student gains membership to a club. Anderson (1993) has further suggested that Catholic secondary education, that caters for the majority of students in the non-government sector in Australia, with its norms of discipline and conformity also give individuals assets which they can take to employment within certain regimes of power and control.

This article, in its consideration of knowledge formation in the market place, will focus primarily on the notion of the *Agora*. Thus, the title of this article carries within it the possibility of changing two perspectives: one of these is that of professional knowledge formation as in the *Agora*, the second more implicitly, changing the educational market place itself.

Mode 2 knowledge and why it is essential for education

Knowledge creation is now a matter for significant contestation and debate as the "Knowledge Society" (Stehr, 1994) emerges and develops. Knowledge has assumed the leading role in social and economic change. What counts as professional knowledge is a much more interesting and complex matter than in times gone by, when it was seen that it was the role of academia and dedicated government agencies to develop such knowledge and communicate it to the cognate profession. It is particularly pertinent for those who have an interest and concern for teacher professional learning.

In their initial work Gibbons, *et al.* (1994) developed our understanding that knowledge creation is not exclusively a matter for scientists and academics working in institutions but may be socially produced and distributed in the form of what they coined as "Mode 2 Knowledge". Such knowledge production is concerned with the identification and solution of practical problems in the lived professional lives of practitioners and organizations which are not encircled by the boundaries of single disciplines with their many rules and customary practices. It is reflexive knowledge in that it results from a dialogic process as conversations in the field. They posed the proposition that the production of knowledge and the processes of research were due for a radical transformation. They saw "Mode 1 Knowledge" as founded upon the orthodoxies of discipline based scientific inquiry and driven by the norms and conventions of those disciplines. In a second work (Nowotny, Scott and Gibbons, 2001) they developed their argument, noting that the great subsystems of modernity: State; Market; Culture and Science itself, once so clearly partitioned were becoming increasingly transgressive. This fuzziness helped to create the transactional spaces in which Mode 2 knowledge could be developed.

Interestingly, the very concept of "fuzziness" is itself deserving of elaboration. A term coined by Kosko (1993) it metaphorically moves us from the black and white of much empiricist science to the shades of grey representing the complexities, nuances and subtleties of the human world. It allows us to develop a greater tolerance for all of the ambiguities lodged therein. Kosko and Isaka (1993) suggested that "fuzzy logic is a branch of machine intelligence that helps computers paint grey, commonsense pictures of an uncertain world" (p. 76). It requires the use of practical, but imprecise rules and allows for a myriad of possibilities rather than a set of fixed solutions and "can often better model the vagueness of the world than can black and white concepts" (p.81).

For too long policies in Education have assumed that there are indeed, fixed solutions, that somewhere there is the elusive "best practice" that can be created, adopted and adapted. Just as for a time there was the notion of "one size fits all" in the clothing industry (absurd as that proposition was) there were thought to be international solutions to matters as wide ranging as literacy instruction, behaviour management and overall school improvement, irrespective of contextual variations. Increasingly, today in Australia, there is a recognition that professional knowledge through formation requires input, not only from academia and government agencies but through the investigations and inquiries of those inside the profession itself. It is noteworthy that many writers have recognised the need to develop professional knowledge *with* the field of practice, rather than *for* the field of practice. The prepositional change is not one to be taken lightly. As Gore and Gitlin (2004) claim "We need to work with teachers to explore the limits and possibilities of research for their work as teachers" (p.52). Furthermore, they believe that this is achieved, not only by engaging in joint research activities but also by exposing and analysing the politics of research and the power relations therein. In this way a genuine parity of esteem within the community of practice, with the purpose of improving learning for all, can be achieved.

Getting inside practice

So, how do we develop professional knowledge within the field of practice? Oliver Sacks in his preface to *An Anthropologist on Mars* (Sacks, 1995) quotes from G.K. Chesterton's spiritual detective, Father Brown, who when asked of his method for investigating phenomena said:

> (Science means) getting *outside* a man (sic) and studying him as if he were a gigantic insect; in what they would call a dry impartial light, in what I should call a dead and dehumanising light. They mean getting a long way off him, as if he were a distant prehistoric monster; staring at the shape of him... When the scientist talks about a type, he never means himself, but always his neighbour; probably his poorer neighbour. I don't deny the dry light may sometimes do good; though in one sense it's the very reverse of science. So far from being knowledge, it's actually the suppression of what we know... I don't try to get outside the man. I try to get inside. (p.*xv*)

Getting inside in the practice of Education, in particular school education, means getting inside the school itself working with those most directly concerned with the enterprise: teachers; students; and their parents/caregivers.

Increasingly, Australian policy makers in the field of Education are acknowledging the power of the kind of professional insight developed within the knowledge creating school. The school, as a knowledge building organization has been discussed widely, notably by David Hargreaves (1999) who first drew our attention to the notion of the knowledge creating school, arguing that schools have within them significant professional knowledge, much of which is tacit and unexamined. But the great fund of knowledge held by practitioners can scarcely be drawn upon if it remains buried beneath the surface. Hargreaves (2003) has since developed his argument, making the case for mobilising and developing the intellectual and social capital held by practitioners into a more coherent and integrated whole. Furthermore he has argued for drawing upon organisational capital in the form of networks and external links in order to inform and improve at both local and regional levels. Importantly, he believes that moving beyond incremental innovation (swimming with the tide) to radical innovation (swimming against the tide) cannot be achieved by central direction, but requires the school itself to be a learning professional life form.

The impact of teachers' practices upon student learning outcomes has now been well documented (Darling Hammond, 1996; Muijs and Reynolds, 2001; Darling Hammond and Youngs, 2002; Rowe 2003). It is the quality of teaching that has the greatest impact upon student learning. However, it can no longer be seen as acceptable that individual "hero" teachers can operate as separate entities within the school. It is essential that those teachers who are identified as having impressive pedagogical practices can and will share these with their colleagues to the advantage of all. Teachers who a make difference have to be models and coaches who will assist others in making a difference also. Rowe (2003) makes the case for quality teacher recruitment, but the majority of those who are teaching in Australian schools are already employed and may remain employed for many years. For the whole school to improve and not just individual classes under the tutelage of individual teachers it is essential that the professional learning of teachers is shared and problematised; that the educational market places is a vigorous and dynamic one. As Warren Little (2002) has observed:

> Research spanning more than two decades point consistently to the potential educational benefit of vigorous collegial communities... Researchers posit that conditions for improving teaching and learning are strengthened when teachers collectively question ineffective teaching routines, examine new conceptions of teaching and learning, find generative means to acknowledge and respond to difference and conflict and engage actively in supporting professional growth. (p. 917).

How then do we go beyond the rhetoric and look to practical examples of professional knowledge formation? This article will discuss two cases: one of a Coalition of Knowledge Building Schools, the other of a state-wide equity program where professional knowledge was documented and "traded" in the form of school learning portfolios.

The coalition of knowledge building schools

Unlike the British Networked Learning Communities the Coalition of Knowledge Building Schools is an alliance that has been formed without funding or formal government recognition. It is a loose association of eleven schools in Metropolitan

Sydney and includes primary and secondary schools from every sector: Government, Catholic Systemic and Independent. The schools range from those serving the most challenging of communities to those who are wealthy and held in high public esteem. What holds them together is a strong commitment to teacher professional learning and school improvement based upon: developing and enhancing the notion of evidence based practice; developing an interactive community of practice using appropriate technologies; making a contribution to a broader professional knowledge base with respect to educational practice; building research capability within and between schools by engaging both teachers and students in the research process: and sharing methodologies which are appropriate to practitioner enquiry as a mean of transforming teacher professional learning (Groundwater-Smith and Mockler, 2003a).

Representatives from each school meet four times a year to report upon their projects and discuss matters which might have been particularly problematic for them. As a group, they are re-defining 'evidence based practice' to be a far richer and more inclusive term than that which has been considered and rightly criticised (see for example, Elliott, 2004). They understand that we need first and foremost to be cautious about the term itself. What may at first glance appear transparent, following close and careful analysis may prove to be opaque. Certainly, they believe that the concept "evidence based practice" is a powerful and useful one; however, they also believe that we need to make some important distinctions both in terms of the context in which the phrase might apply, and in terms of the purposes to which it is to be put. As Groundwater-Smith and Dadds, 2004 argue we can characterize evidence as being used for adversarial purposes, in an attempt to "prove" the viability of a particular social practice; or we can conceive of it being of a forensic kind where the purpose is to understand a particular phenomenon with an intention to "improve" the practice. Clearly this is the disposition of the Coalition.

Space does not permit an enumeration of the ways in which the Coalition has made a contribution to the professional knowledge base. In their presentation to the Joint AARE/NZARE Annual Conference Groundwater-Smith and Mockler (2003b) reported upon eight studies, over four years, presented to various conferences and professional bodies, all of them having been co-written with practitioners in the field. A number of these studies make particular reference to the engagement of students (usually referred to in the British context as 'pupils') in the inquiry process, whereby they themselves develop a sense of agency regarding the ways in which the school may inquire about the conditions under which they are learning (see in particular Needham and Groundwater-Smith, 2003).

Sharing methodologies has been a particularly strong feature of the Coalition. A case in point is where two secondary girls' schools, one Government and one Independent have been successful grantees in a Federal Government Initiative promoting safe schools. The two schools shared methodologies and findings, thus strengthening the insight and understanding of each of them as they investigated the nature of bullying in the context of girls' schools. The publication *Learning to Listen: Listening to Learn* (Groundwater-Smith and Mockler, 2003a) is a concrete example of the ways in which the schools have pooled their innovative research methods and made them more widely available.

In detailing this work of the Coalition the intention had not been to merely celebrate its achievements, but to point to the ways in which practitioners in the field can contribute to professional knowledge formation in Education. It is an authentic market place of ideas and like any market place it is a site where there are issues and debates that continue from one 'market day' to the next. Furthermore, the Coalition does not eschew research evidence collected by the academy, members will bring to the attention of their colleagues papers that they might have found to be particularly valuable. In common with teachers consulted by Cordingley (2001) for the Teacher Training Agency in England the most valued research evidence was that which is collected through genuine partnerships between researchers and teacher in authentic classroom contexts and derived from rigorous and transparent methods that related to authentic questions to do with teaching and learning.

A second and different example of "getting inside practice" in relation to professional knowledge formation is a New South Wales State Government Program with its reporting mechanism of the school learning portfolio.

The priority action schools program

The Priority Action Schools Program (PASP), a $A16 million equity program jointly supported by the NSW Department of Education and Training and the NSW Teachers Federation (the teachers' union) was designed to provide intensive support to 74 primary, central and high schools with concentrations of students from low socio-economic status (SES) communities over the 2003 school year. All schools participating in the program faced issues related to low student achievement, behaviour management and attendance as well as serving communities dealing with significant hardship.

The key tenets of the program were to build individual and school capacity through:

- The creation of professional knowledge developed from practitioner research and evaluation processes;
- Strengthened planning, implementation and evaluation processes;
- Whole school approaches to improved teaching practice; and
- Mentoring, reflection and professional dialogue.

The program valued context based action through:

- The involvement of the whole school community in identifying issues and potential solutions; and
- The provision of support to schools to trial and evaluate local solutions.

Importantly, there were provisions for partnerships with:

- The PASP team of senior DET and Union officers;
- Academics/critical friends;
- Other schools and networks; and
- Other agencies (such as health and housing).

The report upon the project cannot be synthesised here in a way that would do justice to its stretch and complexity (for results of the meta evaluation see Groundwater-Smith and Kemmis 2003). Instead the emphasis will be upon the ways in which the participating schools collected, analysed and interpreted their evidence in the form of a school learning portfolio.

Implicit in the development of a learning portfolio is a recognition that schools are places where teachers learn as do their students. They learn what is expected of them; their craft, their professional responsibilities, their need to develop new strategies in response to new policies; as well as that which arises from their daily interactions with their peers, students and the community. What is less recognised is that schools can also be seen as corporate learning organizations where it is the institution itself that learns, learns to adapt and cope, learns to innovate and learns to be resilient. This perspective was new to many of the PASP schools, but was central to the success of the program.

MacGilchrist, Myers and Reed (2004) have focused upon schools as institutions that are dynamic and organic in their nature. Drawing on notions of multiple intelligence and recent thinking about the nature of organisations, they offer a way of looking at schools as living systems through the exploration of the concept of the *'intelligent school'*. For them, intelligent schools are human communities that are continuously developing their capacity for improvement. The intelligent school, then, is a learning school.

The school, its practices and its culture, can be seen then as the unit which can learn and professionally grow. Much previous work has been undertaken regarding the recording of the individual professional learning growth of teachers. For example Retallick and Groundwater-Smith (1996) sought to provide a rationale and set of processes whereby the individual teacher could document and critique his or her professional learning through the medium of a learning portfolio. The process has now developed further to accommodate to the notions of corporate learning.

Thus the corporate learning portfolio has been defined as: "Evidence based documentation of organisational learning regarding a workplace transformation". PASP schools over the first year of the program were able to create substantial and impressive portfolios using a wide range of data gathering processes and individual and collective reflections. Portfolios contained a contextual framework that traced the history and social geography of the school and the vision that it had for its students and the community. It outlined the plan of operation that would be the focal point of its PASP project. Interventions ranged from: changes in staffing organization with enhanced mentoring and modelling for less experienced teachers; curriculum change with an emphasis upon a more liberatory pedagogy that would allow for genuine debate and interaction between teachers and students, particularly in areas of literacy and information and communication technologies; through to behaviour management. Both qualitative and quantitative evidence was collected as the work progressed. Each school was supported by an academic partner and/or critical friend who also contributed their reflections to the portfolio.

Schools met in local clusters and through two Department of Education and Training sponsored residential forums to discuss their work in progress and their results. At the conclusion to the project the portfolios were submitted to the meta-evaluators who analysed their contents as a means of informing their report. Thus schools themselves, with the support of academic partners and various Department of Education and Training Consultants had a high degree of agency in terms of portraying their challenges and solutions. The knowledge that was generated through the school learning portfolios contributed to both school improvement and overall policies and practices. The meta-evaluators, whose task it was to bring this localised knowledge into a larger and more coherent form were, of course, also engaged in knowledge creation – but knowledge derived from practice rather than driven by theory.

Interestingly, several of the schools are members of the Coalition. Their portfolios have been seen by other member schools to have such power that they too are now documenting their development in this fashion, not only in hard copy form, but also as electronic portfolios with all of the multi-media attributes that such a technology offers.

Conclusion: Changing the educational market place

It is clear that Nowotny, *et al*'s conception of the *Agora,* as a market place for the trade and negotiation of ideas as well as goods and services, is a powerful one when we think about the development and exchange of professional knowledge in Education. As well, the more general understanding of schools being in an educational market place is one that requires careful and critical attention.

What this article has sought to do is to develop an argument for the kind of market place that is one where the trade in ideas and practices is robust and conducted in a fair and transparent fashion that allows for the debate and dissent for which the ancient *Agora* was well known. The rates of exchange are clearly understood and the products ones that are worthwhile and desirable. After all, who amongst us has not gone to a market replete with gew-gaws, baubles and trinkets, slight, flimsy, cheap and tawdry – the sort of thing to turn up in tomorrow's garage or car boot sale? There are such market places in Education, cheap, instant solutions offered up to solve intractable problems. Under such conditions the knowledge formation is not of a kind that is carefully crafted from fine materials by those who well understood the purpose to which it is to be put.

While care must be taken not to idealise Australian educational market places it is the case that there is increasingly an understanding that the field of practice must be recognised and affirmed as an equal and respected trading partner; and that local solutions need to be generated to deal with local problems and challenges. It is to be hoped that this trend will continue and that we will not be overwhelmed by the globalised, glossy shopping mall.

References

Anderson, D. (1993) Public Schools in Decline: Implications of the Privatisation of Schools in Australia, in Beare, H. and Lowe Boyd, W. (eds.) *Restructuring Schools*, London: Falmer.

Cordingly, P. (2001) Teachers' perspectives on the credibility and usability of different kinds of evidence. Paper presented to a symposium on the TTA funded school based research consortia at the Annual Conference of the British Educational Research Association, Leeds, 13th September.

Darling-Hammond, L. (1996) What matters most: A competent teacher for every child, *Phi Delta Kappan,* November, 1996, pp.193–201.
Darling-Hammond, L. and Youngs, P. (2002) Defining 'Highly Qualified Teachers': What does 'Scientifically Based Research' actually tell us? *Educational Researcher,* 31 (9) pp. 13–25.
Elliott, J. (2004) Using research to improve practice: the notion of evidence based practice, in Day, C. And Sachs, J. (eds.) *International Handbook on the Continuing Professional Development of Teachers,* pp.264–290, Maidenhead: Open University Press.
Gibbons, M., Limoges, C., Nowotny, H., Schwartzman, S., Scott, P. and Trow, M. (1994) *The New Production of Knowledge: The Dynamics of Science in Research in Contemporary Societies,* London: Sage.
Gore, J. and Gitlin, A. (2004) Re-Visioning the Academic-Teacher Divide, *Teachers and Teaching: Theory and Practice.* 10 (1). pp.35–58.
Groundwater-Smith, S. and Mockler, N. (2003a) *Learning to Listen: Listening to Learn.* Sydney: MLC Schnol & The Centre for Practitioner Research, Faculty of Education & Social Work, University of Sydney. www.edfac.usyd.edu.au/profdev/learnlisten.html
Groundwater-Smith, S. and Mockler, N. (2003b) Holding a Mirror to Professional Learning, paper presented to the Annual Conference of the Australian Association for Research in Education/New Zeuland Association for Research in Education, Auckland, 29th November-3rd December, 2003
Groundwater-Smith, S. and Dadds, M. (2004) Critical Practitioner Inquiry: Towards Responsible Professional Communities of Practice, in Day, C. and Sachs, J. (eds.) *International Handbook on the Continuing Professional Development of Teachers,* pp.238–263, Maidenhead: Open University Press.
Groundwater-Smith, S. and Kemmis, S. (2004) *Knowing Makes the Difference: Learning from the New South Wales Priority Action Schools Program,* Sydney: New South Wales Department of Education and Training.
Hargreaves, D. (1999) The knowledge creating school, *British Journal of Education Studies,* 47, pp.122–144.
Hargreaves, D. (2003) From Improvement to Transformation. Keynote address presented to the International Conference of the *International Congress for School Effectiveness and Improvement (ICSEI),* Sydney: Sydney Convention Centre, Darling Harbour, 5th–8th February.
Kosko, B. (1993) *Fuzzy Thinking,* New York: Hyperion Press.
Kosko, B. and Isaka. S. (1993) Fuzzy Logic, *Scientific American,* July, pp.76–81.
Marginson, S. (1997) *Educating Australia,* Cambridge: Cambridge University Press.
MacGilchirst, B., Myers, K., and Reed. J. (2004) *The Intelligent School* (2nd Edition), London: Sage Publications.
Muijs, D. and Reynolds, D. (2001) *Effective Teaching: Evidence and Practice.* London: Paul Chapman Publishing.
Needham, K. and Groundwater-Smith, S. (2003) Using Student Voice to Inform School Improvement. Paper presented to the lnternatianal Congress for School Effectiveness and Improvement, Sydney: Darling Harbour Conference Centre, 5th–9th January.
Nowotny, H., Scott, P. and Gibbons, M. (2001) *Re-Thinking Science: Knowledge and the Public in an Age of Uncertainty,* Cambridge: Polity Press.
Nowotny, H., Scott, P. and Gibbons, H. (2003) Mode 2 Revisited: The New Production of Knowledge, *Minerva,* 41, pp.179–194.
Retallick, J. and Groundwater-Smith, S. (1996) *The Advancement of Teacher Workplace Learning.* Wagga Wagga: Charles Sturt University.
Rowe, K. (2003) The importance of *teacher quality* as a key determinant of students' experiences and outcomes of schooling. Background paper to keynote address presented at the ACER Research Conference, Melbourne, 19–21 October.
Sacks, O. (1995) *An Anthropologist on Mars: Seven Paradoxical Tales,* London: Picador.

Stehr, N. (1994) *The Knowledge Society*, London: Sage.
Warren Little, J. (2002) Locating learning in teachers' communities of practice: opening up problems of analysis in records of everyday work, *Teaching and Teacher Education*, 18, pp.917–946

CHAPTER 8

QUESTIONS OF QUALITY IN PRACTITIONER RESEARCH[1]

Universities in the 21st century – the need for safe places for unsafe ideas[2]

Susan Groundwater-Smith

Introduction

Let me explain my subtitle – 1995 was the fiftieth anniversary of the dropping of the atomic bomb by the *Enola Gay*, the B52 bomber that allegedly brought the war in the Pacific to an end. The Smithsonian Air and Space Museum wished to mark the anniversary with an exhibition. This was hugely controversial with, among others, the American Legion and sections of the American Senate characterising the proposed exhibition script as revisionist and offensive. Forty-eight historians and scholars insisted that the Museum not yield to pressures that would undermine the spirit of the proposed script for the exhibition. Numerous resignations followed and the final exhibition was deemed as one that was a sanitised, and clinical account. The dispute was seen as the most violent ever witnessed by a museum. In her discussion of the controversy Elaine Heumann Gurian (a consultant advisor to a number of museums and visitors' centres) insisted that museums should be safe places for unsafe ideas.

When I look at the work of universities in the 21st Century I similarly want to characterise them thus. Of course they should be places where knowledge is created, evaluated and applied using the most rigorous methodologies available; but they should also be places that allow consensual values themselves to be made problematic without fear or favour. Everywhere we turn there are controversial issues in the physical and social sciences and humanities that require scholarly attention. Stem cell research, climate change, and the representation of histories, to name but a few.

The university that is a safe place for unsafe ideas is one where the policies and practices of both today and yesterday can be carefully and systematically scrutinised on the basis of well conducted and well conceived research. We have to be mindful of the constraints that are placed on our work by those who provide our funding, but we cannot be governed by them. Even our students can place intolerable burdens on us if they are understood to be clients to be served rather than as learners to be challenged. Whether, in Australia, we are investigating the history wars, or the literacy debates, or the place of nuclear energy, we must be prepared to baulk at public sentiment when it is based upon populist understandings rather than the fruits of careful scholarship.

The 21st Century sees access to information multiplying year by year. Harvard and the Bodleian libraries provide online gateways to their extraordinary resources. Google Scholar brings journals of every complexion to the academic's desktop. The issue today is not finding, but using information. Universities have an unprecedented responsibility in the development of information literacy among all who participate in them, academics, students and practitioners alike.

Finally, I am willing to be charged with being meritocratic when it comes to considering the role of the university in the 21st Century. If being a meritocracy means working in the most rigorous ways, demanding the highest of standards and working with challenging and difficult ideas then universities have a special and particular responsibility. They cannot be reduced to teaching shops or as industry development centres where form precedes substance and issues of social justice and community wellbeing are marginalised or ignored.

So, summing up this introduction, I am arguing that a 21st Century University should be:

- A safe place for unsafe ideas;
- A place where consensual values need to be rendered more problematic;
- A place where students, at every level, are learners not clients;
- A place where academics are also deep learners as expressed in and demonstrated by their research and scholarship; and
- A place where matters of merit and quality count – centrally, in relation to questions of truth.

Quality research in faculties developing and enhancing professional practice

I take as my starting point the OECD definition of research:

> Creative work undertaken on a systematic basis in order to increase the stock of knowledge, including knowledge of man (sic), culture and society, and the use of this stock of knowledge to devise new applications.

Devising new applications, for me, is what we do when we research *with* the field of practice. These applications, in turn, inform our professional knowledge about practice. The interactions between the two go back and forth in complex ways.

Unfortunately, current metrics and measures used to characterise research 'quality' in universities are immeasurably crude. I believe we need a far more nuanced approach. We need to decide whether we are servants of the academic establishment or prepared to join forces with the field to interrogate and interrupt policies and practices developed by the few for the many.

Anderson and Herr (1999) introduce their discussion of the value and valuing (or non-valuing) of practitioner research with a quote from Donald Schön:

> Introducing the new scholarship into institutions of higher education means becoming involved in an epistemological battle. It is a battle of snails, proceeding so slowly that you have to look very carefully in order to see it

going on. But it is happening nonetheless. (Schön, 1995, in Anderson & Herr, 1999, p. 12)

The 'new scholarship' is taken to mean the kind of inquiry that recognises the distinctiveness of participatory research in which all of the key agents can play a part (Kemmis & McTaggart, 2000). The case made by Anderson and Herr (1999) is one that is clearly recognisable in the Australian context, in that we are faced with simultaneous and often contradictory arguments regarding the worth of collaborative research that engages both the academy and the field. They note that on the one hand administrators and professional development specialists see practitioner research 'as the new silver bullet' that they wish to control and domesticate, on the other hand academics see the value of such inquiry as a 'form of knowledge that leads to change within the practice setting itself, but are less comfortable when it is presented as public knowledge with epistemic claims beyond the practice setting' (p. 14).

In part, we see, the snail-like progress described by Schön as attributable to the academy's determination to hold onto its elite status that will brook no intrusion by the messy and indeterminate world of practice. Practice should remain subordinate to traditional academic discourse. Indeed, I would go so far as to say, the academy, in the main[3], has been quite complicit with the ways in which research assessment exercises of various kinds have been conducted.

Educators in schools, be they teachers, administrators or ancillary staff, are daily confronted by ongoing and relentless demands: demands upon their time; their pedagogical content knowledge; their emotional resilience; their capacity to solve complex problems; the list goes on and on. Of course the divide between the academy and the field is not only one that is experienced in education. Professional practice has been the poor cousin to the disciplinary sciences in our universities since their very inception.

Quality research in professional faculties, for me, is always provisional. It is unfinished business rather than the final solution. It is research that exposes and makes problematic the politics of power.

Knowledge generated *with* the field

As well as asking ourselves questions about practice based-research it is also important that we ask ourselves about the kinds of knowledge that is developed when it is knowledge that is generated with the field.

In a general, rather than a specifically educational sense, a most significant intrusion into the elite world of academia came about with the work of Gibbons, et al. (1994) who developed our understanding that knowledge creation is not exclusively a matter for scientists and academics working in institutions but may be socially produced and distributed in the form of what they coined as 'Mode 2 Knowledge'. Such knowledge production is concerned with the identification and solution of practical problems in the lived professional lives of practitioners and organizations who are not encircled by the boundaries of single disciplines with their conventions and orthodoxies. It is reflexive knowledge in that it results from a dialogic process as conversations in the field.

More recently Nowotny, Scott and Gibbons (2003) have argued that judging the worth of the Mode 2 Knowledge is no longer the exclusive province of the academy 'because there is no longer a stable taxonomy of codified disciplines from which 'peers' can be drawn' (p. 187). They continue by asserting that the 'research game' is being joined by more and more players. Problem generation and problem solving are contextualised within professional practice in the face of 'variously jostling publics' (p. 192).

I would contend that professional knowledge in education will be better served by drawing upon such diverse, rather than narrowly specialised sources. Diversity can more broadly and richly inform and strengthen the educational experience for all who participate in it. Of course, that does not mean that we should eschew quality, but that quality should be determined on ethical rather than technical criteria – a matter to which I shall return.

So what is the knowledge that facilitated practitioner inquiry can build and disseminate and how is it different from the commonsense knowledge that rests upon professional experience alone. Essentially it should be seen as knowledge that is co-constructed. Many writers have recognised the need to develop professional knowledge *with* the field of practice, rather than *for* the field of practice. The prepositional change is not one to be taken lightly. As Gore and Gitlin (2004) claim 'We need to work with teachers to explore the limits and possibilities of research for their work as teachers' (p. 52). Furthermore, they believe that this is achieved, not only by engaging in joint research activities but also by exposing and analysing the politics of research and the power relations therein. In this way a genuine parity of esteem within the community of practice, with the purpose of improving learning for all, can be achieved.

Such writers quite properly focus upon the benefits that can flow to the consequential stakeholders, the students themselves, as a result of research conducted as facilitated practitioner inquiry. It is also essential that teacher learning is clearly recognised as the critical intervening variable. Borko (2004) concludes

> We have much work to do and many questions to answer in order to provide high quality professional development to all teachers. It will take many different types of inquiries and a vast array of research tools to generate the rich source of knowledge needed to achieve this goal. (p. 13)

While one could debate the lack of research agency suggested by Borko, I clearly agree with her assertion that it will take much in the way of research 'types' to assist in and improve practice in ways that have eluded us in the past.

Mitchell & Sackney (2000) have made the case for professional knowledge around school improvement that is founded upon capacity building that 'occurs from an internal search for meaning, relevance and connection' (p. 139). Schools that see themselves as knowledge building enterprises that work in partnership with academic colleagues are in a stronger position to operationalise the outcomes of local inquiries and, indeed, develop authentic contexts for the positive reforms sought for but not often found.

Even so, the distinction needs to be made between the kind of tacit knowledge built from experience and the professional knowledge that is jointly constructed, intersubjectively, between and among practitioners and academics. Professor Ponte posed the difficult question to the recently convened Liverpool Hope University Ethics in Practitioner Research Colloquium the questions 'when is practitioner inquiry good professional development and when is it research?' My answer lies in its transparency as public and contestable knowledge.

It has already been observed, in this discussion that it is socially produced knowledge, that it is reflexive and developed in dialogue with the field, that it has transformational possibilities. Also it is knowledge that has resulted from an authentic desire for truth telling; that recognises and makes problematic the values of those who contribute to it; that acknowledges limitations of the knowledge boundaries; that respects humility over hubris; that basically seeks to do good. It is essentially a form of self knowledge.

Bottery (1996) emphasises this reflexive relationship when he writes of the importance of professional self-knowledge:

> [Self-knowledge] allows professionals to assess their weaknesses and strengths that much better. It allows them to appreciate that some justifications are valid, others are little more than rationalisations for historical accident. It allows them to place themselves within a wider picture, and see that sometimes (perhaps often) legislative change may not be aimed at them specifically, but has a wider target, and that they happen to be in the way. It gives them the opportunity to see that they do not necessarily occupy the centre of any occupational universe, but are part of a much more complex ecology of occupations. Professional action can only be enhanced by such understandings. (p. 191)

Practice based knowledge production that satisfies validity claims

It is not possible, feasible or appropriate to discuss professional knowledge without recourse to a discussion of validity. Anderson and Herr (1999) have suggested that we consider five validity criteria: (1) outcome validity, (2) process validity, (3) democratic validity, (4) catalytic validity, and (5) dialogic validity. Outcome validity refers to the impact that the inquiry has on practice – has it led to a resolution or re-framing of the problem? Process validity points to the appropriateness of the methods that have been adopted to the question being investigated. Democratic validity, as the name suggests, refers to the extent that all stakeholders are consulted and engaged in the inquiry. Catalytic validity points to the transformative potential of the research, while dialogic validity refers to the kind of intersubjectivity that I spoke of earlier. It is in relation to the last of these that Mishler (1990) develops his considerable and powerful arguments in that he forcefully puts the case that trustworthiness' must be a central tenet of research, in his case in medical and mental health studies, and that such trustworthiness is best tested through ongoing discourse among those who participate in it.

To conclude

The purpose of this chapter has been to explore matters of quality in relation to practitioner research and the ways in which these matters relate to the work of the academy. In my introduction I argued for universities to be a 'safe place for unsafe ideas'. In many ways practitioner research is unsafe and dangerous. It requires of us in the academy that we reassign privilege and demonstrate greater trust than has frequently been accorded by the academy to the field and those who participate in it. The erosion of social trust has been well documented and debated by scholars (see, for example Cvetkovich & Lofstedt, 1999; Fukuyama, 1999; Misztal, 1996). In addition, the growing popularity of fundamentalism in varied religious, economic and social forms can be seen as representative of a culture of instrumentalism which seeks to eradicate nuance and provide 'common sense' and simple answers to complex questions. Within education, the erosion of trust and the rise of fundamentalism can be seen in the current fixation on 'standards', measurement and accountability to a set of rather narrow parameters and 'norms', both in schools and Higher Education.

This raises a profound question, requiring public debate and reflection: What is it about our times that prevents us from actively resourcing, respecting and recognising research and inquiry in all of its diverse, illuminating and often indeterminate forms. Perhaps answering this question will require the kind of leap of faith that artists takes when they step outside the known forms of representation and find themselves engaged in new and different conceptualisations of the world in which they live. The 21st Century with its rapidly escalating social, economic, cultural and technological change is a world that cries out for new and robust conceptualisations of practice that will serve its citizens well and allow us to transcend the extraordinarily pessimistic view on educational change and reform proposed by Seymour Sarason (1998).

> What finally convinced me [that change is unlikely] was the recognition that no one – not teachers, not administrators, not researchers, not politicians or policymakers, and certainly not students – willed the present state of affairs. They were all caught up in a system that had no self-correcting features, a system *utterly unable to create and sustain contexts of productive learning*. (...) There are no villains. There is a system. You can see and touch villains, you cannot see a system. (...) The reform movement has been about parts, not about the system, not about how the purposes of parts are at cross-purposes to each other, not about how the concept of purpose loses both meaning and force in a system that is amazingly uncoordinated and that has more adversarial than cooperative features. (Sarason, 1998, p. 141, emphasis added)

There may be no villains, but there is villainy afoot if universities cannot support and be partners in practitioner research. We need to understand how this villainy has entered ways of seeing practitioner research in the academy wherever practitioner research is excluded or derided. In view of the benefits of professional partnership between the academy and schools considered in this paper, we should understand practitioner research as more than a rallying cry – we should understand it as a way of working with the professions that will give and revive energy and purpose in *our* work.

Notes

1 A number of observations made in this discussion paper are based upon a longer and more sustained piece written by myself and Nicole Mockler, 'Research that Counts:

Practitioner Research and the Academy', to be published in the *Australian Educational Researcher*.
2   cf. Elaine Heumann-Gurian.
3   In Australia it is those who have most to gain by conservative metrics and measures who most support them, that is the older and established universities.

References

Anderson, G., & Herr, K. (1999). The new paradigm wars: Is there room for rigorous practitioner knowledge in schools and universities. *Educational Researcher, 28*(5), 12–21 and 40.

Borko, H. (2004). Professional development and teacher learning: Mapping the terrain. *Educational Researcher, 33*(8), 3–16.

Bonery, M. (1996). The challenge to professionals to the new public management: Implications for the teaching profession. *Oxford Review of Education, 22*(2), 179–197.

Cvetkovich, G., & Lofstedt, R. (1999). *Social trust and the management of risk*. London: Earthscan.

Fukuyama, F. (1999). *The great disruption: Human nature and the reconstitution of social order*. New York: Touchstone.

Gibbons, M., Limoges, C., Nowotny, H., Schwartzman, S., Scott, P., & Trow, M. (1994). *The new production of knowledge: The dynamics of science in research in contemporary societies*. London: Sage.

Gore, J., & Gitlin. A. (2004). Re-visioning the academic-teacher divide. *Teachers and Teaching: Theory and Practice, 10*(1), 35–58.

Kemmis, S., & McTaggart, R. (2000). Participatory action research. In K. Denzin & Y. Lincoln (Eds.), *Handbook of qualitative research* (2nd edition) (pp. 590–605). Thousand Oaks: Sage Publications.

Mishler, E. (1990). Validation in inquiry-guided research: The role of exemplars in narrative studies. *Harvard Educational Review, 90*(4), 415–442.

Misztal, B. (1996). *Trust in modern societies: The search for the basis of social order*. Cambridge: Polity Press.

Mitchell, C., & Sackney, L. (2000). *Profound improvement: Building capacity for a learning community*. Lisse: Swets & Zeitlinger.

Nowotny, H., Scott, P., & Gibbons, H. (2003). Mode 2 revisited: The new production of knowledge. *Minerva, 41*, 179–194.

Sarason, S. (1998). *Political leadership and educational failure*. San Francisco: Jossey Bass.

CHAPTER 9

ETHICS IN PRACTITIONER RESEARCH
An issue of quality

Susan Groundwater-Smith and Nicole Mockler

Introduction

Practitioner research, in one form or another, has been with us for around a half a century following the initial influence of Lewin (1947).[1] The process has been seen to serve a variety of knowledge interests (Habermas, 1972) ranging from the technical rational interest – how do we solve this problem?, through the interpretive/hermeneutic interest – how do we understand this practical problem?, to the rarer emancipatory interest – how can we locate this problem in a wider social discourse and address it such that we enhance the opportunity for participative democratic engagement with it? In this contribution, we wish to explore this notion of practitioner research as an emancipatory project with a critical edge, focusing particularly upon the complex links between purpose, ethics and quality. The contribution thus falls into two parts. In the first, we amplify the relationship between practitioner research as a form of critical social inquiry, while in the second we focus explicitly on ethical dimensions and measures of quality.

We argue throughout that practitioner research, with its focus upon local inquiries designed to address and ameliorate local problems, should necessarily be concerned not only with solutions, but with the conditions that produced the problems in the first place. Furthermore, if practitioner research is to constitute part of the base for the justification of policy and practice, then it is vital that there is a shared, recognizable language that allows a vigorous and well-informed debate. As well, we argue that by adopting a stance that foregrounds ethicality, a dimension of quality that we believe to be missing in the Furlong and Oancea paper (2006, cf. p. 15) then those conditions which may have contributed to various challenges and problems in practices in education are more likely to be revealed and open to question.

As well we address the issue raised by Furlong and Oancea (2006) where they argue that 'traditionally it has been assumed that there is a clear distinction between the worlds of research and the worlds of policy and practice – that there are "two communities'" (p. 5). For us, research and practice are indivisible.

Practitioner research as an emancipatory project

Some decade on from Stenhouse's work in the Humanities Curriculum Project (1975) and Elliott's in the Ford Teaching Project (Elliott, 1991), Carr and Kemmis' publication of *Becoming critical* (Carr & Kemmis, 1986) developed the notion of practitioner research as an emancipatory project or what they called 'a critical social science'. In spite of the impact of these seminal writers and the force of their arguments, at the beginning of a new millennium, there continues to be a dominance of treating educational problems as technical, and thus able to be resolved objectively through a rational assessment of evidence gathered within a positivist research paradigm. The effort of much practitioner inquiry has been to identify what ends can be achieved rather than investigate, in any way, what those ends ought to be. This is well recognized by Kemmis (2004) who has indicated:

> The truth is that most of the people it (*Becoming critical*) aimed to challenge and persuade simply continued to do the kinds of positivistic and interpretive social and educational science that they had always done. And they still do. (Kemmis, 2004, p. 2)

As one of us recently argued, what counts as professional knowledge is a much more interesting and complex matter than in times gone by, when it was seen that it was the role of academia and dedicated Government agencies to develop such knowledge and communicate it to the cognate profession (Groundwater-Smith, 2006). In their initial work Gibbons *et al.* (1994) developed our understanding that knowledge creation is not exclusively a matter for scientists and academics working in institutions but may be socially produced and distributed in the form of what they coined as 'Mode 2 knowledge'. Such knowledge production is concerned with the identification and solution of practical problems in the lived professional lives of practitioners and organizations which are not encircled by the boundaries of single academic disciplines with their many rules and customary practices. It is reflexive knowledge in that it results from a dialogic process as conversations in the field. They posed the proposition that the production of knowledge and the processes of research were due for a radical transformation. They were concerned that the separation between the two was problematic as was the division of labour, where practitioners were seen as responsible for applying the knowledge generated by academic researchers. The very problem identified by Furlong and Oancea (2006). As we have argued elsewhere 'the knowledge that drives professional practice and the "theoretical knowledge" valued by the academy are not mutually exclusive' (Groundwater-Smith & Mockler, 2006, p. 107).

All of this is to recognize that in the broader research community there continues to be a debate regarding the worth of educational research as a basis for constructing either policy or practice. Feuer *et al.* (2002) argue strongly for what they term 'a scientific culture of educational research' (p. 4). This they see to be a 'set of norms and practices and ethos of honesty, openness and continuous reflection, including how research quality is judged' (p. 4). To this we would add the necessity that whatever method, it is guided by a series of ethical principles, a concern to which we shall return at a later point. The arguments regarding method, norms and practices certainly can be seen to apply to practitioner research. Such inquiry must be able to stand up to the scrutiny of both the field of practice and the academic community's expectation that it be systematically undertaken and theoretically robust.

Today we are faced, once again, with a regressive stance on what kinds of research should inform educational practice. We need only to look at the Bush policy in the US, articulated through the *Education Sciences Reform Act* of 2002 – a policy that is having ramifications across the English Speaking World, including Australia. The view of science written into law by the Bush administration is clearly a positivist one with its exclusive emphasis upon the employment of randomized controlled clinical trials precisely designed to solve those 'technical problems' to which Carr and Kemmis referred and which others see to only be a thin slice of research in such a complex and interactive field as education where the complexities and exigencies of practice do not readily yield to laboratory conditions with their strict and carefully constructed controls.

As Yates (2004) in her powerful account of these and similar developments indicated, a report by scientific experts from the National Academies in the US was less wedded to one particular form of investigation, setting out instead the following principles that all science should follow and which can be applied across the range of social services, not only education:

- Pose significant questions that can be investigated empirically.
- Link research to relevant theory.
- Use methods that permit direct investigations of the questions.
- Provide a coherent and explicit chain of reasoning.
- Yield findings that replicate and generalize across studies.
- Disclose research data and methods to enable and encourage professional scrutiny and critique. (Feuer *et al.*, 2002, p. 7, quoted in Yates, 2004, p. 25)

The international debate concerning research in education is increasingly being dominated by such agenda as that espoused by the Bush Government. It is unfortunate that practitioner research has barely moved beyond satisfying such technical knowledge interests also; ones that we outlined earlier in this contribution. It has been popularized, domesticated and appropriated as an implementation tool instead of as a liberatory social change method with far reaching implications (Groundwater-Smith & Mockler, 2006).

In Australia this is most recently evident in relation to the Quality Teaching Program (www.qualityteaching.dest.gov.au), a National Government Program that aims to extend teacher professional learning in the key areas of literacy, numeracy, mathematics, science, information technology and vocational education and training. Mediated through state-based agencies, in both the Government and non-Government sectors, the conditions for grantees are highly specific with little room to vary from what is required. Thus the iterative cycle of problem identification, reflection, action, problem reconceptualization so characteristic of practitioner inquiry is effectively denied as there is no provision for a critique of any features of the policy itself. The problem is the Government's problem, not that of the practitioner. As Carr and Kemmis put it so powerfully, action research, within their conceptualization, a critical social science:

> ... not only attempts to identify contradictions between educational and institutional practices, it actually creates a sense of these contradictions for the self-critical community of action researchers. It does so by asserting an alternative set of values to the bureaucratic values of institutions. (Carr & Kemmis, 1986, p. 197)

Of course Carr and Kemmis developed their arguments in a different time and space. In the 20 years that have elapsed since their groundbreaking analysis much has changed in terms of the intervention of the state across the world in a variety of different jurisdictions. For example Judah and Richardson (2006) in writing of action research in Canada regard those engaged in state mandated action research projects as occupying a space between 'a rock and a (very) hard place' (p. 65). It becomes important to the state that those stories told in the public domain are the stories that they wish the public to hear, and that these stories themselves are highly performative.

Our case then is that if there is not some fidelity to the stories that matter to the practitioner but may not be of great account to the state, then there has been a serious omission in ethical terms. While the interests of the state are undoubtedly of significance, arguably of more importance in terms of the broader critical project are the interests of practitioners and the consequential stakeholders. This term is one that particularly appeals to us in that it recognizes that learners in institutions, be they schools, universities or further education facilities deal with the consequences of the policies and practices of others on a daily basis.

Practitioner inquiry, quality and ethics

Elsewhere we have written of ethics as one of the 'three basic tests' of quality for any practitioner research project (Groundwater-Smith & Mockler, 2002). While there has been a significant spotlight shone on the connection between (and indeed, interweaving of) ethics and quality in qualitative research generally over the past 10 years (see Lincoln, 1995; Zeni, 2001; Olesen, 2003; Hilsen, 2006), particularly with regard to feminist and participatory research paradigms, relatively little has been produced relating specifically to the issue of ethics vis-à-vis quality in practitioner research. For example, Eikeland's writing (2006) is directed not to individual researchers and their practice but to the community of practitioner researchers. He is a Norwegian philosopher who has worked both practically and theoretically with action/practitioner research in both public and private organizations. He draws attention to who is actually included in that community and what they do to themselves and others. As he observed, 'It becomes clear that the ethical dilemmas experienced depend very much upon from what position the research is done' (p. 41). Important as his observations are, the missing element for us is the relationship between the ethical dilemmas that he raises and the matter of quality.

Suggestions for criteria for quality are made often in the literature by advocates of practitioner research. For example; in their introduction to practitioner research methods, Altrichter *et al.* (1993) establish four criteria for evaluating the quality of action research. They are:

1. *Considering alternative perspectives:* Have the understandings gained from research been cross-checked against the perspectives of those concerned and/or other researchers?
2. *Testing through practical action:* Have the understandings gained from research been tested through practical action?
3. *Ethical justification:* Are the research methods compatible with both educational aims and democratic human values?
4. *Practicality:* Are the research design and data collection methods compatible with the demands of teaching? (pp. 74–81).

Similarly, Anderson and Herr (1999) have suggested that we consider five validity criteria: outcome validity; process validity; democratic validity; catalytic validity and dialogic validity. Outcome validity refers to the impact that the inquiry has on practice – has it led to a resolution or reframing of the problem? Process validity points to the appropriateness of the methods that have been adopted to the question being investigated. Democratic validity, as the name suggests, refers to the extent that all stakeholders are consulted and engaged in the inquiry. Catalytic validity points to the transformative potential of the research, while dialogic validity refers to the kind of intersubjectivity upon which Stenhouse insisted. It is in relation to the last of these that Mishler (1990) develops his considerable and powerful arguments in that he forcefully puts the case that 'trustworthiness' must be a central tenet of research and a sub-dimension that is clearly of importance to Furlong and Oancea (2006). In Mishler's case trustworthiness applies most critically in medical and mental health studies, and that such trustworthiness is best tested through ongoing discourse among those who participate in it.

While we agree that such criteria (and here we note that these are two sets of many) are both sensible and effective, we wish to argue here for the intrinsic and fundamental relationship between ethics and quality within practitioner research aiming towards an emancipatory goal. Indeed we suggest a hierarchical relationship where ethical issues form the primary criteria for quality in practitioner research, and the establishment of a number of 'implications for quality' which naturally flow from a framework of ethics. Clearly ethics are informed by values which assemble into a values system. On the one hand, in our view, values are those constructs held by individuals, they may differ from person to person, move towards stability and indeed become habitual; they are personal and influenced by social context. On the other hand, ethics are part of a broader social discourse governing the rightness or wrongness of action, and as such belong in the realm of the collective and the public. We should not confuse ethics with efficiency. In the end, ethics is associated with morality, which again is informed by values.

In our view ethicality is a necessary but not sufficient condition for quality. One can undertake studies that are methodologically sound but may employ covert observations (in education it is not uncommon for teachers, as practitioner researchers, to collect data on their students without their knowledge and consent) and thus do not meet ethical validity criteria in that there is no opportunity for members of the community with whom the research is concerned being able to challenge either the observations or the interpretations. The point that we wish to stress is that practitioner research *must* meet ethical criteria if it is to meet norms for quality. At the same time, it is conceivable that enquiries can be conducted ethically, but not engage in sound research principles such as following a coherent and explicit chain of reasoning as outlined by Feuer *et al.* (2002). Clearly the two relate one to the other.

In her work on 'the ethical teacher', Elizabeth Campbell (2003) makes a case for the use of ethics as a primary framework for thinking about teachers and teachers' work generally. Such a framework, she posits, has the potential to provide a renewed sense of professionalism (through providing a focal point for the rethinking of the profession in ethical terms), a basis for renewed school cultures (through using the moral basis of teachers' work as a 'touchstone' for school reform), and a catalyst for renewed teacher education and professional learning. For Campbell, the project of developing ethical teacher professionalism relates closely to the greater project of working towards civil society, through the harnessing of the 'moral purpose' (Fullan, 1993) implicit in the teaching enterprise. In this, she echoes Sachs' (2000, 2003) conceptualization of an 'activist teaching profession', where the aim is to 'improve all aspects of the education enterprise at the macro level and student learning outcomes and teachers' status in the eyes of the community at the micro level' (Sachs, 2000, p. 77).

The notion of ethical teacher professionalism, then, holds a number of important implications for practitioner research and for our discussion of quality therein. In the first place, it sits well with Lewin's assertion that the defining characteristic of Action Research should be that it is 'research leading to social action' (Lewin, 1946, p. 203), and subsequent conceptualizations of the emancipatory nature of practitioner research such as those discussed at length above. Indeed, the enterprise of practitioner research has a reflexive relationship with the ethical or activist professional in that it both provides a tool for engaging with the larger goal of such professionalism and 'can contribute to the larger political project of creating an activist [and ethical] teaching profession' (Sachs, 2003, p. 92).

To return to Altrichter *et al.*'s criteria for quality in practitioner research, while only one relates explicitly to ethics, it could in fact be argued that all four emanate from a framework of ethics. The first through its call to transparency and triangulation, in our opinion a key facet of ethical operation within practitioner research, the second through the call for 'action' emanating from practitioner research, which is highly congruent with Campbell's notion of the ethical professional, and the fourth through an implicit highlighting of the importance of teacher agency within the framework of practitioner research. Similarly, each of Anderson and Herr's validity criteria embrace ethical principles at their core.

For us ethics is not merely a series of boxes to be ticked as a set of procedural conditions, usually demanded by university human research ethics committees and the like, but is an orientation to research practice that is deeply embedded in those working in the field in a substantive and engaged way. Importantly, it has implications for the matter of working critically. Practitioner research that provides only celebratory accounts may meet procedural requirements, but will fail to address the more difficult and challenging substantive ethical concerns in relation to the wider social and political agenda.

We wish to pose here a series of broad, overriding 'ethical' guidelines for practitioner research, some of which are linked to a traditional conceptualization of research ethics, while others flow from the discourse of the 'ethical professional':

- *That it should observe ethical protocols and processes.* Practitioner research is subject to the same ethical protocols as other social research. Informed consent should be sought from participants, whether students, teachers, parents or others, and an earnest attempt should be made to 'do no harm'.
- *That it should be transparent in its processes.* One of the broader aims of practitioner research lies in the building of community and the sharing of knowledge and ideas. To this end, practitioner research should be 'transparent' in its enactment, and practitioner researchers accountable to their community for the processes and products of their research.
- *That it should be collaborative in its nature.* Practitioner research should aim to provide opportunities for colleagues to share, discuss and debate aspects of their practice in the name of improvement and development. The responsible 'making sense' of data collected from within the field of one's own practice (through triangulation of evidence and other means) relies heavily on these opportunities.
- *That it should be transformative in its intent and action.* Practitioner researchers engage in an enterprise which is, in essence, about contributing to both transformation of practice and transformation of society. Responsible and ethical practitioner research operates in such a way as to create actionable, actioned outcomes.
- *That it should be able to justify itself to its community of practice.* Engaging in practitioner research involves an opportunity cost to the community. To do well requires time and energy that cannot be spent in other professional ways. The benefits must be commensurable with the effort and resources expended in the course of the work which necessarily will require collaboration and communication.

Quality, however, should not be taken to be an all-embracing term. It requires close interrogation in relation to matters of evidence, concerns regarding purpose and the nature of the outcomes that are produced. If indeed we are concerned with 'quality assurance' with respect to practitioner research, we must attend to all three. In this final section of our contribution, we suggest some key concerns around each.

Quality of evidence

'Evidence' is not an innocent construct. Indeed, laws of evidence, in practice, are rules about kinds of discourse; what discourse is to count as potent and effective and in what form and, alternatively, what is disqualified. The quality of the evidence lies both in its substance and in its argument. We have only to reflect on the 'history wars' in Australia (Macintyre & Clark, 2003) or the case made for the invasion of Iraq on the grounds of the existence of weapons of mass destruction to see how problematic the issue of evidence is.

To further complicate the matter there is the issue of testimony, whose account counts? Laub (1992) in her searing discussion of it with respect to the holocaust indicated that there are three distinct and separate levels of witnessing:

> ... the level of being witness to oneself within the experience; the level of being the witness to the testimonies of others; and the level of being witness to the process of witnessing itself. (Lamb, 1992, p. 75)

It is also the case that new evidence is emerging all of the time. Beliefs about how the body operates, for example, are constantly being challenged by new evidence arising from research, and not necessarily randomized control trials at that.

Our argument in this contribution is to focus on the quality of evidence that is required to transform practice rather than to inform large systems-based policies, after all as Ball (1997) put it:

> Policies do not normally tell you what to do; they create circumstances in which the range of options available in deciding what to do is narrowed or changed or particular outcomes are set. A response must still be put together, constructed in context, offset and balanced against oilier expectations. (Ball, 1997, p. 257)

In the end, the quality of evidence, for us, will rest upon the ways in which it has been collected and the purposes to which it will be put – in effect, as we argued above, that it first and foremost meets the ethical tests that we have set out.

Thus, evidence collected under duress, evidence collected covertly, evidence that is not validated by triangulation and evidence that has not been debated, in our view is evidence that is invalid.

Quality of purpose

The issue of purpose is significant within any discussion of quality guidelines for practitioner inquiry, predominantly because of the potential for the 'research agenda' to impact in considerable ways upon the collection, analysis and reporting of data and the outcomes and 'action' of the research itself. In terms of quality of purpose, we see three key tensions at play within the arena of practitioner inquiry, namely:

- The autonomy and freedom of internally fuelled projects *vs.* the lure of external funding.
- Teacher research as a catalyst for improved classroom practice *vs.* whole-school inquiry as a catalyst for school improvement.
- Practitioner inquiry for professional transformation *vs.* 'action research' as a vehicle for compliance.

While we wish not to present these tensions as bi-polar dichotomies, we offer them as real and salient issues within schools and a useful 'way in' to this discussion of the agenda and purpose of teacher inquiry.

Sachs (2003) has written at length of the question of 'whose questions get asked?' in the context of school-based practitioner research:

> A central but unacknowledged dimension of school-based research, whether conducted by teachers and academics collaboratively or individually, is the issue of whose questions get put on the research agenda? This issue stands at the core of many successful or failed research attempts. (Sachs, 2003, pp. 83–84)

While her examples are limited to those where an academic-driven agenda has the potential to hijack the practitioner research enterprise, Sachs draws an excellent depiction of the problems inherent in research responding to questions imposed by an outside agenda. Indeed, it is in the realm of this issue that the three key tensions outlined above exist.

The external funding for practitioner research projects such as those which are now common in the UK and Australia in particular can provide opportunities for in-school professional development which would not otherwise exist. There is, however 'no such thing as a free lunch', and teacher researchers can sometimes find themselves caught up in an externally imposed implementation agenda rather than an agenda of personal and community transformation which might otherwise drive the project. The key to navigating this tension, we suspect, is to draw the impetus for the project from the local needs and requirements of the school and teachers while at the same time meeting the requirements of the funding. Such an approach, however, relies on a commitment on the part of the school executive as well as the practitioner researchers to such transformation.

Finally, practitioner research fails the 'quality of purpose' test when it is implemented in a 'top down' way which denies teacher agency and is aimed at serving the school or system hierarchy. While practitioner research can be a highly effective and transformative method of developing professional learning for whole school change, we agree with Sachs' assessment that 'first and foremost, the desire to engage in teacher research must be a choice, it cannot be mandated from the top down' (2003, p. 89). Whether the motivation for such 'top down' impetus is merely a benign belief in the power of practitioner inquiry or a more sinister push for compliance and regulation, such efforts are more likely to breed cynicism and discontent than development and emancipation. The key to navigating these tensions, we believe, lies in working slowly, engaging teachers with a will and interest in practitioner research and encouraging them to share their learnings and new understandings with their colleagues, building trust and adding new opportunities for engagement along the way.

Quality of outcome

Given, then, that purposes for engaging in practitioner research in education settings will greatly vary, with some more oriented to an emancipatory knowledge interest than others, how are we to judge the quality of the outcomes? Our first yardstick for making such judgements is grounded in our earlier discussion of ethical practice and the quality of the discourse. As we have already indicated, understanding, in and of itself, is not sufficient. An important outcome is that the knowledge that has been developed is acted upon. Knowledge must be put to good use. There is an interesting parable to be found in Funder's *Stasiland* (2002) where she details the extraordinary lengths to which the GDR went in order to gather information of the doings of its citizens. And yet with all that 'knowledge' it could not predict the fall of the Berlin Wall. Knowing what is happening in education settings is not enough to change them. There must be a will to step into the twenty-first century and rethink schooling anew.

One of the difficulties in achieving such an outcome is the current inclination to celebrate practice rather than develop an authentic critique. 'Sharing' conferences, where participants come to discuss their achievements in such programs as the Australian Government Quality Teaching Program rarely report ways in which the investigations have challenged existing and established policies that all too often govern practice. A significant quality outcome, in our terms, would be one where the education bureaucracy, itself, has the courage and fortitude to listen and attend to critical insights that those working at the 'chalkface' may have. It is unlikely that we shall see any great departure from celebratory accounts while practitioners feel that their critique will go unremarked, at best, or receive negative attention, at worst. Learning about practice through research is a powerful hammer; we must take care that we do not use it only to crack very small nuts.

A quality outcome for well conducted, ethical, practitioner research in the context of education is an affirmation of the scholarship of teaching. In many ways we see teachers having been deprofessionalized by the KISS principle – Keep it simple, stupid. Too often complex and competing ideas are reduced to ten-minute soundbites. Already there are templates and companions being published to enable teachers to put together strategies to engage students in the kind of higher order thinking advocated as a result of the Queensland Productive Pedagogies and New South Wales Quality Teaching Paper initiatives. In the meta-evaluation of the New South Wales Priority Action Schools Program (PASP), Groundwater-Smith and Kemmis (2003) noted the capacity of teachers to engage in sustained professional conversation and action around practices in some of the state's most challenging schools. The very nature of the program, that gave agency to teachers, created conditions where it was possible, even desirable to work around some of the existing 'roadblocks'.

Conclusion

The conduct of quality practitioner research is in its very nature ethical business. The dynamic which exists between practitioner research and professional practice for educators is such that ethicality cannot be divorced from quality in practitioner research any more than it can be divorced from quality in professional practice. Teaching is or should be moral practice. After all, it is conceivable that one can 'improve' on practices that are unfair and inequitable. One could imagine that a practitioner researcher could become even better at sorting and labelling students through a set of assessment practices that he or she has researched. However for those consequential stakeholders, the students themselves, this could visit upon them incalculable harm. Quality is always troublesome and never easily resolved. It requires of practitioner researchers not only an understanding of the technicalities of research and reflective practice, but an unwavering commitment to ethics and the improvement of the human condition in the context within which they work.

This contribution may be read in two ways: as a discussion regarding a particular lens through which quality in practitioner research may be viewed, that is ethicality; but also as a gentle critique of Furlong and Oancea (2006). For while we find much to agree with in their report, that is after all the basis of this special edition, we also believe that they have not given sufficient prominence to ethicality as a dimension of quality. Certainly, they have attended to ethical issues throughout their study, but in the end it is the technical knowledge interests that they most acknowledge and serve. Taking an emancipatory stance may be a little old fashioned; but it is one to which we strongly adhere and which we hope this contribution strongly defends.

Acknowledgements

This contribution is based in part on 'Practitioner research in education: beyond celebration', paper presented to the Australian Association for Research in Education Focus Conference, James Cook University, Cairns, 4–6 July 2005.

Notes

For a helpful series of essays on action research or practitioner research, both phrases being used interchangeably, see Hollingworth (1997).

References

Altrichter, H., Posch, P. & Somekh, B. (1993) *Teachers investigate their work: an introduction to the methods of action research* (London, Routledge).

Anderson, G. & Herr, K. (1999) The new paradigm wars: is there room for rigorous practitioner knowledge in schools and universities, *Educational Researcher*, 28(5), 12–21.

Ball, S. (1997) Policy sociology and critical social research: a personal review of recent education policy and policy research, *British Educational Research Journal*, 23(3), 257–274.

Campbell, E. (2003) *The ethical teacher* (Berkshire, Open University Press).

Carr, W. & Kemmis, S. (1986) *Becoming critical* (Lewes, The Falmer Press).

Elliott, J. (1991) *Action research for educational change* (Milton Keynes, Open University Press).

Eikeland, 0. (2006) Condescending ethics and action research, *Action Research*, 4, 37–47.

Feuer, M., Towne, L. & Shavelson, R. (2002) Scientific culture and educational research, *Educational Researcher*, 31(8), 4–14.

Fullan, M. (1993) Why teachers must become change agents, *Educational Leadership*, 50(6), 12–13.

Funder, A (2002) *Stasiland* (Melbourne, The Text Publishing Company).

Furlong, J. & Oancea, A. (2006) Assessing quality in applied and practice-based research in education: a framework for discussion, *Review of Australian Research in Education: Counterpoints on the Quality and Impact of Educational Research*, 6, 89–104. Available online at: www.bera.ac.uk/pdfs/Qualitycriteria.pdf (accessed 30 October 2006).

Gibbons, M., Limoges, C., Nowotny, H., Schwartzman, S., Scott, P. & Trow, M. (1994) *The new production of knowledge: the dynamics of science in research in contemporary societies* (London, Sage).

Groundwater-Smith, S. (2006) Professional knowledge formation in the Australian market place: changing the perspective, *Scottish Educational Review*, 37, 123–130.

Groundwater-Smith, S. & Kemmis, S. (2003) *Knowing makes the difference: learnings from the NSW priority action schools program* (Sydney, NSW Department of Education and Training).

Groundwater-Smith, S. & Mockler, N. (2002) Building knowledge, building professionalism: the coalition of knowledge building schools and teacher professionalism, paper presented to the *Australia Association for Educational Research Annual Conference*, University of Queensland, 1–5 December.

Groundwater-Smith, S. & Mockler, N. (2006) Research that counts: practitioner research and the academy, in: J. Blackmore, J. Wright & V. Harwood (Eds) *Counterpoints on the quality and educational research. Review of Australian Research in Education 6* (Melbourne, AARE), 105–118.

Habermas, J. (1972) *Knowledge and human interests* (London, Heinemann).
Hilsen, A. (2006) And they shall be known by their deeds, *Action Research*, 4(1), 23–36.
Judah, M. & Richardson, G. (2006) Between a rock and a (very) hard place, *Action Research*, 4(1), 65–80.
Kemmis, S. (2004) Against methodolatry, paper prepared for a symposium on 'Methodolatry' for the Queensland University of Technology, Provocations Seminar Series, 24 November.
Laub, D. (1992) An event without witness: truth, testimony and survival, in: S. Felman & D. Laub (Eds) *Testimony: crisis of witnessing* (New York, Routledge), 75–92.
Lewin, K. (1946) *Resolving social conflicts* (New York, Harper & Row).
Lewin, K. (1947) Frontiers in group dynamics: social planning and action research, *Human Relations*, 1(1), 145–153.
Lincoln, Y. (1995) Emerging criteria for quality in qualitative and interpretive inquiry, *Qualitative Inquiry*, 1, 27 5–289.
Macintyre, S. & Clark, A. (2003) *The history wars* (Melbourne, Melbourne University Press).
Mishler, E. (1990) Validation in inquiry-guided research: the role of exemplars in narrative studies, *Harvard Educational Review* 90(4), 415–442.
Olesen, V. L. (2003) Feminisms and qualitative research at and into the millennium, in: N. Denzin & Y. Lincoln (Eds) *The landscape of qualitative research: theories and issues* (Thousand Oaks. CA, Sage)
Sachs, J, (2000) The activist professional, *Journal of Educational Change*, 1(1), 77–95.
Sachs, J. (2003) *The activist teaching profession* (Buckingham, Open University Press). Stenhouse, L (I 975) *An introduction to curriculum research and development* (London, Heinemann).
Yates, L. (2004) *What does good education research look like?* (Maidenhead, Open University Press).
Zeni, J. (Ed.) *Ethical issues in practitioner research* (New York, Teachers College Press).

CHAPTER 10

STUDENT VOICE
Essential testimony for intelligent schools
Susan Groundwater-Smith

Introduction

Increasingly, there is an awareness that we cannot continue to debate the nature of schooling without consulting the consequential stakeholders, the students themselves. During the 1960s the *Observer* newspaper in the UK ran a competition asking children of secondary-school age to design the school of their dreams. Edward Blishen used the 1000 entries to put together a book that clearly indicated the difficulties that students were experiencing with their schools (Blishen, 1967). Some 40 years later the *Guardian* newspaper ran a similar competition, K-12. This time they received 15,000 entries, many of them being multimedia. Again a book resulted from the competition which indicated that not much has changed. In their introduction to the book Burke and Grosvenor (2003) wrote: 'There is a history of not attending to the expressed experience of children within schools; everyday neglect in this sense has become institutional'. While, in the main, it is true that schools rarely consult their students and take them seriously, it is the case that there are schools both in the UK and in Australia where there have been systematic policies and practices that have enabled students' voices to be heard and have even given students agency in designing, investigating, analysing and interpreting studies of learning (Needham and Groundwater-Smith, 2003; Groundwater-Smith and Mockler, 2003; Arnot *et al.*, 2004). That being so, there are serious ethical issues to be considered when schools engage in practitioner inquiry where students become integral to the research. These ethical issues revolve around vulnerability and the extent to which young people may be manipulated or coerced. As well, there are matters of various and competing accountabilities and the ways that these are played out in the many and diffuse practices of the school.

Consultation with students: considering the case

It is a truism to suggest that schools could not exist without their students, but it is also curious that as the key stakeholders in the education enterprise they are rarely consulted about the conditions under which they learn. In effect they live in a kind of 'borderland'. Gloria Anzaldua has written most evocatively of borderlands in her meditation upon the existence of those living on the frontiers between cultures and languages, that is Chicanos in an Anglo culture (Anzaldua, 1987: 11).

Culturally determined roles are imposed from the outside and dictate who is acceptable and who is not; what is acceptable and what is not:

> Borders are set up to define the places that are safe and unsafe, to distinguish us from them. A border is a dividing line, a narrow strip along a steep edge. A borderland is a vague and undetermined place created by the emotional residue of an unnatural boundary.

Anzaldua's 'borderlands' are a metaphor for the political and psychological positioning of those denied power. In a similar, if not as heartbreaking a fashion, young people in our schools also occupy a borderland where an unnatural boundary is created between them and those who determine what their experiences will be. Others speak *on* their behalf: they speak *for* them, they speak *about* them, but they rarely speak *with* them. And yet, as Antoine de Saint-Exupery wrote in *The Little Prince*, grown-ups cannot on their own understand the world from the young person's point of view and therefore they need children to explain it to them.

One of the significant dilemmas facing those advocating the need to consult with young people is that, in many cases, it is the young people themselves who are the 'border guards'. As Johnson (2004: 10) has noted in her investigation for the National College of School Leadership, 'school leaders most often refer to elected school councils as examples of pupil participation in their schools'. It is a rare school council that chooses to be transgressive and challenge what is taking place. Rather they work at the behest of those who hold the power. Holdsworth (2005: 7) alerts us to some of the dangers inherent in investing in student leaders at the expense of broader participation:

> I have been concerned that the dominant language has shifted over the years from 'participation' to 'representation' to 'leadership' and that each shift has marked a narrowing of concepts and of increasingly elite ideas.

And yet there are voices who advocate the right of students to be heard, for they are the witnesses to what takes place in schools, both within and outside their classrooms:

> What pupils say about teaching, learning and schooling is not only worth listening to, but provides an important – perhaps the most important – foundation for thinking about ways of improving schools. (Rudduck *et al.* 1996: 1)

Jean Rudduck, Professor Emeritus at Cambridge University, has long been an advocate of the rights of students to be heard. In naming but of few of her many publications on student voice spanning well over a decade (Rudduck and Flutter, 2000, 2004; Flutter and Rudduck, 2004; MacBeath *et al.*, 2003: Rudduck, 2001, 2002), it is clear that she has an enduring concern for students to be more participative in the decisions that govern the place in which they spend so much of their young lives.

Ruddock actually employs the term 'pupils' to describe young people in schools. In the Australian context the preferred term is 'students', that is intended to invest them with greater agency than the former designation would suggest.

Of course it should not be taken that, if and when they are consulted, young people will necessarily wish for more radical or innovative schooling. Howard and Johnson (2000) found, in the Australian context, that young people who were consulted about the possibility of changing the ways in which the early years of secondary school might be operated in order to assist them in making the transition more effectively generally opted for the status quo. It was argued that because the current conditions were the only ones that they knew and experienced, it was unreasonable to ask them to 'imagine how things might be managed differently, because it is asking them to put their present success at risk' (p. 8). Partly the research results could be attributed to the researchers only seeking the views of 'resilient students'. However, the caution is worth observing in that it raises an interesting ethical point, 'What we are to do if students themselves are the conservative forces?'. This is an issue to which I shall return later in this discussion.

Of course, not all young people wish for things to remain the same. This has been illustrated when they have been more broadly consulted, via the mass media, in an investigation of 'the school I'd like'.

The school I'd like

A concern for listening to students is not a discovery of the twenty-first century. During the 1960s, as noted above, the *Observer* newspaper in the UK ran a competition asking children of secondary-school age to design the school of their dreams. Not only did these young people indicate something of the school they'd like, they also told of the features of their schooling that they were unhappy about, even actively disliked. At that time, one 15-year-old girl wrote that 'the institutions of today are run on the principles of yesterday'. So what has changed?

In the *Guardian* follow-up (see above), the editor of the day, Dea Birkett, summed them up in this way: 'I have never read so much that was so full of complaints and criticisms, of schemes for imaginative innovation, and yet that was, as a whole so very sober' (*Education Guardian*, Tuesday, 5 June, 2001). As observed in the Introduction – but it is worth repeating – Burke and Gosvenor commented: 'There is a history of not attending to the expressed experience of children within schools, everyday neglect in this sense has become institutional'.

Introducing a similar competition, in 2005, the *Sydney Morning Herald*'s then education editor, Linda Doherty, reflected that today's students are very different from those who sat in classrooms decades ago. They are sophisticated users of information and communication technologies, engaged in forms of communication unimaginable in their parents' or teachers' own schooldays. It is certainly the generation that has had the greatest engagement with digital technologies. Today's students have never known life without mobile phones, computers, and voice mail (Chester, 2002); they are globally aware and locally savvy. There is very little that they have not seen or heard through the electronic media that is saturated with explicit messages and vision. Young people may be place bound, but they can operate freely in cyberspace.

Of course such competitions have not been the only ways in which young people have been consulted. In a somewhat different context, two Glasgow school leavers, Craig and Kevin (Jones and Smith, 2004: 17) reported on a two-day event that offered students the opportunity to use multimedia, including making a documentary on schooling. They made a number of telling observations upon both their own and their peers' experiences of learning. They suggested that schooling had changed little from the 1920s classroom that they had been researching. They posed the question:

> Why not ask the pupils what they think would help them most to learn, because they're the ones that are going to learn? Not many pupils of our age have this option; most are conditioned to believe that all the rules laid down are correct. They have been battered with this stuff over the centuries; all these artificial pressures have been put on teenagers. Their views aren't encouraged; instead they are dictated to by teachers who take all the responsibility that shapes their character. Even today, school is not really different from the 1920s. They don't have permission to batter us, but we're still in an institutional straightjacket.

While, in the main, it is true that schools rarely consult their students and take them seriously, it is the case that there are schools in the UK, the USA and in Australia where there have been systematic policies and practices that have enabled students' voices to be heard and have even given students agency in designing, investigating, analysing and interpreting studies of learning (Cook-Sather, 2002; Needham and Groundwater-Smith, 2003; Groundwater-Smith and Mockler, 2003; Arnot et al., 2004; Danby and Farrell, 2004; Johnson, 2004). In Sydney, Australia, a network of schools has been working upon the development of authentic inquiry-based processes that involve students at every point in the research.

The Coalition of Knowledge Building Schools as learning network

The Coalition of Knowledge Building Schools (Groundwater-Smith and Mockler, 2003) has as its purpose:

- developing and enhancing the notion of evidence-based practice
- developing an interactive community of practice using appropriate technologies
- making a contribution to a broader professional knowledge base with respect to educational practice
- building research capability within their own and each other's schools by engaging both teachers and students in the research processes
- sharing methodologies which are appropriate to practitioner enquiry as a means of transforming teacher professional learning.

The processes that it has adopted are:

- developing new practitioner research methods; sharing methodologies which are appropriate to practitioner inquiry
- engaging in cross-researching in member schools
- considering forms of documentation
- reporting and critiquing research
- engaging in collaborative writing and reflection.

Altogether, 13 schools (seven government secondary schools, two government primary schools and four independent schools) meet with and visit each other to fulfil these purposes. They see themselves as 'intelligent schools' as understood by MacGilchrist *et al.* (2004) and believe that a significant component of working intelligently is to attend to the testimony of their students.

To demonstrate the Coalition's commitment to taking account of student voice, two studies will be examined: one in which students were central to the investigation of bullying with a need to develop more proactive academic care policies; the other where students considered their own teachers' learning and how it impacted upon classroom practices.

Countering bullying at Independent Girls' School

Independent Girls' School (IGS) has been a foundation member of the Coalition of Knowledge Building Schools. As such, it has become confident not only in consulting its students regarding various practices within the school but also engaging them in the inquiry processes themselves. While the school has given thought in the past to such matters as bullying and intimidation, it perceived that before moving towards more enduring solutions it was important that further evidence be gathered regarding the ways in which the phenomena are understood, in particular by students, in order to inform the development of resources that can be used by them and by their teachers in addressing the various associated issues.

It was strongly believed that in order to gather this intelligence the principal source of information should be the students themselves. Consequently, a student research programme was formed as one that would assist in the organisation and collection of data, the interpretation of results, the formulation of strategies and the development of resources. In effect, the students would act to validate the operational definition of bullying and its consequences and support teacher professional learning to assist them in addressing some of the associated challenges. Importantly the processes that have been adopted have been embedded into the normal practices of the school through curriculum development resource evaluation and student leadership. In this context 'student leadership' is not a term applying to an elected student body, but a role that students may take – the view is that on different occasions and for varying purposes students will be identified, or identify themselves as leaders. While the undertaking of the project has been multidimensional and far-reaching it can be seen that a study of this kind can be a part of the curriculum and not apart from it.

Strategies adopted by the study were:

1 A website on the school intranet, for use by students, has been instituted and used extensively by students – this site has yielded insight into student perceptions of bullying, its nature and incidence within the school. The website has clear protocols for its use. Students refer to behaviours rather than the names of those perceived to be bullying or being bullied. They are aware that staff responsible for academic care do know their identities, but they are able to use pseudonyms on the website.
2 Student focus groups have been conducted, using information from the Senior School Climate Survey data, in order to provide an enriched and informed

perspective from the student point of view. These focus groups have been conducted by trained Year 11 students who have engaged with a significant number of Year 8 and Year 10 students.

3   Students have developed posters for display in various areas of the school in order to raise awareness and understanding of the need for the school community to be one where cooperation is applauded and difference celebrated. These posters have fallen into two categories: the first of these has been at the initiative of the middle school and enjoin cooperation, friendship and the celebration of difference. The second set of posters was developed by the junior school with coaching and support from the older students and featured a similar set of concepts. Another publishing strategy which was enacted was related to gathering designs to support the school's 'Respecting Difference Policy' to be published as a revamped brochure. Students were requested to document and encourage proactive policies. This has been conducted as a 'Speak Out' competition within the middle and senior schools.

4   A number of teaching/learning resources and strategies have been adopted, developed and/or evaluated to be used in relation to affective concerns (relationship building, human skills development). For example an integrated curriculum initiative in personal development, health and physical education (PDHPE), 'The Power in Me', has been designed and enacted. The use of Rigby's maxim 'speaking out makes a difference' as an explicit pedagogical device has been adopted during such occasions as assemblies. The Learning to Learn programme has been adapted to meet identified needs. The 'Snakes and Ladders of Life Game' has been evaluated by Year 5 in 2004 and Year 6 in 2005 and there has been a multimedia approach to developing further insights about bullying as a behaviour through picture book and film analysis.

5   Student leadership groups have met to discuss the results arising from the various strategies and to recommend ongoing action. A particularly noteworthy issue has been the redesign and refurbishment of the senior student common room in order for interaction to be more open and public.

6   Dance, drama and speech programmes are currently under way. These challenge students to question the 'you can't do anything about it' stance. Students in the junior school and Year 8 Empowerment Programme are involved.

Following an analysis of results that also involved teachers, as practitioner-researchers, and the writer of this chapter who has long been the school's 'researcher-in-residence', a group of Year 11 student leaders convened to discuss their impact on school policies and to develop a PowerPoint presentation that would be used for teacher professional development.

Reflecting on teacher professional learning: Outer Western Comprehensive High School

Outer Western Comprehensive High School (OWCHS) is a government school and is established on Sydney's western fringe. It is a more recent member of the Coalition and joined as a result of its involvement in the Australian Government Quality Teaching Program. Having participated in a number of projects, it could see the merit in terms of consulting students with respect to the ways in which learning could be assisted. Thus it was with some enthusiasm that it agreed to take part in a small pilot study to which students might contribute by considering their teachers' professional learning and the ways in which such learning might be improved.

Altogether 13 students participated, seven girls and six boys from Year 12. The group was observed by an officer from the New South Wales Department of Education and Training Professional Learning Unit and a deputy principal.

When asked to comment on their perception of their teachers as learners and how they learn their skills, the group responded with a list of desirable skills: have rapport with students; be able to listen; be able to handle and control difficult students; have good communication skills; speak clearly; be skilled in presenting concepts in a manner that will facilitate learning; be insightful about identifying students experiencing problems in order to prevent those students being demeaned in front of their peers; be friendly; and finally, have a passion for their work.

They believed their teachers learned by making mistakes and from experience in life and in the classroom. When the information that teachers learned from making mistakes was reported back to the School Principal she smiled, as she had only that day talked at the school assembly of the learning that can arise from making mistakes and the importance of taking risks in learning. Students perceived that extended experience in the classroom enabled the teacher to be less nervous. In response to a question asking them to tell a story about a time when they detected that one of their teachers had learned something new and how it impacted on them, several students recounted in detail occasions when they believed that this had happened and the way that the teacher had applied this new learning in the classroom. They discussed the issue of learning through experience and gave the example of a beginning teacher who, they believed, needed to learn and grow and to accept that negative behaviours are not necessarily a personal attack on her but may require the teacher to work out objectively why students react as they do.

When questioned about whether they were aware when their teachers were attending professional learning events, the students affirmed that their teachers would advise them when they would be away attending courses and often described the course they were attending. They shared several examples of occasions when their teachers returned with lessons enriched from these experiences. They assumed that staff development days were occasions when teachers talked about their students and teaching. In response to 'What kinds of things would you like to see your teachers learn?', students stated that they would like their teachers to be more skilled in behaviour management. They understood the balance that a teacher had to maintain between being friendly and maintaining a professional relationship under-pinned by a sense of authority. Students valued teachers who did not 'just put a book in front of you'; they needed interaction. They appreciated teachers who explained the work rather than saying 'just do it'. They wanted their teachers to recognise 'personal learning methods'. However, it was seen that it could be difficult for teachers to reach 'every student when they need to get through the syllabus'.

In this instance, the feedback from the students was intended not only to inform professional learning plans within the school, but also to assist in advising policy more broadly across the system. To this end a number of other schools also participated in this project (for more information see McLelland, 2005). What was revealing was the extent to which the schools themselves responded to the students' perceptions. In the case of OWCHS the information was well received. Consulting students was not new to this school and it was believed that their testimony was dependable and useful. However, as, is suggested by the title to McLelland's paper, 'Why should we tell them what we learn?', referring as it does to the teachers whose learning was being discussed, in other areas the desirability of consulting students was questioned.

Consulting students cannot be seen as unproblematic. The process generates a number of challenges and dilemmas which in turn surface some serious ethical concerns.

The challenges and dilemmas of consulting students

Just as Jean Rudduck has given over a considerable part of her academic life to reflecting upon issues surrounding consulting with students, so too has Michael Fielding devoted much of his time to these concerns (Fielding, 2004). His recent analysis of the very real difficulties in working in this manner reminds us of the range of practical concerns that we must address if we are to move forward:

> [We need to] resist the constant pull for either 'fadism' or 'manipulative incorporation' ... Fadism leads to unrealistic expectations, subsequent marginalisation and the unwitting corrosion of integrity; manipulative incorporation leads to betrayal of hope, resigned exhaustion and the bolstering of an increasingly powerful status quo. (Fielding, 2004: 296)

He asks a series of penetrating questions, among them:

- How confident are we that our research does not redescribe and reconfigure students in ways that bind them more securely into the fabric of the status quo?
- How clear are we about the use to which the depth and detail of data is likely to be put? Is our more detailed knowledge of what students think and feel largely used to help us control them more effectively?
- Are we sure that our positions of relative power and our own personal and professional interests are not blurring our judgements or shaping our advocacy? (Fielding, 2004: 302–304)

In effect we might ask ourselves 'Are we capturing student voice in order to tame the unruly?'. As Cook-Sather (2002: 8) asks in the context of current United States educational reform, are we 'authorising' student perspectives only to later ignore them: 'Most power relationships have no place for listening and actively do not tolerate it because it is very inconvenient: to really listen means to have to respond.'

The more cynical among us might see shades of just this kind of appropriation of student voice in the current work directed towards 'personalised learning' (Hargreaves, 2004: 7). Student voice is seen here as mainly being about

How students come to play a more active role in their education and schooling as a direct result of teachers becoming more attentive, in sustained and routine ways to what students say about their experience of learning and of school life.

There seems little room here for the possibilities of debate and dissent so strongly advocated by Fielding. Indeed, when addressing dissent in the publication Hargreaves notes:

> Dissent on issues that are of evident importance to students is natural and should always be expected and accepted; it does not have to be ignored or suppressed. As John MacBeath has suggested, there are in a school so many voices (some of which may not be verbal) that there are harmonies and discords; strident shrieks, soft whispers and silences, both natural and enforced. Replacing cacophony with just the right acoustic balance is the task of leadership. (Hargreaves, 2004: 9–10)

There is a shadowy elision here. The dialogic encounter may occur, but it will be resolved by those in power, the school leaders; any hint of genuine reciprocity has gone. Is student voice being employed to promote teacher professional development, or to discipline, manage and control both teachers and their students? As Noyes observes (2005: 536) 'Voices are nothing without hearers', the question is, 'Who is doing the listening and to what purpose?'. This brings us, then, to the very significant ethical concerns that require attention in this field of practice.

Ethical concerns

It must first be observed that the ethical concerns of which I write are themselves dilemmas. There are costs and benefits whichever way we turn. If we consult students, we may put them in positions of vulnerability. If we do not consult them, we risk overlooking the important contribution that they can make. If we treat them as vulnerable, we may be patronising them and imagining them to be powerless and irresponsible (Morrow, 2004). If we regard them as invulnerable, we may underestimate their fragility. As Simons (2000) notes, it is a matter of 'damned if you do and damned if you don't'. The fundamental ethical principle is to prevent harm or doing wrong to others; it is a concern to promote the good and to be respectful and fair.

In order to address the ethical concerns in attending to student voice in the intelligent school I pose six questions:

- To what extent are students given the right to exercise informed consent?
- What provision is made to ensure confidentiality and anonymity?
- Who is consulted?
- What are the opportunity costs?
- How is student voice sustained and nurtured?
- How is the information yielded through student voice disseminated and acted upon?

The right to say 'no'

Schools are typically places where students are not asked their permission to participate in whatever is taking place. Indeed they have regulatory influences on children's experiences even when they are home (Danby and Farrell, 2004: 38). They are expected to come to school every day, to write when they are told to write, to calculate when they are told to calculate; to work cooperatively in small groups when they are required to and so on. Informed consent is a fundamental ethical precept, but more often observed in its absence than otherwise. Although parental consent may and should be sought, it is also important that the student is provided with an explanation of the project to make his or her own decision regarding involvement. As Danby and Farrell (2004: 39) documented:

Researcher: How did you feel about actually being asked if you wanted to do it or if you didn't want to do it? [provide consent]
Jacob: I was in heaven.
Researcher: Yeah (laughter) how come?
Jacob: Usually I don't get, uhmm, decisions about those particular things like in school.

Generally, we find that young people are willing participants in school-based inquiry projects, yet they may be easily persuaded and at times naive. It is important that they understand that their participation is voluntary and that they can withdraw.

It is interesting to reflect upon issues related to informed consent when data is being gathered unobtrusively such as was the case in IGS where the postings on the bullying website on the school intranet were made available for the research. Tavani and Moor (2001: 6) in their discussion regarding privacy protection in the context of web-based technologies suggest that the concept of privacy is 'best defined in terms of restricted access, not control ... it is fundamentally about protection from intrusion and information gathering by others'. Students were posting their responses anonymously in a password-protected environment. The site's webmaster was able to monitor responses through his knowledge of student passwords and intervened only when some example of the school's etiquette code was transgressed, such as naming a student rather than the behaviour that caused alarm. None of this information was available to the school-based practitioner-researchers or the researcher-in-residence. All the same, this is an area where we have to exercise caution. As Tavani and Moor (2001: 7) observe, the individual flow of information cannot be controlled, but individual protection can. The web is something of a blurred area in this respect: 'In general, diverse private and public situations can be imbedded and overlap each other in complex ways'.

Confidentiality and anonymity

Working with young people as authentic witnesses to their own experiences in school requires that they engage with the researcher(s) in a space that will guarantee their privacy. Even where the research may be being conducted by their peers, it is important that every care is taken to ensure that they are not overheard and their responses commented upon by third parties. Young people need to feel safe and comfortable when their opinions upon what might be quite contentious issues are being sought. This raises some real issues for practitioner-researchers when they know and are familiar with the students with whom they are working. In the focus group discussion conducted at OWCHS it was noted that the Deputy Principal was present. The purpose of this was to continue to build capacity in the school to undertake this kind of inquiry. The students themselves had already taken part in a number of such discussions and appeared at ease. However, when sensitive issues are being discussed protocols need to be in place to ensure that students may respond freely and without fear of subsequent consequences. The litmus test is to ask 'Whose interests are being served?'. Will the study contribute important knowledge 'without appropriating participants' experiences, understandings and even their miseries to serve our ends' (Keddie, 2000: 80–81)? As Christensen (2004: 166) reminds us in the context of children's participation in research 'viewing power as inherent to research emphasises that research is a practice that is part of social life, rather than an external contemplation of it'.

Who is consulted?

Reflecting back on the earlier cited Howard and Johnson study (2000), it was argued that the very fact that they consulted 'resilient' students led to some unintended consequences for their research in that these were students who opted for the status quo because it had served them well. In considering who is consulted in inquiries involving young people, it is important to take account of issues related to equity and social justice. Are only those students who are likely to put a good face on things the ones who meet the researcher? Have some been excluded because they may have difficulties in formulating their ideas? Perhaps they have speech or learning difficulties, or are just being seen as 'difficult'.

Atweh and Bland (2004: 13) remind us that students' voices are not singular. Perspectives will be mediated by factors such as ethnicity, gender, degrees of cultural and social capital, all working and interacting in complex ways. 'Working with students in collaborative research, adults should be conscious of the differential experiences and expertise that each participant brings to the process of collaboration.' Some of these variations can be dealt with through the employment of mixed methods which not only lend authenticity through triangulation but also allow for voices to be expressed through a variety of media such as in the case of IGS where surveys, focus groups, product analysis and a web-based discussion were all part of the data set.

Opportunity costs

Some studies will take a considerable amount of student time. Good relationships need to be built in order for trust to be established. This is time away from other opportunities. Students need to feel that their contribution has been worthwhile. In the IGS study it was possible to embed a number of data collection strategies into the curriculum itself. Consequently, when students were engaged in developing their information literacy skills they conducted their searches around some of the key questions that the study was investigating. Similarly, they evaluated various visual and written texts as a normal part of classroom practice.

Sustaining student voice

Practitioner-researchers who work with students to provide the conditions that allow them to be heard and respected know well that the process is not one with which to be lightly engaged. It is not a tap to be turned off and on, but rather a continuous and developmental process. There are serious ethical questions to be asked with respect to raising expectations that consultation with students will be ongoing and embedded in the culture of the school. If this is to occur, then schools also need to have ongoing plans for ways in which they can sustain student voice inquiry. Fielding and Bragg (2003: 41) advocate developing students' roles, developing the identity of the work, and involving different staff and developing staff roles. As one Year 10 researcher in their Students as Researchers Project put it:

> We'd like to see the present Year 9 training up new students like we did, so we're continually developing students throughout the year groups on research and presentations . . . We shouldn't be the main people in this because we're eventually going to go. If we take control, they won't know where to start, we need to make sure they have the skills. (Year 10 researcher)

Similarly, continuity is dependent upon staff commitment. Kaye Johnson, Principal of Woodville Primary School in South Australia, has been working with young students in her current school for three years, having done so previously for a number of years in prior appointments. She argues that it has taken three years of strategic action to introduce a culture that enables authentic student participation. However, she notes that 'Although an evenly paced, sequential approach to student participation has been in practice for three years, a significant proportion of staff has not participated in all of it' (Johnson, 2005: 47).

Nurturing an inquiring school culture and the capabilities of those within it to fully participate is clearly a significant but warranted challenge.

Dissemination and action

Finally, in reflecting upon the ethical dimensions of listening to student voice in the intelligent school, it is vital that the matter of how studies are to be disseminated and then acted upon is deeply considered. According to Dewey (1916: 87), education in a democratic society is neither for the individual alone or for the society alone. It is for both. It is 'a mode of conjoint communicated experiences' and rests upon principles of communication whereby the responsibility for learning is a whole-hearted endeavour in which all participate in the interests of decency and democracy. It would be an abrogation of the very tenets upon which student voice is developed, if the inquiries to which they had contributed were distorted or withheld. Dissemination of results must be based upon the kind of dialogic encounter so passionately argued for by Fielding (2004). Similarly, unsettling as it might be, actions arising from the inquiries must be clear and transparent. If students indicate that they have consistently experienced negative conditions for learning, then those conditions must change. If students have been enabled to argue that they have a greater need to participate in decision-making, then some kind of provision for them to be so treated must be put into place. Otherwise the kind of cynicism that Alderson (2000) writes of will be bound to flourish.

Conclusion

Early in this chapter I turned to Gloria Anzaldua who has written so evocatively of borderlands. I found it a powerful metaphor for reflecting upon our need to be more inclusive of student voice when considering the educational landscape. In turning back to an interview with Anzaldua I noted:

> What surprised me most was that the metaphor of the borderlands speaks to its time much more than I thought it would. So that it's being taken up by different people who are in different disciplines, who are in different countries. ... What it does is thrill me and validate me as a writer that people can take my images or ideas and work them out in their own way and write their own theories and their own books. (Anzaldua in Reuman, 2000)

Student engagement in practitioner inquiry in educational research may seem a far cry from the new mestiza, but the social geography of the school is one where many borders, both visible and obscured, apply. Moving in relationships from power *over* students, to power *with* students is no easy matter; but if the consequence is that the borders are more permeable and the interests more mutual, then the effort will have been worth the game.

References

Alderson, P. (2000) 'School pupils' views on school councils and daily life at school', *Children and Society*, 14(2) 121–134.
Anzaldua, G. (1987) *Borderlands/La Frontera: The New Mestiza*, San Francisco, CA: Aunt Lute Books.
Arnot, M., McIntyre, D., Pedder, D. and Reay, D. (2004) *Consultation in the Classroom: Developing Dialogue about Teaching and Learning*, Cambridge: Pearson Publishing.
Atweh, B. and Bland, D. (2004) 'Problematics in young people as researchers: visions and voices', paper presented to the social Change in the 21st Century Conference, Centre for Social Change Research, QUT, 29th October.
Blishen, E. (ed.) (1967) *The School that I'd Like*, England: Penguin Education Special.
Burke, C. and Grosvenor, I. (2003) *The School I'd Like: Children and Young People's Reflections on an Education in the 21st Century*, London: Routledge Falmer.
Chester, E. (2002) *Employing Generation Why?*, Colorado: Tucker House Books.
Christensen, P. (2004) 'Children's participation in ethnographic research: issues of power and representation', *Children and Society*, 18(2) 165–176.
Cook-Sather, A. (2002) 'Authorizing students' perspectives: toward trust, dialogue and change in education', *Educational Researcher*, 31(4) 3–14.
Danby, S. and Farrell, A. (2004) 'Accounting for young children's competence in educational research: new perspectives on research ethics', *The Australian Educational Researcher*, 31(3) 35–48.
Dewey, J. (1916) *Democracy and Education*, New York: Macmillan.
Fielding, M. (2004) 'Transformative approaches to student voice: theoretical underpinnings, recalcitrant realities', *British Educational Research Journal*, 30(2) 295–311.
Fielding, M. and Bragg, S. (2003) *Students as Researchers: Making a Difference*, London: Pearson Publishing.
Flutter, J. and Rudduck, J. (2004) *Consulting Pupils: What's in it for Schools?* London: Routledge Falmer,
Groundwater-Smith, S. and Mockler, N. (2003) *Learning to Listen: Listening to Learn*, Sydney: University of Sydney and MLC School.

Hargreaves, D. (2004) *Personalised Learning – 2: Student Voice and Assessment for Learning*, London: Specialist Schools Trust.

Holdsworth, R. (2005) (ed.) *Student Councils and Beyond*, Northcote, Victoria: Connect.

Howard, S. and Johnson, B. (2000) 'Transitions from primary to secondary school: possibilities and paradoxes', paper presented to the Australian Association for Research in Education Annual Conference, Sydney, December.

Johnson, K. (2004) 'Children's voices: pupil leadership in primary schools', *International Research Associate Perspectives*, Nottingham: National College for School Leadership, Summer edition.

Johnson, K. (2005) 'Students' voices: strategies for promoting student participation in primary schools', in R. Holdsworth (ed.) *Student Councils and Beyond*, Northcote, Victoria: Connect, pp. 44–47.

Jones, C. and Smith, K. (2004) 'Listening to the learner', in M. Selinger (ed.) *Connected Schools*, London: Premium Publishing, pp. 16–25.

Keddie, A. (2000) 'Research with young children: some ethical considerations', *Journal of Educational Enquiry*, 1(2): 72–81.

MacBeath, J., Demetriou, H., Rudduck, J. and Myers, K. (2003) *Consulting Pupils: A Toolkit for Teachers*, London: Pearson Publishing.

MacGilchrist, B., Myers, K., and Reed, J. (2004) *The Intelligent School* (2nd edn), London: Sage Publications.

McLelland, M. (2005) 'Why should we tell them what we learn?', paper presented at the International Practitioner Research/CARN Conference, Utrecht, 4–6 November.

Morrow, V. (2004) 'The ethics of social research with children and young people – an overview'. Available online at www.ciimu.org/wellchi/reports/wsh1/pdfs/pdf%20securitzats/morrows.pdf (accessed 30 September 2005).

Needham, K. and Groundwater-Smith, S. (2003) 'Using student voice to inform', School Improvement Paper presented to International Congress for School Effectiveness and Improvement Sydney, January.

Noyes, A. (2005) 'Pupil voice: purpose, power and the possibilities for democratic schooling: a thematic review', in *British Educational Research Journal*, 31 (4) 533–540.

Reuman, A. (2000) 'Coming into play: an interview with Gloria Anzaldua'. Available online at www.findarticles.com/p/articles/mi_m2278/is_2_25/ai_67532171/#continue (accessed 5 October 2005).

Rudduck, J. (2001) 'Students and school improvement: "transcending the cramped conditions of the time",' *Improving Schools*, 4(2): 7–16.

Rudduck, J. (2002) 'The transformative potential of consulting young people about teaching learning and schooling', *Scottish Educational Review*, 34(2): 123–137.

Rudduck, J. and Flutter, J. (2000) 'Pupil participation and pupil perspective: "carving a new order of experience",' *Cambridge Journal of Education*, 30(1): 75–89.

Rudduck, J. and Flutter, J. (2004) *How to Improve your School: Giving Pupils a Voice*, London: Continuum Press.

Rudduck, J., Chaplain, R. and Wallace, G. (eds) (1996) *School Improvement: What can pupils tell us?*, London: David Fulton.

Simons, H. (2000) 'Damned if you do; damned if you don't: ethical dilemmas in evaluation research', in H. Simons and R. Usher (eds) *Situated Ethics in Educational Research*. London: Routledge.

Tavani, H. and Moor, J. (2001) 'Privacy protection, control of information, and privacy-enhancing technologies', *Computers and Society*, 31(1): 6–11.

CHAPTER 11

CO-OPERATIVE CHANGE MANAGEMENT THROUGH PRACTITIONER INQUIRY

Susan Groundwater-Smith

In his challenging and provocative interpretation of contemporary Australian society, Boris Frankel (2004) seeks to dismantle many of the shibboleths surrounding our characterization of schooling provision, as equitable and socially just. He argues that the political ecology of the continent of Australia is:

> particularly hospitable to three odd and troubling species: the zombies, stalking the political landscape like the walking dead; the Lilliputions, tiny in mind and timid in their expectations . . . and finally the sadists, prowling our workplaces, bureaucracies and parliaments. (p. 9)

He argues that, contrary to the myths we tell about ourselves, there continues in Australia to be deep educational and social inequality both in terms of participation in schooling and the nature of the experienced curriculum. His line of reasoning is supported by, among others, Richard Teese (2006) who makes the case that schools should be pursuing a rigorous agenda of equal outcomes for their students. In addition, he suggests that schools facing challenging circumstances should be ready and willing to be risk takers and innovators and that they should be provided not only with resources, but also an environment where their efforts are recognized and applauded.

Frankel's rather bleak analysis of Australian society is not one that stands alone. More than a decade ago Elliott and MacLennan (1994) pointed to striking similarities between Canadian, British and United States' policies that have been critical of 'educational progressivism and have concentrated upon business values, market discipline and market relations in schools and colleges' p. 165. These policies, too, have brought about distortions in schooling, particularly when it comes to matters of equity and social justice.

It is in this context that somewhat surprisingly the Priority Action Schools Program was developed in the Australian state of New South Wales. This chapter will discuss the genesis of the program and its intention to improve the learning opportunities of young people. The Priority Actions Schools Program (PASP), a joint venture between the NSW Department of Education and Training (DET) and the NSW Teachers Federation (the local teachers union to which almost all teachers in government schools in the state belong) was designed to trial intensive assistance to 74 schools serving communities with deep needs. This group represented approximately one-quarter of those schools in the state who are in receipt of additional funding on the basis of issues around poverty, ethnicity and Aboriginality (a term employed to indicate the proportion of Indigenous students attending a given school). The trial aimed to build school and individual capacity to improve student engagement in learning and student learning outcomes, reduce disruptive behaviour and suspensions and improve attendance and retention in the context of fostering co-operation between schools, the Tertiary and Further Education Sector (TAFE) and other agencies and community organizations.

PASP was conceived of as a knowledge based program in that schools were required to create and share professional knowledge. The program aimed to model for schools a culture of collaborative enquiry with opportunities for dissemination and the nurturing of teacher professional learning. The evaluation strategy, articulated in the guiding principles for evaluation, placed knowledge creation and knowledge transfer at its core.

Designing a program with an equity of educational outcomes focus

Currently educational policy development in Australia is primarily a matter for the individual states and territories, although, increasingly the federal government is seeking to intervene in relation to the development of a national curriculum, national testing and standards for teachers as they progress through their careers. Frankel (2004), whose colourful quotation opened this chapter, observed that social justice and equity concerns were not prominent in the policies of the then federal government; however, they remained of primary concern at the state level in all jurisdictions. This balance may change with the recent change of federal government; however, it is too early to make a determination in relation to any such change.

The objectives of the Priority Actions Schools Program were to support schools to build their capacity to:

- improve students' educational outcomes;
- improve student behaviour and attendance;
- support teachers through mentoring and induction programs;
- support whole school approaches to improved teaching practice;
- reduce high student turnover and increase retention to complete schooling;
- reduce the impacts of socio-economic disadvantage; and
- maximize interagency and community support. (NSW Department of Education and Training, 2002)

Schools identified on a number of criteria were invited to submit expressions of interest, outlining strategies they would use in pursuit of these objectives. Each school's set of strategies was to be designed as a 'local solution' to local problems and issues. Funding was delivered to schools at the start of 2003 after negotiations with the state team managing the Program to identify how these additional resources to the schools might be used – including for additional teaching, executive or support staff.

The Priority Action Schools Program was structured as a 'knowledge building program'. Each school was required to conduct a systematic evaluation of its own work, assisted by an academic partner experienced in school-based research. Each school would build a *school learning portfolio* documenting its work. The meta-evaluators worked in a co-operative relationship with the state PASP team in a similar way to the academic partners who worked with each PASP school.

Together with their academic partners, schools explored a variety of strategies in pursuit of the objectives of the Program, including strategies aimed at developing:

- pedagogy;
- improved learning outcomes for students;
- whole school vision and culture building;
- staffing solutions;
- organization for learning;
- interagency work and parent and community involvement;
- student well-being and student support; and
- teachers' professional development.

The program was underpinned by the notion of 'pressure and support' (Beveridge et al., 2005). Where schools were expected to undertake action inquiry by first identifying the particular challenges they faced and then designing an appropriate means of addressing them. They were then to document their findings in partnership with an academic associate who would act as a practitioner research facilitator.

The pressure element was not in relation to an expectation that schools would conform to a 'one size fits all' solution, but rather that they were expected to be able to explain what they were doing, why and how they were doing it and how effective their strategies were. The pressure was intended to provide a form of professional accountability. Schools were supported to develop a culture of collaborative enquiry by engaging in a range of professional learning opportunities implemented by the NSW Department of Education and Training State Team.

Each learning portfolio was analysed by the author of this chapter, Susan Groundwater-Smith, and by Stephen Kemmis. As well, the evaluators made a number of site visits and attended all team meetings at which the senior DET officers and union officers were present. The evaluators engaged with practitioners at all levels: in the classrooms, in the schools, in the communities, in the universities from which the academic partners came, and in the bureaucracy itself. Thus PASP was both a knowledge building program and one that contributed to teacher professional learning in the context of an inquiry that has a social justice focus – that is a normative concern about what *should be*, as well as what *is*, where teachers are enjoined to be courageous learners as encouraged by Newman (2006).

Escaping old bonds of practice: two examples

Changing educational practices is never an easy matter. In spite of being faced with often quite extraordinary challenges, it is the case that bringing about effective change in entrenched behaviours is difficult. Richardson and Placier (2001) have gone some way to assisting us in understanding this conundrum by offering two contrasting strategies for change, one they describe as an 'empirical-rational approach' (p. 905) where teachers are instructed by consultants, academics and bureaucrats about how they ought to go about their practice; the other is a 'normative-reeducative' approach (p. 906) that gives the practitioner agency in developing improvement strategies based upon systematic practical inquiry Richardson, 1994). The PASP was clearly founded upon the latter.

In offering two examples from the case record of the PASP, the writer is mindful of respecting the confidentiality that has been required by the study. Therefore each example, is in effect, a composite of the work of several schools. In the first case, Moorok Central School is located in a remote area of the state and caters for children from Kindergarten to Year 10; in the second case Garrick Public School is on the metropolitan fringe and provides an education for young people from Kindergarten to Year 6. The composites were formed by examining the portfolios of several schools located in similar areas and dealing with similar challenges.

Moorok Central School

One must first be appreciative of the fact that rural New South Wales has been subject to a prolonged drought that has placed great pressure on the social resilience of its most remote communities. As economic pressures increased those most able to leave have done so, leaving behind those who are increasingly impoverished and marginalized, many of whom are Indigenous Australians. The Human Rights and Equal Opportunities Commission (HREOC) conducted a national inquiry into rural and remote education (HREOC, 2000) and found that a range of social and structural factors limited access to quality education, among them: town size, distance to the nearest school, quality of roads and limited curriculum breadth due to school size; staff turnover, and student alienation resulting in participation, attendance, retention and achievement far below the national average. These conditions prevailed during the first year of the PASP and continue to this day.

In common with many small towns in remote New South Wales, Moorok has experienced the closure of a number of its businesses and services, including the local motel, pharmacy and real estate agency. Tradespeople such as plumbers and electricians have left, or are in the process of moving out. Many of the students experience significant learning difficulties, partly exacerbated by irregular attendance and health problems. All the same, the school is seen by a majority of its students as a place of safety, shelter and sustenance. All of these matters were documented carefully and poignantly in the school's learning portfolio. Indeed, it was suggested that this was itself a new experience, that is to say an opportunity to articulate the complex social challenges faced by the school in the context of being located in a remote community.

A major challenge for the school has been to retain its teachers and provide them with opportunities for professional learning. With no readily available relief teachers who could come in when called upon on an irregular basis, it was decided that the school would use some of its PASP funding to appoint additional staff to the school's complement. This has been no small achievement. Staffing government schools in New South Wales has been highly regulated. Because the program was undertaken in consultation with the New South Wales Teachers Federation it was possible to reach working agreements on variations that went outside the normal procedures. As a result of additional staff, teachers were able to be relieved from their classes and be engaged in examining the scope and sequence of the curriculum, seeking for greater integration and relevance. This is a particularly important strategy in a context of high staff turnover in such schools and a number of relatively inexperienced teachers, which means that much planning is of a stop-start nature, and much of it not integrated. Having additional staff also meant that a program that would mentor and nurture early career teachers could be put into place.

In relation to its community, the school sought to have closer links with ways in which local Indigenous culture could be better understood, acknowledged and incorporated into the practices of the school. Not only were local Indigenous elders consulted, but also local identities such as artists and musicians were invited into the school to share poetry and music.

While in this first year of the PASP the school concentrated upon its teachers' learning, particularly with respect to more inclusive and relevant pedagogy, it also acknowledged that students needed assistance in developing study habits that were more likely to lead to improved learning. Many of the young people had circumstances at home that made sustained study very difficult. Moorok Central School established a learning centre that was a quiet and congenial space, staffed by a teacher who would act as a facilitator for learning rather than engaging directly in instruction. As well, as a means of overcoming the limited curriculum choices of a relatively small school, arrangements were made to increase distance education opportunities through the learning centre.

Much of the evidence collected by the school to inform its learning portfolio related to descriptions of processes and documents that had been developed. Importantly the program provided opportunities for teachers to be professionally engaged with one another, returning to first principles as they reflected on practice. In summing up the impact of one year of PASP upon teaching and learning at Moorok Central School practitioners were rightly suspicious of 'silver bullets', and right to caution that significant changes may not occur in complex organizations like schools over several years, let alone a single year.

Garrick Public School

Whereas Moorok Central School faced the challenges attendant upon its physical isolation, Garrick Public School suffered an isolation of a different kind, that of being spurned and shunned especially by media representations. Located on the metropolitan fringe it was a school serving a community described by Vinson (2003) as one of those 'so concentrated in their degree of disadvantage of life opportunities ordinarily available to most people [that they] are crushed by the negative social spiral' (p. 1). He later continues:

> There are causal associations between poor neighbourhoods and other social problems that are more than the consequences of macroeconomic forces and individual or household characteristics. The larger and longer running the area health problems the stronger the cumulative impact becomes causing a drain on services with resultant lower quality outcomes such as educational performance, housing services and health care ...neighbourhoods affect life

chances during early childhood and late adolescence, the very times when a just society would be most anxious to open up life opportunities to children and young people. (p. 56)

Vinson conducted a study of entrenched social disadvantage by tracing the circumstances of neighbourhoods by postcode and found it to have become more concentrated in fewer areas in the last 25 years. Garrick is one such area.

Garrick Public School, catering for the first six years of schooling, draws its student body from the surrounding Department of Housing estate that predominantly provides for families in crisis. A large proportion of the families are under the care of a single parent who most likely is not in the paid workforce. Both mental and physical health difficulties plague the community with a notable number of its adult members suffering the consequences of substance abuse. As well as a number of families with Indigenous backgrounds many come from those where English is a second language. Breaking through to literacy is particularly problematic in that few children had any experience of early childhood education prior to attending school.

In developing its first solutions to what seemed like intractable problems the whole staff withdrew for a weekend conference. Its first emphasis was to reorganize staffing with the appointment of a male teacher's aide; additional staff responsible for assisting in literacy development and a change in the work organization of assistant principals who would undertake mentoring of the many early career teachers in the school. As well, a community liaison officer was appointed with a brief to keep in contact with families at risk. Also the school recognized that it had a small cohort of talented students who were often overlooked within a context of crisis management. It was decided that some extension programs should be provided for these students.

Working on a premise that students learn best when they feel safe, secure and have their basic nutrition needs met, the school instituted a breakfast program in conjunction with local providers of health and well-being services. Previously a number of children had come to school both tired and hungry. Providing breakfast appeared to reinvigorate the children and made for a pleasant start to the day.

An interesting development was that of seeking for a common, agreed language that students and teachers would employ when faced with a learning difficulty or block; students have been encouraged to 'self talk' about how they might tackle a problem, saying to themselves such things as 'have I tried to remember what I have been told?' 'can I help myself before I ask someone else?'. In reference to this development teachers wrote of 'not keeping learning as secret business; we explain not just the "what" of learning; but the "why" as well'.

In their reflections teachers not only noted increased academic engagement, but also wider community engagement. They had not been fully appreciative of the ways in which their former communication patterns had failed. The practice of sending notes home to parents who themselves suffer significant literacy problems is unlikely to be helpful. Phoning and visiting in a blame-free context appeared to have much more productive results. As one entry put it:

> We have found as the year has progressed that the only way to ensure constant contact and cooperation is to keep up the level of contact by phone or house

visits as many of the community cannot read, so written attempts at communication are futile. We have learnt that it is a community-wide problem. We now view the way in which we communicate in a different light. We have become far more sympathetic to the needs of our parents.

As well as recording drops in student absenteeism, the school has also been able to document reductions in staff absenteeism. Not only have the students been more engaged, but teachers have evidently also been more professionally engaged. In the past the school believed its teachers to be experiencing significant burnout; as a result of their sense of their own efficacy it would seem that they are finding their work more satisfying and rewarding. A major learning for teachers has been that consistency in approaches to student learning pays dividends. 'Children are very perceptive and have a well-established sense of what is fair and just'.

Tools and strategies

It is clear from these case studies that the tools and strategies adopted by the PASP were critical to its implementation. The key concept was that of the *School Learning Portfolio* as a professional learning and accountability mechanism that could document processes of professional knowledge creation.

The school as a knowledge building organization has been discussed widely, notably by David Hargreaves (1999) who argued that schools have within them significant professional knowledge, much of which is tacit and unexamined. But the great fund of knowledge held by practitioners can scarcely be drawn upon if it remains buried beneath the surface. Hargreaves (2003) has since developed his argument, making the case for mobilizing and developing the intellectual and social capital held by practitioners into a more coherent and integrated whole. Furthermore, he has argued for drawing upon organizational capital in the form of networks and external links in order to inform and improve at both local and regional levels. Importantly, he believes that moving beyond incremental innovation (swimming with the tide) to radical innovation (swimming against the tide) cannot be achieved by central direction, but requires the school itself to be a learning professional life form.

How then is knowledge created in a school, with its many participants, factions and territories? PASP believed that the school itself needs to be seen as an intelligent organization. MacGilchrist et al. (2004) have focused upon schools as institutions that are dynamic and organic in their nature. Drawing on notions of multiple intelligence and recent thinking about the nature of organizations, they offer a way of looking at schools as living systems through the exploration of the concept of the *'intelligent school'*. For them, intelligent schools are 'human communities' that are continuously developing their capacity for improvement. The School Learning Portfolio required the schools to conceive of themselves as just that. Each school examined its history, its philosophy, the challenges that it was currently facing and the strategies that it chose to employ to ameliorate these. Each provided evidence of the ways in which successes had been achieved and which barriers continued to stand in their way.

The pressure and support that was provided by senior officers of the DET, the academic partners and the meta-evaluators ensured that schools stayed on track.

This was not a draconian process but nevertheless was relentless. It was important that agreement had been reached with the teachers' union who endorsed the processes and also provided resources in the form of a seconded official who worked closely with the DET team and the meta-evaluators.

The insights that evolved did not develop through change mechanisms that tell teachers what they should do and how they should do it; but rather have come about as a result of coherent, school based inquiry that has identified what is required and sought to develop appropriate interventions. It is action research writ large.

Action research on a large scale

Lawrence Stenhouse, the founder of the Centre for Applied Research in Education at the University of East Anglia, is one who struggled long and hard with the question of 'what counts as research?' Stenhouse's minimal definition of research is that it is systematic selfcritical inquiry, based upon a stable and deep curiosity (1981). As well, he has written of research as 'systematic inquiry made public' (1979). Stenhouse has argued that curiosity is both powerful and dangerous because it has the potential to lead to social change. It proposes heresy, is transgressive even, and threatens that faith in those embedded and enduring practices which conspires to keep so many of our institutions and professional practices so little changed. At the same time it gives a better informed context for action than just a belief in change would lead us to. It is for this reason that the Stenhousian position accords so well with the principles of the Priority Actions Schools Program.

Importantly, the processes that have been adopted are not individualistic. They have informed collegial professional learning about current conditions, past histories and future prospects. It is a co-operative process of problem solving by those who are participating. Together they seek to get a grip on the action processes and develop new action scripts through co-operative reflection. The notion of the 'script' is a dramaturgical one and is used here metaphorically. Thus the schools in the program worked together to construct scenarios of what exists and what needs to change and from these develop their action scripts. For example, in the case of Moorok Central School scenarios evolved around the concern for providing ways to relieve staff so that they might engage in more substantive professional learning in a context where short-term substitute staff was hard to find. The proposed script was to appoint a full-time teacher to the school who would be accepted by the students and could move in and out of classrooms as the need arose. Such new action scripts are tried out in practice, evaluated and adjusted or rejected. Furthermore, action and reflection are seen to reinforce each other, which results in a cyclical or narrative development. Reflection must not be disconnected from action; otherwise one runs the risk of estrangement, utopianism, dogmatism, scientism or fundamentalism. Reflection in and on action in the context of practice can be said to be a form of practical philosophy. Those 74 schools participating in the PASP may not have seen themselves thus engaged, but indeed they were.

> Practical philosophy aims at being a philosophy that engages with the conditions of all people, women and men, poor and rich, Others and us. It is a kind of philosophy that is interested in the empirical world as a way of grounding its conclusions in interaction between thinking and acting. (Griffiths, 2003: 21)

The action research basis of PASP assumed that those involved in it would constitute a group with common objectives and goals, interested in a problem that emerges from a given context. It has been research that has at its heart the public good (Jenson, 2006) in the development of professional knowledge. What has been argued for is a continuous process of testing theories in action and pursuing questions of significance. In some respects it can be counted as experiential learning where the experience is that of undertaking the inquiry. Fenwick (2003) points out that experiential learning

> ... focuses on the messy problems and tenacious practices of everyday life which run counter to the logic, language and disciplines of the academy, particularly those privileging the rational and, increasingly, the linguistic and discursive ... We need ask, is there a more generative way to meld educative intents with non institutional experience? To promote fuller participation of people in learning experience without normalizing it? (p. 13)

There can be no question that PASP schools have been pursuing 'messy problems and tenacious practices'. What was unusual about the program was its reach and scope, all conducted in a national, indeed international, context: where professional work is increasingly fragmented through work intensification; where detailed guidelines, procedures and checklists are created to circumscribe professional autonomy and discretion; and, where public trust is constantly eroded as governments and the media conspire to strip teaching of its professionalism by ever burgeoning surveillance in the form of standards development, audit measures and unrealistically high expectations.

As Mulford (2005) argued in terms of school leadership, organizational and student learning in schools:

> To have these advances [for school reform] fall to the same fate as the latest gimmickry, short-term political opportunism or impossibly high expectations benefits no one, especially the practitioners, those in and responsible for schools, for they are the people most likely to ensure the long-term improvement of schools, the children in them and the communities they serve. (p. 321)

In their conclusion to the report upon the Priority Action Schools Program, Groundwater-Smith and Kemmis quoted a participating school:

> Almost without exception, teachers spoke eloquently and passionately about their concept of teacher professionalism; the challenges they were confronting in their everyday work, the efforts to address these challenges and their re-invigoration as a result of the directions of their school, generally since 2001 and specifically under the PASP of 2003.
>
> As one noted: 'I used to think of teaching as a trade; you came to work, did your job and went home. Now I am treated as a professional and I act accordingly. This has been liberating for me'.
>
> And another observed: 'Teachers are feeling free and able to take risks to such an extent that the openness has led to people working more together. (p. 103)

Returning to Teece (2006) and his invocation that schools facing challenging circumstances should be ready and willing to be risk takers and innovators and that they should be provided not only with resources, but also an environment where their efforts are recognized and applauded, it can be argued that the Program, as a large-scale action research project, has clearly met this test. With few exceptions, teachers who have participated should feel that they can walk tall and that they have made a difference in what might otherwise be seen as an indifferent world.

References

Beveridge, S., Groundwater-Smith, S., Kemmis, S. and Wasson, D. (2005). 'Professional learning that makes a difference', *Journal of In-Service Education*, 31 (4): 697–710.

Elliott, B. and MacLennan, D. (1994) 'Education, modernity and neo-conservative school reform in Canada, Britain and the United states', *British Journal of Sociology of Education*, 15 (2): 165–185.

Fenwick, T. (2003) 'Community based learning and the development of really useful knowledge'. Conference paper presented at the International Conference of the Centre for Research in Lifelong Learning. Glasgow, June, 2003.

Frankel, B. (2004) *Zombies, Lilliputians and Sadists: The Power of the Living Dead and the Future of Australia*. Fremantle, WA: Curtin University Books.

Griffiths, M. (2003) 'Action for social justice in education', Open University.

Groundwater-Smith, S. and Kemmis, S. (2005) *Knowing Makes a Difference: Learnings from the NSW Priority Action Schools Program*. Report presented to the New South Wales Department of Education and Training, Sydney, NSW. Available on the web https://www.det.nsw.edu.au/reviews/pasp/index.htm Accessed 12 June, 2007.

Hargreaves, D. (1999) 'The knowledge creating school', *British Journal of Education Studies*, 47: 122–44.

Hargreaves, D. (2003) 'From improvement to transformation'. Keynote address presented to the *International Conference of the International Congress for School Effectiveness and Improvement (ICSEI)*. Sydney: Sydney Convention Centre, Darling Harbour, 5th–8th February.

Human Rights and Equal Opportunity Commission (2000) *Emerging Themes. National Inquiry into Rural and Remote Education*. Canberra: Commonwealth of Australia.

Jenson, J. (2006) 'Research and the public good', *Social Work Research*, 30 (4): 195–7.

MacGilchirst, B., Myers, K. and Reed, J. (2004). *The Intelligent School* (2nd edn). London: Sage Publications.

Mulford, B. (2005) 'Quality evidence about leadership for organisational and student learning in school', *School Leadership and Management*, 25 (4): 321–330.

Newman, M. (2006) *Teaching Defiance: Stories and Strategies for Activist Educators*. San Francisco: Jossey-Bass.

NSW Department of Education and Training, Initial briefing to District Superintendents and Teachers' Federation Organisers, 9th August, 2002.

Richardson, V. (1994) 'Conducting research on practice', *Educational Researcher*, 23 (5): 5–10.

Richardson, V. and Placier, P. (2001) 'Teacher change', in V. Richardson (ed.) *Handbook of Research on Teaching* (4th edn). Washington, DC: American Educational Research Association, pp. 905–47.

Stenhouse, L. (1979) 'Research as a basis for teaching. Inaugural lecture, UEA', in L. Stenhouse, (1983) *Authority, Education and Emancipation*. London: Heinemann Educational Books.

Stenhouse, L. (1981) 'What counts as research?' in *British Journal of Educational Studies*, 29 (2). Reprinted in J. Rudduck and D. Hopkins (eds) (1985) *Research as a Basis for Teaching*. London: Heinemann Educational Books, pp. 8–24.
Teese, R. (2006) 'Getting smart: The battle for ideas in education', *Griffith Review*, February.
Vinson, T. (2003) *Black Holes of Entrenched Disadvantage in Australia*. http:///.jss.org.au/media/pdfs/black_hole_address.pdf (accessed 20th May, 2007).

CHAPTER 12

LEARNING OUTSIDE THE CLASSROOM

A partnership with a difference

Susan Groundwater-Smith and Lynda Kelly

Introduction

This chapter connects inquiry and professional learning in the fresh context of Museum Education. It speaks to a long-standing partnership that involves schools, a university and a natural history museum in Sydney. It portrays the evolution of methods that have captured student understanding and experience to inform the museum of approaches to educational practices. Young people have acted as consultants to the museum, informing design principles in both real and virtual contexts and also ways in which they can be engaged and active agents when visitors to the museum.

The chapter portrays several instances of consultation and draws out the conditions that have made the partnership powerful. It also examines parallels with more orthodox partnerships between schools and academia. It argues for communication that understands and is respectful of the different cultural contexts within which each partner operates.

Designing for learning in the Australian Museum

A generative partnership

Before outlining the range of projects undertaken with the Australian Museum (AM), it is necessary to explain the partnership between it, the Coalition of Knowledge Building Schools (CKBS) and the Practitioner Research Special Interest Group (PRSIG) established in the Faculty of Education and Social Work at the University of Sydney.

Over the past five years the Museum and the Coalition have been in a cooperative relationship designed to enhance learning outside the classroom. A significant synergy has developed between Australasia's oldest natural science museum and a group of schools who have made a commitment to building professional knowledge regarding educational practices (Groundwater-Smith and Mockler 2003b).

The work of the Coalition is well-documented: it is a network of schools with a commitment to action research, which is systematic inquiry conducted by practitioners and transparent and available for critique, with the aim of improvement. It meets under the auspices of the PRSIG in the Faculty of Education and Social Work. The Coalition sees itself as:

- Developing and enhancing the notion of evidence based practice.
- Developing an interactive community of practice using appropriate technologies.
- Making a contribution to a broader professional knowledge base with respect to educational practice.
- Building research capability within and between schools by engaging both teachers and students in the research process.
- Sharing methodologies which are appropriate to practitioner enquiry as a mean of transforming teacher professional learning.

Currently there are 13 schools in the Coalition: 3 Independent Girls Schools, 3 Government Girls High Schools, 2 Government Boys High Schools, 3 coeducational Government High Schools and 2 Government Public Schools (catering for primary-aged students). All but three are in metropolitan Sydney in suburbs to the north, west and east of the centre. Two are in regional towns, one in a remote rural area. They embrace both wealthy and well-provisioned schools and others that face serious socio-economic challenges. In addition, the Coalition has well-developed ongoing relationships with several environmental education centres, evidence of commitment to learning outside the classroom. Most recently, the Coalition has been joined by a respite care school that takes groups of children experiencing difficult circumstances into a residential care education programme focused upon developing empathy and resilience.

Learning and research at the Australian Museum

Museums present different contexts for learning, particularly when compared with places such as schools, universities and libraries. They have been described as free-choice learning environments (Falk and Dierking 2000) and are visited by a broad range of people. Museums have always seen themselves as having some kind of educational role. The earliest museums were founded on the premise of 'education for the uneducated masses' (Bennett 1995), 'cabinets of curiosities' established to 'raise the level of public understanding ... to elevate the spirit of its visitors ... to refine and uplift the common taste' (Weil 1997: 257). Current discourse has identified the need for a conceptual change from museums as places of education to places of learning, responding to the needs and interests of visitors and users.

Audience research is a discipline of museum practice that provides information about visitors and non-visitors to museums and other cultural institutions, influencing the ways museums think about and meet the needs of audiences and stakeholders. The long history of audience research in the cultural sector demonstrates the interest museums have had in their visitors over time. Studies have been conducted since the late nineteenth century, with one of the first visits to the Liverpool Museum in the UK in the 1880s (Kelly 2005). Over the past 15–20 years, increasing emphasis has been placed on increasingly quality-based research into museum learning, answering complex questions and working with a range of audiences (Kelly 2007).

The AM was established in 1827 and is Australia's oldest natural history and anthropological museum. Its mission is 'Inspiring the exploration of nature and cultures'. The primary functions are to make information, collections and research available to a wide range of audiences through undertaking scientific research and managing a vast range of collections in the areas of zoology, mineralogy, palaeontology and anthropology. Also, public communication and learning through physical exhibitions, public programs, publishing, regional outreach and online delivery of services are ways in which the Museum communicates with various audiences. The Museum established a permanent audience research function in 1994, undertaking many evaluation and research projects, both with specific Museum exhibitions and programmes and broader research questions. A recent focus has been working with young people through a close relationship between Museum and Coalition.

Learning projects

Our partnership commenced in 2003. The initial study utilised a variety of innovative methodologies to examine those features of the AM that contributed to, or made more difficult, museum learning (Groundwater-Smith and Kelly 2003). Young people in several of the Coalition schools were introduced to concepts of learning beyond the classroom and subsequently photographed aspects and experiences that 'helped' or 'got in the way' of their learning. Photographs were assembled in annotated posters, subsequently analysed, with the resultant data presented to· the Museum to inform future exhibition designs and pedagogical practices.

Several Coalition schools also contributed, the following year, to the trialling of self-guided tours whose purpose was to enable independent school visits. Again the emphasis was upon young people acting as consultants to the Museum.

More recently a major project was undertaken, 'Designing for Learning in the Museum' (Groundwater-Smith 2006). The project fell into two parts. The first of these was where Coalition schools were invited to send submissions to a competition 'The Museum I'd Like'; the second was to send student delegates to a two-day *Kids' College* where the young people would hear about and evaluate the current plans for the refurbished museum and would suggest ideas for development. The following observations give a sense of the nature of the contributions to them, 'What I want to get out of my time at the Museum.'

Messages were posted on large sheets by members of the various groups. The largest number referred to understanding how the Museum operates and how they might learn from its collection.

- 'A greater knowledge of how a museum works and the care they take to create the "right" history'.
- 'I want to know more about the Museum and know the Museum managers'.
- 'I want to have fun. Learn a bit about the Museum and science. See a lot of interesting things associated with science'.
- 'I'd like to learn, but in a fun way such as picture learning, not paper and pen learning and loads and loads of talk'.

- 'I want my voice to be heard. (I want) a behind the scenes look at the Museum. More fun learning than boring learning. New exhibitions. A tour of the Museum'.
- 'I would like to learn a little bit more about the exhibitions and other things by having a look round a bit more'.
- 'I want to learn about the variety of different objects here, how they work and what they do'.

For some there was a sense of privilege in having access to things not normally experienced by Museum visitors, '(I'd like) to see interesting things that you won't usually see. Looking at things that aren't things that everyone will see.' 'Things that are only a little known about but people are curious about.'

Also some students relished the prospect of obtaining some specific insights:

- 'I would like to know how exhibitions are thought of.'
- 'What I would like to get out of the Museum experience is why the objects that are on display are on display there'.
- 'I want to know how they pick and design exhibitions'.
- 'Understanding how a museum is put together and run'.
- 'How the Museum achieves its goals, completing everything with great success'.

Others saw this as both a social experience and one that would make a contribution to the Museum, 'Being out of school, enjoying my time here, getting to know other people, putting my knowledge into the Museum.' A further theme was 'What I can contribute to these two days.'

All of these messages were posted on the first day. They came from all groups. In the main the focus was upon the contribution of knowledge, thoughts and ideas, particularly with respect to young people.

- 'I can contribute by helping the Museum see what kids would like in a Museum'.
- 'Ideas, new programs for the public. Kids want to touch things, not look. The Museum should let children touch'.
- 'I can contribute the voice of a child, so the exhibitions can reach Australia's children'.
- 'My ideas (thoughts) and help them make the Museum more appealing to children'.
- 'A young person's perspective on the Museum and its representation of Australian History'.
- 'The voice of the child so that exhibitions can be for children and for adults'.

Clearly the young people involved in both phases had provided the museum with rich consultative data of considerable value in informing the designing-for-learning process. Following consultation with Museum staff, it is seen that the information is commensurate with the Museum's Vision Statement, 'To inspire an exploration of nature and cultures'. In other words, the data collected from both the *Museum I'd Like* and the *Kids' College* informed the ways in which the AM can inspire an exploration of nature and cultures such that young people will be substantively engaged in learning.

Developing an *E-College* seemed a natural progression. Learning through social media and digital resources is increasingly a core function in the learning repertoire of today's students. The *E-College* was designed to be conducted over a full day, based on feedback from the previous participants. In preparation, a booklet was prepared for each participant with their name on the cover and a digital photograph. These booklets would be used for reflections throughout the day and were the major source of data along with the observations of museum personnel working as group facilitators.

The aims of the *E-College* are set out below:

- To understand how young people aged 12–18 are using the web and new media and where they fit into their lives.
- To seek feedback about how these technologies might be used at the Museum both in the physical and virtual spaces.
- To explore e-learning, its tools and artefacts as they relate to the Australian Museum and young people as a social medium.

The critical questions to be addressed by the *E-College* were as follows:

1 What is it like to learn using computers and digital technologies?
2 How might the AM employ digital technologies to enhance engagement in learning in two specific contexts (Search and Discover and The Fossil Collection) and more generally?
3 What should the AM do to make its website more inviting for young people?
4 What message would you like to leave with the AM as a result of the *E-College*?

While the purpose of this chapter is principally to explore the partnership between the Museum and the Coalition, it is not possible to cover all findings of this study. However, for a flavour of the student responses we report one such here.

Several students made a distinction between visiting the Museum itself and visiting its website. Patrick, who had participated in the earlier *Kids' College* and was one of two students from a remote school and whose travel had been subsidised by the Museum had this to say:

> Last time I came here we focused mainly on new technology and we were constantly saying we needed more screens, games and interactive displays, but since then I have been thinking: I can do that at home, I can watch movies, play games, etc. at home. If I come to the museum I want to be able to get information, read it and be able to learn from it. It is good to have these things (screens, etc.) but I guess, like all things, in moderation.
>
> The website needs to suit all audiences. I got the feeling that you were trying to find bright colours, games, etc. that could be good, but it is unlikely that the reason we are at a museum site in the first place is to play the games. We can do that anywhere. If we are there we are probably looking out what we want but we are not the only people that use the museum. A section on the site, for information of some kind. So it needs to be easy to read and access without being too dry.

All the projects discussed hitherto were ones initiated by the Museum and enthusiastically engaged with by the schools. In 2008, a new direction emerged, one where a school has sought government funding for a Quality Teaching Project in relation to learning in the Museum. The partnership can be seen to be emerging as a truly reciprocal one! This last project is still very much a work in progress. Designed to cover two years, it rests upon the development of integrated teaching and learning units using the Museum as a principal resource.

Further 'Colleges' are also being planned to investigate with schools student perceptions and understandings of issues around sustainability and climate change.

As we have already indicated, it is not possible to nominate all of the complex learning arising from these projects: learning for young people; learning for the partners; and learning for the profession. However, we believe that some clear lessons can be derived from the significant synergy that has developed between the Museum, the schools and the academics.

We now briefly explore other AM issues.

Spaces and experiences that enhance learning

Contemporary understandings of learning in museums have indicated that substantive engagement for young people is not merely a whim of the educational imagination, but is critical to transforming learning productivity positively (Piscitelli and Anderson 2001). Such transformative learning can be characterised as authentic, that is: that young people need to feel welcomed and supported; that the museum exhibits/exhibitions relate to their lives and highlight ways in which learning can apply to them; that they have some control over their learning and will be involved in problem solving and inquiry tasks; that they are set challenging but achievable goals; that they can question and reflect upon what they have learned; that they can exercise judgement; that their curiosity is stimulated; that they can share new knowledge with others in a multi-directional flow; that they can understand and employ the language of learning; and they can interact with the new media.

As Lemerise (1995: 403) put it, '(Young people) say loud and clear that they like being with their friends and they want to do things with them ... Alas the museum is generally seen as a place where there is not much to do other than look and listen.' All the data collected in the collaborative studies and reported upon in this chapter points to young people's desire to be engaged in active and interactive learning. They want to be in spaces that are colourful, vital, so that all their senses are brought into play. They want to have a sense of agency where they can follow a variety of learning pathways employing a variety of media.

How tame learning sites such as museums can appear to be to young people when they themselves inhabit such an interactive and compelling digital environment with access to mobile phones, instant messaging and the worldwide web, which encourage two-way active participation. Having grown up in a technology-rich world, adolescents, commentators have argued, have dispositions much like those of native language learners: they take their culture (and language) as natural. Prensky (2001) has aptly referred to them as 'digital natives' who are in contrast to other generations who have not grown up in a digital world. Learning digital media for them is like learning a second language.

For young people, operating in a media-rich environment is 'fun'. It is not merely by chance that the word 'fun' appeared many times in the various studies.

But it is not only a form of entertainment that these young people are seeking. They are also curious about how the Museum goes about its business of collecting and preparing collections for exhibitions. The experience of hearing stories from Museum experts was for the students a highlight of their experiences when they were being consulted. A significant issue was in relation to *how* these stories might be told. Lindauer (2005) suggested that museum staff generally adhere to implicit curriculum theories that guide their practice, these being: didactic (unelaborated information dissemination); Tylerian (information developed in logical scope and sequence order); constructivist (recognising what the visitor brings to the learning); and narrative. In the case of the last of these, she argues that a narrative curriculum theory incorporates answers to who, what, where, why and how something takes place in a manner that a good story requires. Narrative is now acknowledged as a critical component when engaging learners (Kelly 2007). The illuminative story not only serves to illustrate a concept or idea, but also stimulates further questioning and inquiry.

The young people we sampled want to find information that meets their needs, but they also want to be entertained. They want access to taboos and controversies, but they want to be comforted and reassured. They want the boundaries to be pushed out, but they want to feel safe. They need, as Cameron (2003) has reported, to transcend their fears, but not to avoid them. Paradoxically, they want the museum to be a site incorporating the most modern of technologies, but also one that continues to embody the traditional. In effect the traditional becomes the exotic.

The Museum cannot assume that the young people who visit are only wanting to be superficially entertained; or are all the same. This extended consultation reveals clearly that they *are* desirous of dealing with complex and challenging concepts. They want the fun, but also the depth. They want to be provoked, not merely informed. They want to hear questions to which there may not be ready answers. They are not empty vessels waiting to be filled. They bring with them a multiplicity of experiences and insights. Participants from a remote town such as Broken Hill have very different experiences to those who have grown up in Sydney's multi-cultural inner city.

The ways in which consulting young people can inform pedagogical and organisational practices

It is becoming increasingly clear that as Burke (2008: 1) puts it:

> New approaches to pedagogy are emerging in both the educational and cultural sectors and there are important questions arising about the roles of professionals and the rights of learners to participate in the making of meaning. We know from research that children from a very early age can participate in conversations (visual and textual) about matters of design that influence their lives and new research methodologies are developing that allow this to be realised and documented.

An important element that holds these studies together is the understanding that young people can provide legitimate insights into educational enterprises designed for them, whether within or outside schools; in real time or digital space. It is generally agreed that improvement in engagement can come about when their views are systematically collected and interrogated (Falk and Dierking 2000; Piscitelli and Anderson 2001). Paradoxically, they are rarely consulted.

It is increasingly understood that young people, in order to participate productively in social and academic life, need to be active agents in that life. Unlike the adults who surround them, today's young people have been born into a digital world; they know it, they understand it and they can navigate within it. Old models of teaching and telling are no longer sufficient. As Cornu (2004) has observed in relation to schools, knowledge is now networked and requires an understanding of a collective intelligence over and above individual enterprise. The same holds true for Museums, which have such a vital role to play in developing enjoyable and engaging learning among their visitors.

It is clear, from the above, that this study gives much credence to the salience of 'student voice', that is, the importance of listening and responding to young people. A large British project, *Consulting Pupils about Teaching and Learning*, has run over the past three years (Rudduck and McIntyre 2007). It is argued that the present climate is one where there is unprecedented support for the idea of listening to young people. Importantly, they argue that the place where this should start is the classroom itself, where teachers take seriously their students' views and find ways of meeting their concerns. They believe that consulting with young people has many positive results. Their argument holds equally true for large learning institutions, such as the AM, that take the responsibility for learning outside school classroom seriously.

Frequently, however, consultation has tended to take place after the teachers and museum educators designed and delivered the curriculum. What is remarkable about the work of the AM and the Coalition is that increasingly the voices of young people are built into the design process itself. The purpose of the *E-College* was not so much to evaluate existing products, although that did take place, but rather to imagine what digital products might look like and how they might be used.

As Valdecasas, Correia and Correas (2006: 35) note:

> Presently, many museums do not make use of opportunities to 'dialogue' with their visitors in a creative fashion, i.e. they do not foster visitor curiosity nor enhance their sense of wonder via a conceptual dialogue that allows the visitors to develop questions and work on answers to them. Some exhibitions [and we would argue websites] nowadays speak in an almost uni-directional manner to their visitors.

Brown *et al*. (2005: 2), in considering ways of adding value to online collections for diverse audiences, have argued that school students have a need to be able to develop the characteristics of experts while still being novices:

> (They, the young people) need to be able to discover, analyse and synthesise information that addresses identified topics, but their domain knowledge and

skill levels are such, like the general public, they still need a degree of scaffolding to engage their interest and provide the conceptual frameworks required to assimilate new knowledge.

These are surely important messages for schools as well.

It is worth considering a significant difference between Museums and schools in the ways in which they view and understand young people. For the Museum the young person is thought of as an 'audience'; albeit one which wishes to learn; for the school the young person is positioned as 'student'. Indeed, in schools, other than the most senior years, the young person is there as a State requirement. Schooling is compulsory and schools are places where young people are constantly subject to the surveillance of the State through testing and assessment regimes, just as their teachers are through various inspectorial devices. The custodial nature of schooling shapes much of its practices, just as the client-focused nature of the Museum requires paying careful attention to the ways in which young visitors can be enticed through its doors, both real and virtual. Arguably schools might consider becoming more seductive and enticing places where, as Erica McWilliam (2008) suggests, radical doubt can flourish and contribute to a more original and creative learning environment. After all, Museums are not intended only as places for transmitting knowledge of culture, natural history and the like; they are also places for provocation and questioning.

The ways in which such partnerships can contribute to ongoing teacher professional learning

So far we have focused upon ways in which the Museum has benefited from its partnership with members of the Coalition. Implicit is that schools also are beneficiaries in that many of the observations apply as much to learning in the classroom as in the Museum. Student engagement is recognised as contingent upon the ways in which their learning experiences are connected to their life-worlds and contemporary youth culture.

It is our contention that forming sound partnerships can provide fruitful outcomes for students and teachers. Too much attention in teacher professional learning is directed towards technicist strategies whereby courses, developed to meet government requirements, are delivered in short bursts with little real application to the classroom. It is not entirely the case that compliance with regulatory frameworks is the enemy of authentic professional learning, but certainly it is possible to see the two concepts as uncomfortable bedfellows.

Certainly, it is much easier to measure and quantify the kinds of 'spray on' (Mockler 2005), 'drive by' (Senge et al. 2000) or 'hit and run' (Loucks-Horsley 1999) professional development experiences that are relatively easy to control and 'deliver' to teachers. Yet questions abound about the effectiveness of such approaches. The partnership arrangements that have been spelled out in this chapter are far more encouraging in that practitioners are active agents in their own professional growth.

Loucks-Hocsely et al. (1987) set out the conditions for effective teacher professional growth including:

- collegiality and cooperation;
- experimentation and risk taking;
- participant involvement in goal setting, implementation, evaluation and decision making;
- designs built on principles of adult learning and the change process.

Clearly, this partnership with a difference has provided those conditions for both parties.

Conclusion: why this can be counted as a successful partnership

We are mindful that this account is being celebratory. But it is difficult to deny the power of the ongoing relationship between the Museum, the Coalition and the PRSIG. For it to have endured for so long, to have been so generative of innovative practices, to be looking forward to new projects, it must surely be deemed successful. We would argue that such success lies in a number of factors:

- the relationship's having an authentic purpose;
- the relationship's having continuity;
- the benefits being reciprocal;
- partners taking collective responsibility;
- the promotion of consultation, collaboration and democratic decision making;
- an active support of innovation and change;
- opportunities to think outside the square;
- a continuing exercise of trust and respect.

In the most recent iteration of the work of the partnership, the development of an integrated, holistic curriculum in the middle years in a single sex boys' school, we asked the boys to reflect on the project as a kind of game involving more than one person. They were asked to nominate the game and their reason for selection. Among the responses one boy reasoned:

> It has been like a treasure hunt. You have to find out information if you are to succeed. In the same way we have been following the clues that we have got from our teachers and the people from the museum, and in the end you get to the glory and the gold.

References

Bennett, T. (1995) *The Birth of the Museum: History, Theory, Politics*. London: Routledge.
Brown, S., Gerrard, D. and Ward, H. (2005) 'Adding value to on-line collections for different audiences' in J. Trant and D. Bearman (eds) *Museums and the Web 2005 Proceedings*, Toronto: Archives and Museum Informatics, published 31 March 2005. (Available at www.archimuse.com/mw2005/papers/brown/brown.html, accessed 5th January, 2008.)
Burke, C. (2008) 'The view of the child and young person in museum and gallery design', paper presented at *the International Conference on the Inclusive Museum*. Leiden. The Netherlands, 8–11 June.

Cameron, F. (2003) 'Transgressing fear: engaging emotions and opinion – a case for museums in the 21st century', *Open Museum Journal*, 6:
Cornu, B. (2004) 'Networking and collective intelligence for teachers and learners' in A. Brown and N. Davis (eds) *Digital Technology, Communities and Education*, pp. 40–5. London: Routledge Falmer.
Falk, J. and Dierking, L. (2000) *Learning from Museums: Visitor Experience and the Making of Meaning*. New York: Alta Mira Press.
Groundwater-Smith, S. (2006) 'Millennials in museums: consulting Australian adolescents when designing for learning', invitational address presented to the *Museum Directors' Forum*, National Museum of History, Taipei, 21–22 October 2006.
Groundwater-Smith, S. and Kelly, L. (2003) 'As we see it: improving learning in the museum', paper presented to the *British Educational Research Association Annual Conference*, Edinburgh.
Groundwater-Smith, S. and Mockler, N. (2003a) 'Holding a mirror to professional learning', paper presented to the joint *Australian Association for Research in Education/New Zealand Association for Research in Education Conference*, Auckland, New Zealand, 29 November-3 December. (All AARE Conference papers can be found at www.aare.edu.au.)
Groundwater-Smith, S. and Mockler, N. (2003b) *Learning to Listen: Listening to Learn*. Sydney: MLC School and Faculty of Education, University of Sydney. (Available at www.edfac.usyd.edu.au/profdev/learnlisten.html.)
Kelly, L. (2005) 'Evaluation, research and communities of practice: program evaluation in museums', *Archival Science*, 4(1–2): 45–69.
Kelly, L. (2007) 'Visitors and learners: adult museum visitors' learning identities', unpublished Ph.D. thesis. Sydney: University of Technology.
Lemerise, T. (1995) 'The role and place of adolescents in museums: yesterday and today', *Museum Management and Curatorship*, 14(4): 393–408.
Lindauer, M. (2005) 'From salad bars to vivid stories: four models for developing "educationally successful" exhibitions', *Museum Management and Curatorship*, 20: 41–55. Loucks-Horsley, S. (1999) *Designing Professional Development for Teachers of Science and Mathematics*. Thousand Oaks, CA: Corwin Press.
Loucks-Horsley, S., Harding, C., Arbuckle, M, Dubea, C., Williams, M. and Murray, L. (1987) *Continuing to Learn: A Guidebook for Teacher Development*. Andover, MA: Regional Laboratory for Educational Improvement of the Northeast and Islands and National Staff Development Council.
McWilliam, E. (2008) 'Making excellent teachers' in A. Phelan and J. Sumsion (eds) *Critical Readings in Teacher Education*. Rotterdam: Sense Publishers.
Mockler, N. (2005) 'Trans/forming teachers: new professional learning and transformative teacher professionalism', *Journal of In-service Education*, 31(4): 733–46.
Piscitelli, B. and Anderson, D. (2001) 'Young-children's perspectives of museum settings and experiences', *Museum Management and Curatorship*, 19(3): 269–82.
Prensky, M. (2001) 'Digital native, digital immigrants'. *On the Horizon*, 9(5):
Rudduck, J. and McIntyre, D. (2007) *Consulting Pupils about Teaching and Learning*. London: Routledge.
Senge, P., Cambron-McCabe, N., Lucas, T., Smith, B. and Dutton, J. (2000) *Schools That Learn*. London: Nicholas Brealey.
Valdecasas, A., Correia, V. and Correas, M. (2006) 'Museums at the crossroad: contributing to dialogue, curiosity and wonder in natural history museums', *Museum Management and Curatorship*, 21: 32–43.
Weil, S. (1997) 'The museum and the public', *Curator*, 16(3): 257–71.
Watson, S., Dodd, J. and Jones, C. (2007) *Engage, Learn, Achieve*. (Available at www.le.ac.uk/museumstudies, accessed 20 December 2007.)

CHAPTER 13

LIVING ETHICAL PRACTICE IN QUALITATIVE RESEARCH

Susan Groundwater-Smith

On "seeing" ethical practice

In her confronting and challenging book *Regarding the pain of others*, Susan Sontag (2003) analysed images of war and asked us: When we look at the same photographs do we feel the same things? She argued that we see through the prism of our prejudices and expectations; that we have a capacity for both intimacy and dissociation. The capricious viewer can choose to stay and watch, or go and forget. Sontag's work may seem a far cry from the concept of living ethical practice in qualitative research, but there are many invisible threads that can hold the two together. What do we believe ethical practice to be and how can we live it in our work? This chapter is written from the standpoint of my own experience, as one who has retired from full-time academic work but continues to engage in participatory action research (PAR) with field-based practitioners, more often than not as a consultant. Thus, viewing my practice is mediated by my personal position and what governs it.

In her vivid discussion Sontag argued that the intention of the photographer may be to shock the viewer into taking into consideration the terror and violence of war, but that such an assumption is often but not always overridden by a vicarious sense of detachment which erodes empathy and instead evokes the opposite, that is apathy. For many academic researchers the governance of the ethical conduct of their inquiries is managed, not by *their* own ethical stance but by the determinations of the university's human research ethics committees, whose intentions may differ from those of the researcher. Deferring to such committees may not be a matter of choice, but is more often than not determined by the university's policies, more concerned with risk management than with an authentic desire for the researcher(s) to behave ethically. Of course, I concede that not all committees function in this way. As Gorman (2007, p. 23) explained, a human research ethics committee's work should be designed to improve rather than inhibit the inquiry:

> If we accept that good research benefits society then it follows that the work of ethics committees also benefits society and researchers.... Positively engaged with, the ethics review process will enhance rather than detract from the research.

Nonetheless, usurping the autonomy of ethical academic researchers may very well have the effect of detaching those researchers from serious ethical considerations of their work, instead positioning them to find ways of conforming to the requirements of the governing committee. Thus they see ethics as another bureaucratic hurdle to be satisfied.

So how do I "see" my own ethical practice when engaged in facilitating practitioner research as a form of PAR, and where I do not come under the surveillance of a university human research ethics committee? To answer that question I turn in the first instance to some work I undertook with Nicole Mockler (Groundwater-Smith & Mockler, 2008) where we argued that the most vital test of quality in action inquiry is that of the ethical principles which have underwritten the work. We proposed a series of guidelines that would inform ethical professionalism, these being (a) that the research should observe ethical protocols and processes, (b) that it should be transparent in its processes, (c) that it should be collaborative in its nature, (d) that it should be transformative in its intent and action, and (e) that it should be able to justify itself to its community of practice (pp. 85–86). In effect, my ethical position is one that seeks to be accountable to those with whom one is most directly working, ensuring that they are not left vulnerable or exploited and that they are fully appraised of the consequences of decisions they may make in the pursuit of their inquiries. One may think about it as enacting a kindness to all who participate. To make this position clear it is important first to explain more fully the nature of PAR and the ways in which I strive to live my ethical practice.

Facilitating Participatory Action Research

As its name suggests, PAR is characterised by its orientation to producing a knowledge of practice in ways that can contribute to a deep understanding of that practice, so that authentic improvement can take place. Of course, we always need to be wary of what the term "improvement" implies – improvement for whom and under what conditions? After all, working within a collaborative framework itself produces many dilemmas in relation to power and authority and the expectations and rewards that go with occupying different roles. Goldstein (2000, p. 523), in her revealing discussion regarding her project to work collaboratively with an early career classroom teacher, observed:

> Any collaboration can be difficult. And when university researchers enter classrooms, some problems are bound to arise because of the issues of power and status inherent in these relations. Though the university researcher may see herself as little more than the classroom teacher she once was (as I often did), the view from the classroom is quite different.

The school-based practitioner may have been motivated by a desire to improve communication in the interests of caring for the children in her classroom in order that all may have a voice; whereas Goldstein, as the academic partner/facilitator may have shared that desire, but also was conducting the study as part of her doctoral candidature. For other academics there may be the additional pressure to conform to some kind of research selectivity exercise demanded by the university that requires them to publish in nominated journals which play little part in the communal professional debate and which arguably make little impact on practice.

Many who write of PAR emphasise its transformative and emancipatory nature, from small micro-studies through to large national investigations via social movements (see Fals Borda, 2000: Freire, 1996). Regardless of its scope and size, the work requires conditions that will allow for genuine dialogue and for social outcomes that are just and equitable. In essence it is informed by social relations whose intent is to fulfil a concern for

> doing the moral good – The emphasis is on the enhancement of ethically authentic action and the development of situated knowledge rather than on the accumulation of general (generalisable) theoretical knowledge. (Ponte & Smit, 2007, p. 3)

Those concerned with undertaking action research are familiar with the spiral of observation, reflection, theory building, planning and executing action and its study, followed by re-observation, further reflection and so on. In its most stripped-down sense, action research could be characterised as a form of systematic problem solving. But PAR has in addition a number of other key features. It has been identified by Kemmis and McTaggart (2005) as being: a social practice. participatory, practical and collaborative, emancipatory, critical, reflexive and transformative; thus it transcends any instrumental purpose based upon merely "acting".

To place these high ideals into some kind of perspective that will allow me to discuss living ethical practice it is important for me to draw attention to particular features of the context in which much of my work occurs. As a result of my appointment as Honorary Professor at the University of Sydney, over a decade ago I established, with Professor Judyth Sachs, the Centre for Practitioner Research (CPR) whose aims were to validate and value the research-based knowledge created by practitioners in the field, and to develop cross-disciplinary networks to facilitate the production and circulation of new knowledge. Its purposes were seen to be related to fostering, supporting and enhancing practitioner research in its many modes and guises.

As time went by and the University's regulatory frameworks changed, the Centre was re-designated as a Special Interest Group (SIG) and continues its work to this day. Under the umbrella of the CPR and more lately the SIG, a Coalition of Knowledge Building Schools (including government and non-government, primary and secondary, metropolitan and regional schools) was formed (see Mockler & Groundwater-Smith, 2011, for a detailed discussion of the history of the coalition, its aims and range of activities). The Coalition is affiliated with the University of Sydney, but each individual member undertakes inquiries with the support of school resources or specific project funds. Over time I have worked with each of the schools, often in association with other academic partners, as a facilitator of their PAR. In this capacity it has been my role to (a) identify and collate research discussion papers that inform the given school of recent and relevant research in the field in which it has an interest; (b) work with school-based committees (which may include students and parents) advising on qualitative research methods; (c) engage directly in the inquiry when a third party is advisable; (d) act as a critical friend in response to participant reflections; and (e) support writing and publishing the research for a broader audience such as conference delegates. It is in this context that I live my ethical practice and encounter a range of challenges and dilemmas.

Ethical challenges and dilemmas arising from facilitating Participatory Action Research

To give substance to my argument that living ethical practice produces very real dilemmas, not only for me but for my field-based colleagues, I narrate two case studies. One is set in a comprehensive co-educational high school in metropolitan Sydney; the other is in a facility for the support of young people requiring brief respite care.

Site A

The school is located in a community that faces challenging socioeconomic circumstances. Salaries are relatively low, few adults are engaged in ongoing training and most are in unskilled occupations. A number of the students have a Lebanese background, with some Pacific Island and a smattering of Vietnamese students, and recent refugee arrivals from West Africa, Afghanistan, Iraq and Burma. Boys outnumber girls in the ratio 2:1. The area is a well-established residential community, the school having been built some 50 years ago, with several industrial precincts and a regional airport. On the basis of its low socioeconomic status the school receives school communities partnership funding aimed to improve student engagement and attainment.

A group of teachers in the school have identified Year 9 as a pivotal point in the students' schooling, when they are in danger of becoming increasingly academically and even socially disengaged. The teachers were determined to develop a project whereby the students would have greater agency. Using partnership funding the team of teachers worked to develop a consultative model within which students would be enabled to research the conditions of their learning and make recommendations for the ways in which they could be encouraged to be active participants in learning and teaching in the classroom. The participating teachers were familiar with significant writing in the field of "student voice", such as that of Bragg and Fielding (2005) and Cook-Sather (2006); as well, they were cognisant of the need to develop pedagogies to engage students living under such challenging circumstances (Munns. 2007).

The project that was developed was designed to maximise student participation so that they might develop an informed critique of the school's practices and engage in an authentic dialogue with staff. Following a series of Year 9 meetings when all students were advised of the project and given opportunities to document their perceptions of the school, a research steering committee of 20 students was established. The team were conscious that they should not only be advised by students who generally conformed to the school's policies, but also be inclusive of students who were at times actively resistant.

Over a period of months the research steering committee met and learned something of qualitative inquiry methods ranging from focus group discussions to using visual media. As Thomson (2008, p. 4) observed:

> [Student] voice is not only about having a say, but also refers to the language emotional components and non-verbal means used to express opinions. Undertaking research which attends to voice may thus mean listening to things that are unsaid and/or not what we expect.

158 *Living ethical practice*

Add to this the argument put by Maguire (2005, p. 3):

> Children have good social radar for assessing the situations and contexts in which they find themselves. Thus children's perspectives and voices are important signifiers of their conceptualizations of the situatedness of their learning, their interests, needs and perceptions.

The steering committee's work resulted in them running a series of inquiry "stations", where all members of Year 9 recorded their responses to a number of salient prompts and questions. It is not the purpose of this case study to spell out the detail of the project, which continues to run and which the teachers themselves will be documenting, but to bring to attention a specific dilemma that has arisen and impacts upon my own sense of ethical practice and how I might best live it. In their analysis, students focused upon the many negative messages that were implicit, and sometimes explicit, in their interactions with their teachers. They perceived that their teachers did not know them and their circumstances well, that they did not encourage them in their learning, and that the classroom activities were often undemanding and thus not very engaging.

A critical stage for the project was one where the steering committee students would present their findings to the school staff at an afternoon meeting. For a number of the students this proved to be a significant challenge. After all, they were going to confront a status quo in which teachers were perceived to have the power, and they would be delivering some painful messages. Thomson (2008) cited Arnot and Reay (2007), who noted that students are already schooled in the norms and expectations of those they wish to critique. At a meeting with the students, the team and I were concerned about the students' couching of their messages in highly negative terms. Students were determined to put to staff their perceptions that teachers failed to respect them or interact with them in positive and productive ways. Here we had a paradox. The students themselves appeared to be formulating their presentations in exactly the manner that they so disliked when coming from the staff. Our shared ethical dilemma was whether to honour the students' rights to voice their negative sentiments – with the result that some harm might be done as teachers become cynical and resistant – or to appropriate their voices and have them deliver a message that would have less impact, but also produce fewer defensive reactions. The team grappled with this issue, believing that a rejection of the students' findings would reduce the potential for lasting impact. Perhaps if the students presented their idea with a "positive spin" then the hope was that the teachers would be more responsive. Students were convened in smaller groups to consider these matters, weighing up the pros and cons of the ways in which to present their idea. The consensus was that they would share with staff their school experiences as they saw them, in all their rawness and difficulty.

Our apprehensions were confirmed. While many teachers heard and understood the difficulties of the students a number were cynical and critical. An important linchpin in the subsequent proceedings, however, was that the school was formulating its Positive Behaviours Implementation Strategies (PBIS), a process that required consultation with students. The school's pastoral team saw that the steering committee's work had indeed laid the foundations for student participation, and this lent weight to the students' findings. Being on the horns of a dilemma means that we can find both costs and benefits in either direction. In this case, although we had significant concerns for the students in the longer term their persistence in the face of our caution paid off.

Site B

The setting for this case is a facility that provides respite care for young people from across the state. They may need support because there has been a death or serious illness in the family or because the family is facing challenging circumstances, either socioeconomically or as the result of an event such as a house fire or even a flood. Sometimes all factors can come into play. Along with a well-designed evening and weekend recreation program, the facility also provides schooling that needs to take account of the short-term nature of the stay. In recent years the school has moved from what had been described as a "holiday program" to an educational program with an emphasis upon emotional literacy. The program encourages students to locate and understand their emotions and the ways in which they impact on their learning potential. My role in the facility was to assist a team of teachers within the school to reflect on their professional learning and to find strategies to evaluate their practices. This was achieved by regular meetings and discussions with teachers, documenting their insights arising from critical incidents in their learning in the form of journal entries, as outlined by Tripp (1993). Critical incident analysis is an approach to identifying and managing the challenges in everyday practice in order to better understand them and find alternative ways of responding to them. They are not necessarily dramatic moments, but rather ones that present themselves, after reflection, as particular practical concerns that can arise not only from classroom practice but also, maybe, from staff interactions, or from attending a particular professional learning course. Teachers also documented their most significant change stories in a way that allowed them to use narrative and metaphor to write about changes in direction in terms of pedagogy and/or their philosophies of practice.

The school had undertaken to informally survey the home schools of the children on their return, to see what impacts the program had made. Feedback had suggested that the students returned with a more positive orientation to their learning and engagement.

However, from time to time there was pressure on the facility to provide what was seen as "harder" evidence of the impact of the program on the students. This, of course, is no easy matter. Each new cohort of young people varies in terms of its composition and the nature of the contexts from which the students have come, as well as the length of their stay. As an academic partner to the facility, I have over several years been able to work extensively with the staff and leadership within the small school and have found their commitment quite remarkable. But this personal testimony was not seen as sufficient.

The dilemma that arose for me was the result of the school seeking an acceptable measure that could be used to indicate the value that the stay had added to the lives of the young people. A measure considered by the school executive was the "Messy" or Matson Social Skills Survey, originally designed to assess social skills of students with an intellectual disability. It was later modified to have a broader social skills application. The problem with the survey, that is based upon self-report, is that it focuses on negative behaviours, for example "I threaten people or act like a bully" or "I pick on people to make them angry" or "I make fun of others" and so on. Of the 62 questions, 41 are framed in this way. My view was that the survey was inappropriate for young people who were already vulnerable and whose self-concept was fragile, to say the least. This was a view that was shared by a number of the staff. Interestingly, the school psychology literature cites the survey as a social tool, but does not develop a critique of it in terms of its consequences for those responding to the items.

Although I and others strongly expressed a view that the survey was inappropriate, it was not my prerogative to influence the final decision regarding the use of the survey. Senior management was well qualified in the field of educational measurement and believed the instrument to be appropriate to the purpose to which it was to be put. The case is included here as an instance where I, as the academic partner, faced an ethical dilemma in a context where my judgement had little impact. Although I could have chosen then to withdraw from the role as facilitator and critical friend I decided that my continuing presence could be used to create conditions where further discussions could take place. So while the survey was employed, so too did broader debates take place among the staff regarding appropriate ways to provide evidence of the impact of the facility on young people, their capabilities and their self-regard. My contribution, then, shifted from providing advice regarding the employment of an appropriate instrument to becoming the fulcrum for ongoing dialogue beyond any particular cohort of young people.

In effect, in both these case studies I found myself engaged in making particular moral judgements, in the first instance in relation to the possibility of exposing young people to the consequences of voicing their negative stance to the staff of their school. Fielding (2004, pp. 302–304) asked a series of penetrating questions to be considered when employing student voice. Among them:

- How confident are we that our research does not redescribe and reconfigure students in ways that bind them more securely into the fabric of the status quo?
- How clear are we about the use to which the depth and detail of data is likely to be put? Is our more detailed knowledge of what students think and feel largely used to help us control them more effectively?
- Are we sure that our positions of relative power and our own personal and professional interests are not blurring our judgements or shaping our advocacy?

In the second case, the judgement related to the effects on young people of engaging in a form of self-report that over-emphasized a pessimistic construction of the self. Both these case studies relate to my ethical disposition in the facilitation of PAR, and are genuine dilemmas. A crucial feature of a dilemma is that one has two choices for undertaking an action; one can do either but cannot do both. In the Year 9 case, the team and I could have intruded upon the students' decisions to present their findings in a fashion that might bring opprobrium upon their heads but failed to honour their agency and autonomy; in the second instance, I could have recognised the right of the school-based practitioner to select a strategy that would meet the needs of those asking for a particular kind of accountability by providing "rigorous" evidence but would have not done a kindness to the young people completing the survey.

Elsewhere I have discussed other examples of the kinds of ethical concern that a consultant supporting PAR faces. In a chapter concerning my professional self (Groundwater-Smith, 2006) I addressed the ways in which I was unsettled by the angry and disruptive behaviours of a number of students in the face of efforts to prepare them for mandatory state tests. I acknowledged that I could not "unknow" my own experiences or the values that infuse them, but that I could and should make my values more explicit and transparent such that they too could be challenged. This example was clearly a matter of my values, but also there are cases of actual practice. In the opening to a chapter on researching ethically (Groundwater-Smith, 2010) I outlined an instance where I had not sufficiently established the boundaries of confidentiality, with the result that information was distributed and discussed before it had been appropriately cleared by those participating in the inquiry.

Living ethical practice in the context of engaging with others in PAR is not so much a matter of being constrained by regulatory frameworks, but rather is to do with ensuring that the quality of our work is such that we can uncover and reveal the very real and complex concerns that govern social practices. As Kemmis (2007, p. 21) noted:

> The quality of practitioner research is not just a matter of the technical excellence of practitioner research as "research". It is a matter of addressing important problems in thought and action, in theory and practice – problems worth addressing in and for our times, in and for our communities, in and for our shared world. It is a matter of addressing important problems for education, for the good of each person, and for the good of our societies.

Conclusion – regarding the wellbeing of others

I commenced this chapter with a reflection upon the work of Susan Sontag with regard to observing the pain of others. Here, in my conclusion I propose that living ethical practice requires of us that we put ourselves and our academic egos to one side and think instead of the wellbeing of those who are often vulnerable and lacking in power. John Stuart Mill (1806–1873) has been quoted as writing:

> A person may cause evil to others not but his actions but by his inaction and in either case he is justly accountable to them for the injury. (Mill, n.d.)

In the case that I have cited here the ethical relationships are problematic, even blurred. But they are not sundered or irreparable. To ensure that they are not injurious, ongoing dialogue and negotiation is essential. That then is my bedrock in living ethical practice: that I strive to be ever sensible to the needs and rights of those with whom I work and hold them in due regard beyond rhetoric and into action.

References

Arnot M., & Reay, D. (2007). A sociology of pedagogic voices. *Discourse, 28*(3), 327–342.
Bragg, S., & Fielding, M. (2005). "It's an equal thing . . . it's about achieving together": Student voice and the possibility of radical collegiality. In H. Street & J. Temperley (Eds.), *Improving schools through collaborative inquiry* (pp. 205–235). London: Continuum.
Cook-Sather, A. (2006). Change based on what students say: Preparing teachers for a paradoxical model of leadership. *International Journal of Leadership in Education, 9*(4), 345–358.
Fals Borda, 0. (2000). People's space times in global processes: The response of the local. *Journal of World-System Research 6*(3), 624–634.
Fielding, M. (2004). Transformative approaches to student voice: Theoretical underpinnings, recalcitrant realities. *British Educational Research Journal, 30*(2), 295–311.
Freire, P. (1996). *Pedagogy of the oppressed.* London: Penguin.
Goldstein, L. (2000). Ethical dilemmas in designing collaborative research: Lessons learned the hard way. *Qualitative Studies in Education, 13*(5), 517–530.
Gorman, S. (2007). Managing research ethics: A head-on collision? In A. Campbell & S. Groundwater-Smith (Eds.), *An ethical approach to practitioner research* (pp. 8–23). London: Routledge.
Groundwater-Smith, S. (2006). My professional self. In P. Aubusson & S. Schhuck (Eds.), *Teacher learning and development* (pp. 179–194). Rotterdam: Springer.
Groundwater-Smith, S. (2010). Researching ethically? In J. Higgs, N. Cherry, R. Macklin & R. Ajjawi (Eds.), *Researching practice: A discourse on qualitative methodologies* (pp. 75–87). Rotterdam: Sense.
Groundwater-Smith, S., & Mockler, N. (2008). Ethics in practitioner research. In J. Furlong & A. Oancea (Eds.), *Assessing quality in applied and practice based research in education* (pp. 79–92) London: Routledge.
Kemmis, S. (2007). Participatory action research and the public sphere. In P. Ponte & B. Smit (Eds.), *The quality of practitioner research* (pp. 9–28). Rotterdam: Sense.
Kemmis, S., & McTaggart, R. (2005). Participatory action research: Communicative action and the public sphere. In N. K. Denzin & Y. S. Lincoln (Eds.), *The Sage handbook of qualitative research* (3rd ed., pp. 559–603). Thousand Oaks, CA: Sage.
Maguire, M.H. (2005). What if you talked to me? I could be interesting. Ethical research considerations in engaging with bilingual/multilingual child participants in human inquiry. *Forum: Qualitative Social Research, 6*(1) Available:http://www.qualitative-research.net/index.php/fqs/article/view/530, accessed 25 January 2011
Mill, J.S. (n.d.). At BrainyQuote.com. Available:http://www.brainyquote.com/quotes/quotes/j/johnstuart118013.html, accessed August 25, 2010
Mockler, N., & Groundwater-Smith, S. (2011) Weaving a web of professional practice: The Coalition of Knowledge Building Schools. In B. Lingard, P. Thomson & T. Wrigley (Eds.), *Changing schools: Alternative models* (pp. 294–322). London: Routledge.
Munns, G. (2007). A sense of wonder: Pedagogies to engage students who live in poverty. *International Journal of Inclusive Education, 11*(3), 301–315.
Ponte, P., & Smit, B. (2007). Introduction: Doing research and being researched. In P. Ponte and B. Smit (Eds.), *The quality of practitioner research* (pp. 1–8). Rotterdam: Sense.
Sontag, S. (2003). *Regarding the pain of others.* New York: Farrar, Strauss and Giroux.
Thomson, P. (2008). Young people: Voices in visual research. In P. Thomson (Ed.), *Doing visual research with children and young people* (pp. 1–20). London: Routledge.
Tripp, D. (1993). *Critical incidents in teaching: Developing professional judgement.* London: Routledge.

CHAPTER 14

CONCERNING EQUITY
The voice of young people[1]
Susan Groundwater-Smith

Why bother – the rationale for consulting young people in schools

In the preamble to the *Melbourne Declaration on Educational Goals for Young People* (Department of Education, Employment and Workplace Relations, 2008), Ministers of Education from every Australian state and territory wrote:

> As signatories to the Melbourne Declaration, Australian Education Ministers seek to achieve the highest possible level of collaboration with the government, Catholic and independent school sectors and across and between all levels of government. Australian Education Ministers also seek to achieve new levels of engagement with all stakeholders in the education of young Australians. (p. 5)

Highlighting 'all stakeholders' is intended, here, to remind us that young people in our schools who are rarely counted as such, are the 'consequential stakeholders,'[2] for they bear the consequences of the multitude of decisions that are made on their behalf.

The two critical goals that are articulated in the *Melbourne Declaration* are:

Goal 1:

Australian schooling promotes equity and excellence

Goal 2:

All young Australians become:
- successful learners
- confident and creative individuals
- active and informed citizens. (2008, p. 7)

Each of these goals is spelled out in the original document. In support of the Declaration a 4-year plan was articulated and endorsed by all Australian Education

Ministers in March, 2009. The key strategies and initiatives are included in eight inter-related areas:

- developing stronger partnerships
- supporting quality teaching and school leadership
- strengthening early childhood education
- enhancing middle years development
- supporting senior years of schooling and youth transitions
- promoting world-class curriculum and assessment
- improving educational outcomes for Indigenous youth and disadvantaged young Australians, especially those from low socioeconomic backgrounds
- strengthening accountability and transparency.

Admirable as each one of these strategies is, one has to wonder how they might look to the young people who are to experience them. Do 'partnerships' include partnerships with students in discussions of quality teaching and school leadership in a myriad of contexts? Do students have a voice in discussions of world class curriculum and assessment? Do young people from Indigenous backgrounds and areas of social disadvantage perceive that they have a voice in the improvement of educational outcomes? How do they perceive accountability and transparency in the system? Most importantly, why should they have a voice at all?

At the beginning of the second decade in a new century, in this era of an 'education revolution'[3] it may be said that it is the instrumental and material discourses that govern us. Seemingly more attention is paid to buildings, computers, testing regimes and discussions around 'choice' and less is given to student engagement in decision making in the schools that they attend.

Currently, Australia does not have national human rights laws, in spite of it being a founding member of the UN and playing a prominent role in the negotiation of the UN Charter in 1945 and partaking in the drafting of the Universal Declaration of Human Rights. Nonetheless, it is inescapable that it has obligations to consider issues of human rights in education. It has a Human Rights Commission and has ratified a number of features of various rights treaties. It can be argued that there is an absence of human rights' principles in the prevailing political debate, in the legal system, and in the lack of protection for the vulnerable and disadvantaged in the Australian community.

Equity, as a human right, brings with it an entitlement, *inter alia*, to be treated with dignity and respect; to participate fully and democratically in matters with which the persons are concerned; to be enabled to monitor, advocate and take action; and, to engage in freedom of expression, assembly and movement. In terms of young people in our schools equity encompasses the right for them to be heard, and that means not only the few who already have the cultural, social and intellectual resources to be visible and audible, but also those who are dealing with difficult and challenging conditions and are often marginalised and silenced.

The right of young people to be heard

Children, as human beings, are said to possess the same rights as all people. This is recognised by The United Nations Convention on the Rights of the Child (1989) to which Australia is a signatory. The Convention sets out a broad range of rights in addition to the universal human rights shared by all. Children are defined under Article 1 of the Convention as including 'every human being below the age of eighteen years'.

The Convention is comprehensive and entitles children to a broad range of rights including, *inter alia*, the right:

- to express views in all decisions that affect them and the opportunity to be heard in any court or administrative proceedings;
- to freedom of expression and the right to seek, receive and impart information of all kinds;
- to have their best interests treated as a primary consideration in all actions concerning them, including decisions in relation to their care and protection;
- to free education available on the basis of their capacity; and
- to enjoy the highest attainable standard of health and I an adequate standard of living.

In particular, Article 12 states that every child has the right to say what they think in all matters affecting them, and to have their views taken seriously.

In this way the Convention recognises that children have particular needs and vulnerabilities which require special protection beyond the rights to which adults are entitled. All Australian states and territories have Children's Commissioners, with the exception of South Australia which has a Children's Guardian.[4]

Many young people in Australian schools are able to enjoy their rights. However, the rights of some children who are most vulnerable are yet to be recognised and met. For example, these include: children experiencing serious socio-economic disadvantage, sometimes resulting in homelessness; children experiencing violence, bullying or harassment; and children who live with a disability, including those living with mental illness. There are also certain groups of at-risk children who are less likely to be able to enjoy their full range of rights. These groups include Aboriginal and Torres Strait Islander children; children in out-of-home care; children in detention including those in immigration detention; and children living in rural and remote areas of Australia.

How sobering it is to read the following:

> If I could make one change to support children and young people, it would be for kids' views to be taken seriously and treated with respect. (Calvert, 2008)

> Kids aren't as naïve as you think. I think the reason that people don't listen to kids is that they're kids. (Cossar, Brandon & Jordan, 2011, p. 4)

> Children do not have an official or defined role to play in mainstream politics and policy making. It is easy, therefore, for decision makers to overlook including children in these processes. And, if children are invited to 'sit at the table' their voices are rarely truly heard. (Australian Human Rights Commissioner, 2010)

Participatory research that engages young people as active, informed and informing agents with respect to such social provisions as education can well be constructed as a radical means of interrupting this dominant discourse where so many young people receive so little attention. For through its power they are no longer silenced and rendered invisible.

But we cannot be sanguine about how this might operate. Young people are typically positioned by the adults and the professional and political agendas that surround them. These, in turn, are mediated by where children are placed in the social order and the spaces that they occupy. Wyness (2009, p. 395) suggests that 'while professional adults are committed to creating and sustaining children's spaces, they are equally concerned to locate these spaces within the more conventionally defined structures of children's places'.

Cruddas (2007) mounts a pointed critique upon the received notions of student voice as they have prevailed in the UK over a number of years. She sees that much of the emergent practice has been appropriated for the purposes of meeting statutory requirements to 'give children and young people a say' (p. 480) and argues instead for the notion of 'engaged voices' whereby young people and adults operate within an intertextual, provisional discursive space that may allow the unsayable to emerge. Much of what purports to employ the voices of young people as a form of authentic dialogue is conducted within spaces where the power relationships are significantly distorted in favour of the adult. At worst this contributes to existing technologies of power, at best to paternalism and tokenism.

Participation – how?

Participation by young people in forms of social inquiry can take shape in different ways and at different levels. Shier's (2001, p. 110) model is particularly useful in considering young people's engagement in participatory research because it embodies the nature of commitment required for a project to be successful. He argues that there are five levels of participation, namely: (a) children are listened to, (b) children are supported in expressing their views, (c) children's views are taken into account, (d) children are involved in decision-making processes, and (e) children share power and responsibility for decision-making. He goes on to argue that at each level of participation there are three stages of commitment: openings, opportunities and obligations.

Openings are where there has been a commitment or statement of intent to work in a certain way. It is only an opening, because at this stage, the opportunity to make it happen may not be available. At the second stage, an *opportunity* occurs when the needs are met that will enable the young people to operate at this level in practice. These needs may include resources such as the provision of time, skills and knowledge, maybe through training, development of new procedures or new approaches to established tasks. Finally, an *obligation* is established when it becomes the agreed policy of the organisation or setting that the young people should operate at this level. Later this article will illustrate the ways in which these three stages of commitment were created, in the context of two National Partnership[5] projects designed to address equity issues in a manner that might be described as radical.

In his sobering paper in the *Griffith Review*, Teese (2006) wrote that schools in difficult circumstances are still viewed much as they have been over the 30 years since the Whitlam reforms. He argues for a radical approach, giving these schools 'an opportunity not available elsewhere – to experiment and innovate in the interests of the children attending them and the system as a whole' (opening para). Could it be that the National Partnerships Program with its extended timeline and financial underwriting could provide just such an opportunity for experimentation and would such innovation lead to young people having greater access to equitable outcomes while at the same time making an overall contribution to equity and social justice across the schooling system?

The National Partnership Program is an opportunity for the school to:

- provide a range of school-level and broader level reforms that address educational disadvantage associated with low socio-economic status;
- implement reforms to better support student learning needs and well-being and to foster successful transition to further education, work and active participation in the community; and
- be better equipped to address complex and interconnected challenges facing students from disadvantaged communities.

For some schools this has meant developing projects that build upon students' perspectives on the ways in which teaching and learning is conducted and the impacts upon them, not only in terms of achievement, but in relation to their enjoyment of and engagement in schooling.

Developing a project that authentically provides students with a voice is neither easy nor comfortable. Fielding (2011), who has contributed so powerfully to our understandings that lead us from students as clients to students as change agents, stages the development thus:

- Students as data source;
- Students as active respondents;
- Students as co-enquirers;
- Students as knowledge creators;
- Students as joint authors; and
- Students sharing commitment for the common good.

In the two cases reported below we can see that this road is indeed a challenging one.

The genesis of the case studies

The two case studies portrayed here are extracted from ongoing work undertaken by the author as an academic partner to the schools employing a complex framing of facilitation. Her purpose in facilitating the innovative practices of the schools that were involved was to take facilitation beyond the commonplace understanding of providing assistance and move it into the realm of transformative partnerships between the academy and the field of practice, with all of the challenges and uncertainties that such a relationship entails. Facilitating practitioner inquiry and action can be all too easily read as a process that is transactional; that is the provision of resources and skills to be handed on from one party to another rather than providing each of the partners with an opportunity to engage in deep professional learning.

Case 1: 'our gee'ed up school'[6]

During 2010 I was able to work for a full year with a team of teachers in school included in the Australian National Partnerships Program for schools serving low-SES communities. The school in question intended to start a student voice project with a specific year group. This year group would be apprenticed as co-researchers in a 'collaborative inquiry' investigating the reforms in teaching and learning that were needed for improvement in student engagement. There was some discussion over which year group should be involved. Year 9 was chosen because this was considered to be the year when apathy and active resistance become entrenched. Also, the team considered that the metacognitive benefits of reflecting on teaching and learning would be beneficial to students as they moved closer towards senior high school studies.

In attempting to apprentice students as co-researchers in considering school reform, it was hoped to reorientate the school towards a genuinely person-centred school, away from being a performance-driven environment. The team wondered whether the search for significance by students had led to their disengagement when they had felt 'insignificant' to the organisation because of their poor results. It was considered that perhaps this poor self-worth perpetuated the cycle of poor results and whether focusing on the affective *before* the cognitive would ironically end up generating better results because of increased student engagement.

Additionally, it was hoped that 'resistance' could be 'authorised' through this project. Students could critique and make suggestions about their learning and their school. The thought was that, potentially, when resistance is authorised, passive resistance (in the form of challenging behaviour) would no longer be deemed as necessary; 'ownership' of their learning could reduce apathy. In authorising resistance and allowing students to voice their opinions, it was hoped to partially reorient relationships between teachers and students from control to voice. Under these circumstances a steering committee comprising some 20 Year 9 student volunteers, that included some students who hitherto had been quite disengaged from their schooling, was established.

Time and space do not permit a detailed account of the processes that were employed. Suffice to say the research steering committee met with the team and myself as their critical friend on a regular basis. They were trained in research methods and undertook a series of research days with their peers. In Term 3 (early September), students presented their findings to staff at a staff meeting after school. They had previously determined that they would demonstrate their findings creatively, including a video, animation and a classroom simulation during the staff meeting. Their main recommendations to teachers were: know students individually; encourage students, respect students; and make learning fun.

There were mixed reactions of staff to the presentation, with some teachers expressing support, while others were more sceptical. This potentially could be as a result of staff not feeling part of the project and therefore feeling personally undermined by student recommendations. It could also be a result of teachers' concerns about the limits of giving students a voice. Teachers may have felt that students would exercise their agency without respect for teachers.

It is interesting that both students (during the research days) and teachers (after the staff presentation) expressed their dissatisfaction at the negativity and lack of respect of the 'other'. Both students and teachers struggled with the idea of who was 'responsible' for this state of affairs. As students discussed notions of blame, they reasoned:

- Sometimes [students] need to see that their misbehaving caused the teacher to not do any fun work and arguing doesn't make it better.
- Respect needs to go both ways and sometimes it does but other times the respect is scarce.
- Most of the negative feedback was criticising teachers, and although students would have to try to understand teachers, the teachers should be putting in more effort to repair their reputations.

While there was some acknowledgement from the students of their need to take greater responsibility, mutual and reciprocal responsibility for the positive reconstruction of the teacher/student relationship seemed to be the key idea that emerged from their reflections. From the practitioner research team's perspective, greater student agency can lead to increased student commitment, confidence, critical awareness and cognitive reflection.

2011 saw a continuation of the project. As the steering committee members from 2010 moved into Year 10 they were reluctant to relinquish their roles and responsibilities. This was resolved by them becoming mentors to the incoming group. While they are now less involved they nonetheless keep a 'watching brief' on the new developments that are underway.

Among the changes to the work of the steering committee has been an additional emphasis upon designing surveys and scenarios that are being responded to by the whole year group. A risky new step has also been introduced with students working in four small groups observing those teachers whose lessons they believed to be most engaging. Teachers provided informed consent and the observations were collected through note-taking and video-recording. Afterwards a sample of the class was withdrawn for a focus group discussion regarding the lesson and the ways in which the teacher worked to make learning engaging. Subsequently the teacher was also interviewed. Each student researcher group informed the steering committee of what they had observed and how their observations contributed to ways in which they might characterise engaging teaching and learning. In this way, information was shared from multiple perspectives, in a sense to complete the jigsaw. Currently these studies are being incorporated into a report to staff.

Effective participation by young people in advising their teachers of the ways in which their professional practices facilitate or impede learning cannot be taken lightly. If consulting young people is to be seen as a powerful means of enhancing teacher professional learning, then it cannot be a short-term, tokenistic strategic tool, but rather the means by which trust and openness are fostered, valued and celebrated and where all who participate in it see themselves as members of an equitable society. Indeed, in articulating their views and critiquing the power structures surrounding them, students are being enabled to 'rewrite' their world, no easy matter. Furthermore, this is a costly business involving significant amounts of teacher time and opportunity costs for students working outside their classrooms.

170 *Concerning equity*

In the second case to be reported, the project is in its early stages, laying down the groundwork for the incorporation of student voice. It too is in a school that is a beneficiary of the National Partnerships Program and is in the non-government sector.

Case 2: from cruising to moving

Not all schools facing difficult socio-economic circumstances are characterised by open resistance. It may be that low levels of student engagement are more a result of a sense of 'Why worry? We're ok!' when manifestly achievement, as measured by high stakes testing, is not what it might be. Borrowing a phrase from Stoll and Fink (1998), such schools could be said to be 'cruising' as compared to moving, or strolling, or struggling or sinking.

As with all National Partnership Projects there is an emphasis on capacity building that will both enhance achievement, but also develop engagement beyond the procedural and towards a more substantive model. In terms of students, procedural engagement is related to students being on task and generally complying with what is required of them in the classroom. Substantive engagement requires students to be highly operational, that is: being fully participative in classroom activities; being able to employ a wide range of cognitive strategies; having a capacity to synthesise and evaluate; being able to sustain effort; and being self-regulated.

> This second case is one where there was a determination by a new and vigorous executive to interrupt the seemingly low motivation of students to invest their energy and effort in deeper and more profound learning. Taking along with them a number of staff, they desired to move towards a goal where 'doing' school would be seen as a worthwhile enterprise. Prior to establishing something akin to the steering committee outlined in the earlier case, it was decided that there would be a period of 'reconnaissance' where a team of teacher researchers would investigate the current conditions by drawing upon the perspectives of the young people, in particular those in Years 9 and 10. Ten teachers elected to become part of the project and have met on a number of occasions to develop their inquiry skills. At this point they have developed three separate but interdependent projects.
>
> The goal of the first was to develop a deeper understanding of what makes for effective learning from the perspective of the students. The team wanted to understand what makes the learning enjoyable, fulfilling, memorable, and important. Thus two groups of 7 students from Year 10 were identified for focus group inquiry. In advance, they are asked to 'prepare' by bringing an artefact (e.g., photograph, work sample, product, journal entry etc.) that reminds them of a time when they have learned really effectively, when they were really proud of their achievement. They were asked to 'tell the story of the learning'. Students were given prompts, for example: 'What was happening at the time; How would you rate the level of enjoyment; What did you learn and why was it important to you; How would you apply this learning to another situation?' and so on.
>
> A second group is exploring the experiences of a sample of those students who appear to sit in the middle of the bell curve of achievement and who are

perceived as often 'invisible' in the classroom. At present these Year 9 students are responding to a survey and a set of scenarios regarding engagement and working with the team to make sense of the results. Thus, the students will assist in the interpretation of the results. It is also intended to hold discussions of the results with more senior students and ask them to reflect on whether these results hold true for them to this day and why or why not.

A third group is also working on a survey with another sample of Year 9 students, with three stages to their inquiry: firstly students respond to the items, secondly they are interviewed in pairs regarding the results, and finally the participating students will meet in focus groups to discuss emerging issues.

In this second case we see the school progressively focusing upon the students' experiences and perspectives as understood by the young people themselves. While, normally, schools are sites where the many voices of teachers are heard, in that noisy acoustic the sounds of the students' voices tend to be muted other than when they are expressing resistance. Here we see that the school has found a way forward for the expression of students' experiences to be represented by the students themselves. As Fielding and Moss (2011) argue, this is the beginning of a journey, reclaiming education as a democratic project and community responsibility that can disturb and disrupt the status quo that is normally anything but equitable for young people.

In a sense these cases can be read as provocations asking readers to consider rethinking the challenges and possibilities of student voice and agency. They cannot be characterised as research studies designed to provide the kind of evidence that might be used in an adversarial manner, that is to prove that a particular practice is the most viable and appropriate; but rather as examples of teachers' working with students in ways that permit a forensic examination of the outcomes such that school practices are better understood and conditions ameliorated.

Student advice – equity and ethics

It has already been argued that ensuring that we attend to the views, attitudes and aspirations of the full complement of students is a matter of equity, but in the name of equity we must remain cautious. No-one puts it better than Michael Fielding (2004) when he writes:

> How confident are we that our research does not redescribe and reconfigure students in ways that bind them more securely into the fabric of the status quo? ... How clear are we about the use to which the depth and detail of the data is likely to be put? Is our more detailed knowledge of what students think and feel largely used to help us control them more effectively? ... Are we sure that our positions of relative power and our own personal and professional interests are not blurring our judgements or shaping our advocacy? (pp. 302–303)

Clearly, equity as a concept does not stand alone – equity has a sibling relationship to ethics. If the goal is one directed to social justice then the means to reach that goal have to be undertaken in an ethical manner. Ethics is not just about feeling good, or about a particular regulation or social code, or about following the law;

it is about behaviour that is motivated by understandings of, among other things, respect, fairness, compassion, tolerance, honesty, courage, integrity and prudence.

These attributes align with the then Howard Federal Government's publication of its *Values for Australian Schooling* which remain in place today, these being:

- Care and compassion;
- Doing your best;
- Fair go;
- Freedom;
- Honesty and trustworthiness;
- Integrity;
- Respect;
- Responsibility; and
- Understanding, tolerance and inclusion.

Such values are not only intended for students, but are there to be embraced by the whole school community. In order to address the ethical concerns in attending to student voice in our schools in terms of an equity agenda, I have posed six questions (Groundwater-Smith, 2007, p. 122):

- To what extent are students given the right to exercise informed consent?
- What provision is made to ensure confidentiality and anonymity?
- Who is consulted?
- What are the opportunity costs?
- How is student voice sustained and nurtured?
- How is the information yielded through student voice disseminated and acted upon?

Informed consent can mean the right to say 'no'

Young people become accustomed to the fact that they have little or no choice about attending schools and conforming to what is required of them. Their daily attendance is expected; they read, write, calculate, inquire and interact with one another to the orders and specifications of others. Schools even have regulatory influences on children's experiences when they are at home where they are expected to comply with homework demands. In such a fundamentally coercive context, informed consent as a basic ethical precept is more often observed in its absence than otherwise.[7]

Generally, we find that young people are willing participants in school-based inquiry projects, yet they may be easily persuaded and at times naïve. It is important that they understand that their participation is voluntary and that they can withdraw. We should pay them the courtesy of explaining to them why they are being consulted and how it is that they have a stake in the process.

Confidentiality and anonymity

Again, the very culture of schooling is one where young people function in a public context; in effect, they are constantly on display. Their teachers generally expect to know who said what and when. Having opportunities to provide anonymous responses are often treated with some suspicion: 'Will the young people betray us?'; 'Can they be trusted to tell "the truth" when we don't know their names and they are not accountable for what they may say?'. The litmus test is, 'whose interests are being served?' Will the inquiry contribute important knowledge about schooling processes and the ways in which they may be enhanced?

Who is consulted?

As it has already been argued, it is often the case that when it is proposed to consult students the school will choose to select those who will be seen as good ambassadors and who will advocate for the school. They are the students who are seen as leaders and may be members of student representative bodies. Atweh and Bland (2004) remind us that students' perspectives will be mediated by factors such as ethnicity, gender, and degrees of cultural and social capital, all working and interacting in complex ways: 'Working with students in collaborative research, adults should be conscious of the differential experiences and expertise that each participant brings to the process of collaboration' (p. 13). Some of these variations can be dealt with through the employment of mixed methods which not only lend authenticity through triangulation but also allow for voices to be expressed through a variety of media where surveys, focus groups, product analysis and a web-based discussion may be all part of the data set.

Opportunity costs

As was discussed in the first case study, asking students to contribute to school-based inquiry, especially when they are substantially engaged as consultants and active researchers, will take a considerable amount of student time. Ideally it should be possible to embed a number of data-collection strategies into the curriculum itself. In recent work that has involved clusters of schools across Australia investigating the implementation of values in the curriculum, one school chose to dedicate a whole class to the research across seven schools. Students in Year 8 (13–14 year olds) interviewed their peers, created and analysed surveys and undertook observations using a range of digital applications. Effectively, this enterprise took a day out of each week for a school term. The activity was seen to be inclusive of the following key learning areas: Mathematics/Technology, English, and Human Society and its Environment. Good relationships needed to be built both within and between schools in order for trust to be established and the requisite skills acquired. Nonetheless, enterprises of this kind take time away from other opportunities. Students need to feel that their contribution has been worthwhile.

Sustaining student voice

Developing a school culture that recognises and respects young people's contributions to policies and practices, as a form of ethical obligation, takes time. It also takes a commitment on the part of staff to ensure that the processes and procedures become embedded in school practices. If this is to occur, then schools also need to have ongoing plans for ways in which they can sustain student-voice inquiry.

Fielding and Bragg (2003) advocate: developing students' roles; developing the identity of the work; and involving different staff and developing staff roles. School improvement cannot be seen as the responsibility of the few. It requires commitment and engagement across the spectrum.

Dissemination and action

According to Dewey (1916), education in a democratic society is neither for the individual alone or for the society alone. It is for both. It is 'a mode of conjoint communicated experiences' (p. 87) and rests upon principles of communication whereby the responsibility for learning is a whole-hearted endeavour in which all participate in the interests of decency and democracy. Communicating the results of inquiry may make for the emergence of some uncomfortable truths (Groundwater-Smith & Mockler, 2009) but the suppression or distortion of these in order to put the school and its practices in a better light would be a significant betrayal.

Conclusion – making it happen

In his inaugural address to the Centre for an Ethical Society, Sir Gerard Brennan (2006) spoke to the matter of public policy, arguing:

> Public policy would be directed to achieving the common good – a society in which every person would have an opportunity to develop his or her capacities and to live in dignity – freely, peacefully and with the ability to participate in social life. (p. 2)

Such a society would necessarily be an equitable society. In sum, our schools are places where this can happen; where it should happen and where it will happen. However, this cannot be a matter of mere assertion. If improvement to school practices, which are sustainable and authentic, can be achieved through the voice of young people, then schools need to address pedagogical and governance procedures as well as those concerned with school leadership. Pedagogy is not to be solely confined to discussions of teaching and learning processes in order to fulfil curriculum outcomes, but also needs to embrace the concept of 'social pedagogy' as an understanding that relationships that are inclusive and harmonious are central to the well-being of all and based firmly within a policy of human rights. Governance, that is the ways in which matters are managed, accords status and respect to all who participate and thus leaders, both student leaders and staff leaders, have a responsibility to create those conditions that will not only permit this to happen, but will nurture and develop transformative practice.

Notes

1. This article is based upon a presentation to: *Equity in Education Connecting for Change*, Australian College of Educators National Conference 13–15 July, 2011, University of Technology Sydney.
2. This is a term that I have chosen to use in my writing, but is drawn originally from the then Queensland Board of Teacher Registration.

3 A term used by the Rudd Labor Government in Australia when it formed government following the 1977 election.
4 While a Children's Commissioner works to improve and ensure better services for all children a Children's Guardian works solely to help improve the services for children in the care of a department.
5 The National Partnerships Program, a structure of state and territory financial relations with the Commonwealth government, is aimed at achieving economic and social reform across various areas including education. The reforms in literacy and numeracy contained in national partnership agreements are aimed at 'closing the gap' for low SES and Indigenous students. http://smarterchools.gov.au/Pages/default.aspx
6 For a full account of the first year of this project see Mayes & Groundwater-Smith, 2010. Part of this account is extracted from that presentation and was principally written by Eve Mayes.
7 Although parental consent may and should be sought, it is also important that the student is provided with an explanation of the project and permitted to make his or her own decision regarding involvement.

References

Atweh, B. & Bland, D. (2004) *Problematics in young people as researchers: Visions and voices*, paper presented to the Social Change in the 21st Century Conference. Centre for Social Change Research, QUT, Brisbane (29 October).

Australian Human Rights Commission. (2010) *An Australian Children's Commissioner. Discussion paper*. Retrieved June 1, 2011 from: http://www.hreoc.gov.au/human_rights/children/2010_commissioner_children.html

Brennan, G, (2006) *Inaugural address*, presented at the National Launch of the Centre for an Ethical Society, Pitt Street Uniting Church, Sydney, 21 November, 2006. Retrieved June 1, 2011 from: http://www.ces.org.au/Other%20 stuff/X00002%20IA%20G%20Brennan.pdf

Calvert, G. (2008) *UNICEF Roundtable*, NSW Parliament House 9th September. Retrieved June 1, 2011 from: http://kids.nsw.gov.au/kids/resources/speeches.cfm?itemID=9C114D12C247D76977926CCE37DEBF56#ixzz1NytAMLkh

Cossar, J. Brandon, M. & Jordan, P. (2011) *'Don't Make Assumptions': Children's and young people's views of the child protection system and messages for change* (Norwich, UK: University of East Anglia, Centre for Research on the Child and the Family, for The Office of the Children's Commissioner).

Cruddas, L. (2007) Engaged voices – dialogic interactions and the construction of shared social meanings, *Educational Action Research*, 15(3), pp. 479–488.

Department of Education, Employment and Workplace Relations. (2008) Melbourne Declaration on Educational Goals for Young Australians (Canberra: Ministerial Council on Education, Employment, Training and Youth Affairs). Available online from: http://www.deewr.gov.au/Schooling/CareersandTransitions/CareerDevelopment/RelatedLinks/Pages/MelbourneDeclaration.aspx

Department of Education, Employment and Workplace Relations. (2011) *Values Curriculum Resources, National Framework for Values Education in Australian Schools*, available from: http://www.valueseducation.edu.au/values/default.asp?id=8758

Dewey, J. (1916) *Democracy and Education* (New York: Macmillan).

Fielding, M. (2004) Transformative approaches to student voice: Theoretical underpinnings, recalcitrant realities, *British Educational Research Journal*, 30(2), pp. 295–311.

Fielding, M. (2011) Patterns of partnerships, in N. Mockler & J. Sachs (Eds), *Rethinking Educational Practice through Reflexive Inquiry* (Rotterdam, NL: Springer), pp. 61–76.

Fielding, M. & Bragg, S. (2003) *Students as Researchers: Making a difference* (London: Pearson Publishing).

Fielding, M. & Moss, P. (2011) *Education and the Common School* (London: Routledge).

Groundwater-Smith, S. (2007) Student voice: Essential testimony for intelligent schools, in A. Campbell, & S. Groundwater-Smith (Eds), *An Ethical Approach to Practitioner Research* (London: Routledge), pp. 113–128.

Groundwater-Smith, S. & Mockler, N. (2009) *Teacher Professional Learning in an Age of Compliance* (Rotterdam, NL: Springer),

Mayes, E. with Groundwater-Smith, S. (2010) *Year 9 as Co-researchers*, paper presented to the annual conference of the Australian Association for Research in Education (AARE), Melbourne (28 November–2 December).

Office of the United Nations High Commissioner for Human Rights (1989) *Convention on the Rights of the Child 1990*, opened for signature on 20 November 1989, 1577 U.N.T.S. 3 (entered into force 2 September 1990) ('Convention'), article 1.

Shier, H. (2001) Pathways to participation: Openings, opportunities and obligations, *Children & Society*, 15(2), pp. 107–117.

Stoll, L. & Fink, D. (1998) The Cruising School: The unidentified ineffective school, in *No Quick Fixes: Perspectives on schools in difficulty* (London: Falmer Press), pp. 189–206.

Teese, R. (2006) Condemned to innovate, *Griffith Review*, Edition 11, Getting Smart: The Battle for Ideas in Education, available online from: http://griffithreview.com/edition-11-getting-smart/condemned-to-innovate/all-pages

Wyness, M. (2009) Adults' involvement in children's participation: Juggling children's places and spaces, *Children and Society*, 23(6), pp. 395–406.

CHAPTER 15

WEAVING A WEB OF PROFESSIONAL PRACTICE
The coalition of knowledge building schools

Nicole Mockler and Susan Groundwater-Smith

Introduction

In this chapter we outline the formation, processes and purposes of a dynamic hybrid network of schools working to create usable professional knowledge in a context of change. The Coalition of Knowledge-Building Schools, based in New South Wales, Australia, was formed in 2000 and over the past ten years has grown steadily and developed procedures for working collegially. Here, we trace the different phases of the Coalition's expansion and identify a number of turning points in the evolution of the network. We explore processes used for the invention and re-invention of professional knowledge within the community of practice, across varying social, geographic and educational contexts.

This chapter seeks to identify the conditions for building a joint enterprise through events and publications and highlights a range of strengths and challenges in creating this joint enterprise. As strengths, we examine issues of diversity and flexibility, academic support and goodwill. Among the challenges, we highlight matters associated with sustainability, capacity building and the need to remain 'critical'. We conclude not by offering a model but by suggesting a number of principles upon which successful hybrid networks can be established and maintained.

Network or web?

In his account of orb web construction, Zschokke (2009) outlines the moves that the spider makes in building its web. Briefly, the spider bridges an open space by attaching a dragline and traversing the gap; it then tightens the thread and uses it as a means to cross back to the other side. Slowly, but strategically, the spider establishes what is known as a 'proto-web', a star-shaped structure in which the threads come together in a hub enveloped within a frame, paying particular attention to balance. It then progresses to amplify the frame and to construct a 'sticky spiral' that will ultimately attract and capture its prey.

In seeking a metaphor for the establishment of the Coalition of Knowledge-Building Schools, the manufacture of a web most closely approximates the ways in which the community has been established – although clearly not with the purpose of preying upon its members! In our account of the history of the Coalition (developed below), it is clear that there were a number of steps analogous to the work of the spider. Initially, a modest bridge was built between a small number of participating schools. The Centre for Practitioner Research (CPR[1]) in the Faculty of Education and Social Work provided a hub and frame that would enable the web to be built and strengthened. The stickiness of the threads paralleled the agreed-on principles by which the Coalition would function.

The hub and frame: the Centre for Practitioner Research

The CPR was established in 1998, following the then Faculty of Education's successful hosting of the Inaugural International Practitioner Research Conference.[2] At that time, it was co-directed by Judyth Sachs and Susan Groundwater-Smith. It has always been unfunded and was seen as associated with the Division of Professional Learning's service to the community.

The two aims of the CPR were

- to validate and value the research-based knowledge created by practitioners in the field, and
- to develop cross-disciplinary networks to facilitate the production and circulation of new knowledge.

Its purposes were seen to be these:

- To foster, support and enhance practitioner research as a mode of inquiry to understand and improve practice in universities and schools locally, nationally and internationally.
- To contribute to the creation of situated knowledge regarding educational practices.
- To investigate and critique the outcomes of practitioner research.
- To encourage the development, validation and documentation of new methodologies in practitioner research.
- To act as a forum for the discussion of practitioner research via conferences and electronic and print media.
- To establish international affiliations with universities and schools similarly engaged.

The CPR's range of activities included conducting free-to-the-public 'twilight seminars', developing professional practice links with networked learning communities in the United Kingdom and mainland Europe and reaching out to other sites for learning beyond the classroom (such as the Australian Museum), and building and nurturing the Coalition of Knowledge-Building Schools. In any one year, these activities were seen to make a significant contribution to the education community. For example, twilight seminars would adopt a theme and pursue it with well-respected academics who were keen to make links between the academic and professional communities. One year the theme was focused upon the nature of identity formation, with bi-monthly meetings focusing upon

- professional identity in changing times;
- practitioner enquiry and professional identity formation;
- the public intellectual and social capital formation;
- the shift from pastoral to political identity;
- institutional identity and professional partnerships; and
- national identity formation in the context of polarised debates about the history curriculum.

Throughout the life of the CPR and, later, the Practitioner Research Special Interest Group (PRSIG), a wide variety of publications and conference presentations have been developed, often in association with school-based practitioners working in member schools of the Coalition or with such Friends of the Coalition as the Australian Museum. A number of these are inserted in the evolving history of the Coalition and its manifold activities outlined later in this chapter. Additionally, in partnership with MLC School, Burwood, Australia, the CPR published a resource (Groundwater-Smith and Mockler 2003b) designed to assist those engaged in practitioner research and drawing upon the wisdom and experience of members of the Coalition. *Learning to Listen: Listening to Learn* is in use by those supporting practitioner research in the United Kingdom, Netherlands, Austria, Singapore and the United States, as well as throughout Australia. Thus it may be seen that the CPR and PRSIG provided a robust frame and hub for the development of a web of interconnectivity between the members of the Coalition of Knowledge-Building Schools.

Developing the 'proto-web'

The initial dragline came as a result of the Innovative Links between Universities and Schools for Teacher Professional Development project, established as part of the Australian National Schools Network in the context of a school reform agenda in the early 1990s (Hartley and Whitehead 2006). Both Judyth Sachs and Susan Groundwater-Smith were able to establish sustained links with a range of schools with a commitment to ongoing teacher professional learning and to engage in what became known as facilitated practitioner inquiry whereby academic partners assisted in modest action research projects in schools (Groundwater-Smith 1998). The very beginning of the web was taking place.

The next important bridging line came through the Innovation and Best Practice Project, or IBPP (Cuttance et al. 2001). The IBPP, one of the largest educational research projects ever undertaken in Australia, was a large-scale research and development project that specifically focused on innovation in schools. Each of the 107 participating schools developed and implemented a significant innovation aimed at improving learning outcomes for students. Each school researched and provided a report on its innovation, with a specific focus on its success in improving student learning outcomes. Several of these were supported by academics from the CPR who sought to connect them to other schools with similar ambitions. At this point, the participation of Nicole Mockler, initially in the role of a practitioner researcher and later as a full-time academic, became critical as she served to further amplify the work of the partnership.

From these projects, a small number of schools were identified that clearly had an interest in engaging in systematic inquiry. Following some early meetings, these schools came together to form the nucleus of the Coalition. By 2002, seven schools (three independent and four government) had gathered together to more formally outline their shared purposes, which were

- to develop and enhance the notion of evidence-based practice;[3]
- to develop an interactive community of practice using appropriate technologies;
- to make a contribution to a broader professional knowledge base with respect to educational practice;
- to build research capability within their own and each other's schools by engaging both teachers and students in the research processes; and to share methodologies that are appropriate to practitioner inquiry as a means of transforming teacher professional learning. (Groundwater-Smith and Mockler 2003b: 1).

By the time of this writing (2009), the Coalition had 13 members[4] – four independent girls schools (three metropolitan and one regional), two metropolitan comprehensive boys schools, one metropolitan comprehensive girls school, three coeducational high schools (one being regional), two metropolitan primary schools and one residential respite care school (accommodating young people from across the state of New South Wales). In addition, it is affiliated with what have been deemed 'Friends of the Coalition', namely the Australian Museum and Taronga Zoo Education Centre. It counts among these members some of the state's most privileged residents and those living in the most challenging of circumstances, all meeting in a climate of cooperation and goodwill. The Coalition's recently established website (www.ckbschools.org) includes further information about member schools, academic partners and 'Friends' of the Coalition.

Knowledge building within and beyond the coalition

By its very name, it is possible to detect the mission of the Coalition of Knowledge-Building Schools – that is, to create usable professional knowledge for employment within the participating schools and beyond into the wider educational community. In part this ambition was inspired by the David Hargreaves publication titled 'The knowledge creating school' (1999), in which he argued for schools to be sites for the generation of professional knowledge designed to enhance effective teaching and learning. Hargreaves (1999: 124) argued that such a school

- audits its professional working knowledge;
- manages the process of creating professional knowledge;
- validates the professional knowledge that is created; and
- disseminates the created professional knowledge.

Further, Hargreaves (1999: 126–127) outlines the conditions and factors that will favour knowledge creation in schools, *inter alia:*[5]

- A culture of and enthusiasm for continual improvement
- An awareness of the external environment
- A sensitivity to key stakeholders (including students)
- Coherent and flexible planning
- Flatter management structures
- Recognition of the expert knowledge held by teachers
- Knowledge creation as a whole school enterprise
- Regular opportunities for reflection, dialogue and enquiry
- A readiness to 'tinker', experiment and engage in partnerships and alliances
- A willingness to include diverse opinions
- An ethical culture embodying freedom and responsibility.

These factors and conditions can be seen as working principles for the Coalition members as they go about their business. In any one year, a number of the schools will be engaged in a diverse range of projects that they share with their colleagues through breakfast meetings once a term and through an annual one-day conference. This diversity is best illustrated by drawing upon an example of an email sent to members by the convenor following the most recent meeting.

> First of all a 'big thank-you' to N. She has done a great job with the website and I know spent many, many hours on it . . .
> We had a chance to hear about the Teachers' College and contribution that it made to planning in terms of both the actual and virtual museum. V. did a great job of reprising the report and you all have a copy to read at your leisure. L. indicated that at the end of the year the museum will be able to report on actions taken. She also foreshadowed that later in the year she would like to invite around 15 teachers to assist in working on the website, in particular a Teachers' Blog. At first she thought it might take a half a day; but the meeting indicated that release is for whole days and that the schools would be willing to work with the AM. A little later we also heard about the successful visit of G. Boys High School Pacific Island students, where the boys requested that the museum keep their cultural history safe!
> A. Boys High School . . . have worked with the museum on a number of exhibitions, Dinosaurs, Surviving Australia and Climate Change and a team comprising science, history, English and maths teachers worked to develop interdisciplinary units of inquiry using technologies, in particular Marvin, an animated program originally developed for indigenous students. Interestingly this application has also been used by S. H. in their Quality Teaching Indigenous Program (QTIP) project – it is another example of cross-over work that Coalition members have been so creative in implementing . . .
> N. told us of the G.P. High School cluster's successful values project. Along with the High School, several primary schools, varying in size and location, have worked to engage in writing and publishing projects. I suggested that they take a look at the *Special Forever* environmental communication project managed by the Primary English Teachers Association (PETA) and the Murray-Darling Basin Commission – perhaps there would be the possibility of publishing beyond the cluster – it sounded very exciting and hopefully at our day conference we can look more closely at the products . . .

M. shared the G. Boys High School story in which boys have been active participants in developing the Positive Behaviours Intervention System (PBIS) for the school. The overall scaffold of all being safe, respectful learners (including teachers) was fleshed out by the boys and resulted in a matrix using students' own language. She showed us some great pictures from the launch where African and Lebanese drummers performed as well as rappers and a Pacific Island Haka. M. also outlined a peer reading program where year 10 students are trained by TAFE to act as tutors for years 7–9.

J. from St. M. College was able to report on the ongoing nature of their action research focus that is tied to the school's core values in relation to 'love of learning'. Currently there are eight projects underway, ranging from the effective use of laptops to J.'s own work on cultural diversity and inclusion. How, for example, does one teach about the Renaissance to Thai students with different cultural histories; and how does one learn from them? Currently she is interviewing Kenyan students and looks forward to reporting more of the progress at the next Coalition meeting . . .

We missed our primary school members and look forward to their contributions at our November day-long meeting where our focus will be on values education and where we are anticipating some contributions from students.

Turning points in creating the web

The strength of the web depends in part upon the moments when a new thread is cast and a turning point created. We would assert that a number of these can be identified. Early discussions and alliances, by happenstance, were conducted with a small number of independent girls' schools. Clearly, this could be seen as somewhat limiting. In seeking a broader representation of interests, several schools that had participated in past projects through the Australian National Schools Network and were known to the convener were approached.[6] In Australia's complex education environment where the funding of schools is highly contentious and there is a degree of ill will between the sectors, it was encouraging to find that such a diverse range of schools could see the benefit of working together. Other than the first meeting of each year that is held at the University of Sydney, the remaining meetings are conducted by host schools. Having representatives from privileged, generously funded schools spend time in schools of their colleagues, some of which were highly challenging physical environments, proved to be a new experience.

A second turning point occurred with the involvement of the Australian Museum and, subsequently, Taronga Zoo Education.[7] This engagement provided schools with opportunities to consider issues of education beyond the walls of the classroom and to more closely examine what it is to be a professional and engage in inquiry-based professional learning. Sachs (2007) observed that the Coalition provided teachers with rich professional learning opportunities that allowed them to focus on themselves as learners in the context of a learning community composed of colleagues similarly committed to taking a critical orientation to their practice. Working with the museum was particularly generative in the development of presentations and publications (Groundwater-Smith 2006a; Groundwater-Smith and Kelly 2003; Kelly and Groundwater-Smith 2009).

Indeed, it might be argued that the policy of making public the work of the Coalition has been a particularly distinctive feature, with presentations ranging from discussions of the employment of student voice in school-based research (Groundwater-Smith 2006b; Needham 2006; Needham and Groundwater-Smith 2003) to adopting mixed methods in research design (Groundwater-Smith et al. 2006). Publications have also focused upon documenting particular projects and initiatives within member schools (Elliott and Mockler 2008; Mockler 2001; Mockler and Groundwater-Smith 2010), on the broader professional learning implications of practitioner inquiry (Groundwater-Smith and Hunter 2000; Groundwater-Smith and Mockler 2002a, 2003a; Mockler 2005), on the ethical dimensions of quality in practitioner inquiry (Groundwater-Smith and Mockler 2006, 2007) and on the formation and development of the Coalition itself (Groundwater-Smith and Mockler 2002b, 2009).

So what kind of knowledge is being built here?

The strength of the web: challenges and tests

At this point in the evolution of the Coalition, it is possible to identify a range of strengths and challenges that impact upon the web: interestingly, but perhaps not surprisingly, the strengths and challenges of the Coalition can be conceived as 'flip sides' of each other, where each strength presents with a corresponding vulnerability or challenge, and for this reason we shall deal with the strengths and challenges together here.

The Coalition is an enormously diverse network, as noted earlier, where schools with radically different profiles and student populations come together, transcending some of the common barriers and obstacles to cooperation that can be observed within Australia and elsewhere. In addition, the contribution made by the Friends of the Coalition – both academic partners from a range of universities and the Australian Museum and Taronga Zoo Education – brings greater diversity to the web. While this diversity enables unusual conversations and collaborations to take place, it also demands of all participants an openness to one another's circumstances and life worlds and a willingness to 'inhabit each other's castles', to borrow Bridget Somekh's (1994) metaphor. This is particularly so when one considers the socio-economic diversity and its implications of this in terms of school resourcing and funding. The emphasis placed on the common aim of engaging deeply and critically with inquiry processes to the mutual benefit of students and teachers within schools assists Coalition members to transcend these barriers to a large degree, although this challenge is ever present.

Though the unfunded nature of the Coalition might be regarded by some as a challenge, in our view it is in fact a great strength. Within the audit culture that is currently so strong within Western societies, funding is often linked strongly to measures of compliance. As an unfunded web or network, the Coalition is accountable to no external body and, while members feel a strong sense of accountability to one another and their own school communities, this commitment comes with no external compliance agenda. As such, the Coalition operates based on goodwill. The willingness of members to contribute their time, share their ideas and experiences, and join together in collaborative projects with the intent of maintaining and focusing their capacity to critically inquire into practice, is a very evident strength.

The links between schools and universities fostered in the Coalition provide a foundation of academic support within which members operate. Schools can and do invite academic partners to support them from time to time in the gathering and analysis of evidence, and academic partners within the Coalition operate as resource people for members, supporting them in their professional learning and inquiry. This is not, however, a one-way street. Elsewhere (Groundwater-Smith and Mockler 2011), we have written of the potential of such endeavours to work as professional learning opportunities for all members, with university-and school-based colleagues operating within a reciprocal learning relationship.

The issue of sustainability is a critical and challenging one for the Coalition. Kemmis (2009: 35) has argued that practices will not be sustainable if they do not meet criteria necessary for their continuation in one or more of five dimensions:

- discursive sustainability (the comprehensibility of the practice);
- social and political sustainability (the inclusiveness of the practice in the interests of social harmony);
- material and environmental sustainability;
- economic sustainability; and
- personal sustainability (the practice does not drain the personal knowledge, capacities, resources and energy of its members).

We would argue that, indeed, the Coalition satisfies all five of these criteria in one way or another.

The Coalition has demonstrated a capacity to be self-sustaining for a decade now – an undeniable strength of the web – but we are also aware that sustainability cannot be taken for granted. Although in some member schools it is evident that a great deal of capacity building has taken place and that what Cochran-Smith and Lytle (2009) have termed 'inquiry as stance' has become embedded within the culture of the school, in most schools involvement in this work hinges upon the commitment of a small number of teachers. In the past, when key actors have departed from schools, a slow decline in involvement has occurred that has often seen schools slipping away. While in a number of cases this has given rise to involvement with new schools as those key actors have taken up roles in schools that they then brought into the Coalition, over the last few years we have worked to encourage schools to broaden their base of active participants.

The final challenge for the Coalition is that of becoming and remaining critical. Although sharing ideas and experiences is important, elsewhere we have written about the 'celebratory tendencies' inherent in some practitioner research contexts (Groundwater-Smith and Mockler 2005). For us, it is important that a willingness to celebrate the successes of practitioner inquiry is matched with a willingness to face some of the 'unwelcome truths' (Mockler and Groundwater-Smith 2009) that may come to light and to maintain a critical stance where development and learning is valued above celebration. The quality of relationships developed and sustained between schools over an extended period of time has helped to underwrite this criticality and, as a network, we are committed to remaining vigilant on this issue, asking the kinds of questions of one another that require honest and critical responses.

Lessons from the coalition: developing and sustaining communities of practice

As the Coalition of Knowledge-Building Schools approaches the end of its first decade, it is timely to reflect on the principles of operation that have enabled it to succeed and expand. In Groundwater-Smith and Mockler (2007), we developed a rationale for understanding 'quality' in practitioner inquiry through using the lens of ethics. We posed a series of ethical guidelines:

- That it should observe ethical protocols and processes
- That it should be transparent in its processes
- That it should be collaborative in its nature
- That it should be transformative in its intent and action
- That it should be able to justify itself to its community of practice. (Groundwater-Smith and Mockler 2007: 205–06)

A strong concern for ethical processes and practices and a commitment to transformation is at the heart of the Coalition's work. As individuals and organisations, we share a common commitment to listening to and privileging the voices of students, to critically examining our own practice in order to develop it, and to creating pathways for equity and justice through education. These common commitments are what enable us to transcend our differences and the challenges we face as a community of practice, in the interests of knowledge creation both within and beyond the community itself.

We first wrote about the Coalition as an emerging community of practice many years ago now (Groundwater-Smith and Mockler 2002a), based on Wenger (1998: 73). Three key dimensions of practice provide the basis for the development of an authentic community of practice. They are (1) joint enterprise, (2) mutual engagement and (3) shared repertoire. We have quite deliberately worked to build and share each of these. Joint enterprise is developed through the collaborative work undertaken within schools and supported by academic partners and across schools with the Australian Museum and Taronga Zoo Education. Over time, we have built a negotiated understanding of purpose and process that is articulated in different ways in different contexts but is nevertheless common. Mutual engagement is built primarily through our once-a-term gatherings and annual conference, where we share our work broadly and open it up to one another's critique and questioning. Shared repertoire is partly about shared histories and discourses; this has built slowly over time as our experiences as a network have been shared and, just as importantly, documented.

Finally, membership of the Coalition is predicated not upon a mere interest in practitioner inquiry or knowledge creation but rather an *active and sustained commitment* to the work. As personnel and priorities change within schools, this commitment can either strengthen or weaken over time. One of the original three members of the Coalition left the network four years after its formation when the key staff member retired from the school. When a school's priorities shift such that this work becomes less important than other priorities, sometimes so does the commitment to the Coalition. Additionally, Coalition meetings are not a place where one can hide: members are accountable to one another, and part of that accountability is about being transparent about what is happening in schools and what is not. Members make a commitment to engage in inquiry and, while it is not uncommon for the intensity of this work to 'ebb and flow' throughout the course of the school year in any one school, membership requires a sustained and demonstrated commitment without which schools tend to self-select out of the network.

Conclusion

In her moving contribution to the tribute to the life and work of Orlando Fals Borda, the late Shirley Grundy argued for universities to reclaim their right to engage in partnerships with 'grass roots communities'. Grundy (2007: 81) concluded:

> In Australian Universities in the early 21st century the 'audit culture' is killing us softly and hastening the death of participation in social and intellectual life. Yet, as I suggest, participatory action research and the action of those of us who pursue it can help reform the audit culture and curb the current demise of higher education in Australia.

In some senses, the impact of cultures of audit and measurement have had just as deleterious an impact upon schools. Cultures of compliance demand that emphasis be placed on that which is easily measured, often to the detriment of that which is important. The Coalition of Knowledge-Building Schools provides a small oasis in this desert, where schools and teachers who share a commitment to understanding and developing their practice and to the transformative capacities of schooling come together to share that which is, in our view, critically important but not so easily measured.

Notes

1. Renamed the Practitioner Research Special Interest Group (PRSIG) in 2006 in accordance with university policies regarding the naming and functioning of centres.
2. This conference built upon one held at the Institute of Education, Cambridge, UK, at which both Sachs and Groundwater-Smith presented keynote addresses.
3. This term is one that the Coalition has embraced in its broadest sense, seeking to problematize its current usage and redefine it to mean evidence that is gathered in a forensic rather than adversarial sense. For further discussion, see Groundwater-Smith and Mockler 2002b.
4. It also has an additional nominal member from remote New South Wales whose students take part in consultations with the Australian Museum.
5. In the interests of brevity, these have been paraphrased.
6. The Australian National Schools Network at this time was in abeyance, having had its funding reduced considerably owing to a change of federal government policy.
7. While we have made anonymous the schools and participating teachers, it is not possible to do the same for these two institutions, in that they are each 'one of a kind'.

References

Cochran-Smith, M. and Lytle, S. (2009) *Inquiry as Stance: Practitioner Research for the Next Generation*. New York: Teachers College Press.

Cuttance, P., Department of Education, Training and Youth Affairs, and The Innovation and Best Practice Consortium (2001) *School Innovation: Pathway to the Knowledge Society*. Canberra: Department of Education, Training and Youth Affairs.
Elliott, G. and Mockler, N. (2008) 'Practitioner inquiry for whole school change: possibilities and pitfalls.' Paper presented at the Annual Collaborative Action Research Network Conference, Liverpool, October.
Groundwater-Smith, S. (1998) 'Putting teacher professional judgement to work.' *Educational Action Research*, 6(1), 21–37.
Groundwater-Smith, S. (2006a) 'Millennials in museums: consulting Australian adolescents when designing for learning.' Invitational address presented to the Museum Directors' Forum, National Museum of History, Taipei, October.
Groundwater-Smith, S. (2006b) 'Professional knowledge formation in the Australian educational market place: changing the perspective.' *Scottish Educational Review*, 37(Special Edition), 124–131.
Groundwater-Smith, S. and Hunter, J. (2000) 'Whole school inquiry: evidence-based practice.' *Journal of In-Service Education*, 26(3), 583–600.
Groundwater-Smith, S. and Kelly, L. (2003) 'As we see it: improving learning at the museum.' Paper presented to the Annual Conference of the British Educational Research Association, Edinburgh, Scotland, September.
Groundwater-Smith, S. and Mockler, N. (2002a) 'Building knowledge, building professionalism.' Paper presented to the Annual Conference of the Australian Association for Research in Education, University of Queensland, Australia, December.
Groundwater-Smith, S. and Mockler, N. (2002b) 'The knowledge building school: from the outside in, from the inside out.' *Change*, 5(2), 15–24.
Groundwater-Smith, S. and Mockler, N. (2003a) 'Holding a mirror to professional learning.' Paper presented to the Annual Conference of the Australian Association for Research in Education and the New Zealand Association for Research in Education, Auckland, New Zealand, November/December.
Groundwater-Smith, S. and Mockler, N. (2003b) *Learning to Listen: Listening to Learn*, Sydney: University of Sydney Faculty of Education and Social Work/MLC School.
Groundwater-Smith, S. and Mockler, N. (2005) 'Practitioner research in education, beyond celebration.' Refereed paper presented to the Australian Association for Research in Education Focus Conference, Cairns, Australia, July.
Groundwater-Smith, S. and Mockler, N. (2006) 'Research that counts: practitioner research and the academy.' In J. Blackmore, J. Wright and V. Harwood (eds) *Counterpoints on the Quality and Impact of Educational Research. Review of Australian Research in Education*, (6), 105–118.
Groundwater-Smith, S. and Mockler, N. (2007) 'Ethics in practitioner research: an issue of quality.' *Research Papers in Education*, 22(2), 199–211.
Groundwater-Smith., S. and Mockler, N. (2009) *Teacher Professional Learning in an Age of Compliance: Mind the Gap*. Rotterdam: Springer.
Groundwater-Smith, S. and Mockler, N. (2011) 'Sustaining professional learning networks – the Australasian challenge.' In C. Day and A. Lieberman (eds) *International Handbook of Teacher and School Development*. London: Sage.
Groundwater-Smith, S., Martin, A., Hayes, M., Herrett, M., Layhe, K., Layman, A. and Saurine, J. (2006) 'What counts as evidence: mixed methods in a single case.' Paper presented at the AARE Annual Conference, Adelaide, Australia, November.
Grundy, S. (2007) 'Killing me softly: the audit culture and death of participation.' In *Action Research and Education in Contexts of Poverty: A Tribute to the Life and Work of Professor Orlando Fals Borda* (pp. 71–82). Bogota: Universidad de la Salle.
Hargreaves, D. (1999) 'The knowledge creating school.' *British Journal of Education Studies*, 47(2), 122–144.
Hartley, D. and Whitehead, M. (2006) *Teacher Education: Globalisation, Standards and Teacher Education*. London: Taylor and Francis.

Kelly, L. and Groundwater-Smith, S. (2009) 'Revisioning the physical and on-line museum: a partnership with the Coalition Of Knowledge-Building Schools.' *Journal of Museum Education*, 34(1), 55–68.

Kemmis, S. (2009) 'Understanding professional practice: a synoptic framework.' In B. Green (ed.) *Understanding and Researching Professional Practice*. Rotterdam, Netherlands: Sense Publishers.

Mockler, N. (2001) 'Professional learning portfolios: a tool for the reflective practitioner.' Paper presented at the Australian Association for Research in Education Annual Conference, Fremantle, Australia, December.

Mockler, N. (2005) 'Trans/forming teachers: new professional learning and transformative teacher professionalism.' *Journal of In-Service Education*, 31(4), 733–746.

Mockler, N. and Groundwater-Smith, S. (2009) 'Seeking for the unwelcome truths: action learning beyond celebration.' Paper presented at the Pedagogy in Practice Conference, Newcastle, Australia, July.

Mockler, N. and Groundwater-Smith, S. (2010) 'Professional learning side by side.' In A. Campbell and S. Groundwater-Smith (eds) *Connecting Inquiry and Professional Learning in Education: Joining the Dots*. London: Routledge.

Needham, K. (2006) 'Zen and the art of school improvement: a case study of using students as researchers into their own learning.' Paper presented to the joint Collaborative Action Research Network/Practitioner Research Conference, Utrecht, Netherlands, November.

Needham, K. and Groundwater-Smith, S. (2003) 'Using student voice to inform school improvement.' Paper presented to the International Congress for School Effectiveness and Improvement, Sydney, Australia, January.

Sachs, J. (2007) 'Learning to improve or improving learning: the dilemma of teacher continuing professional development.' Keynote address presented to the International Congress for School Effectiveness and Improvement Conference, Slovenia, January.

Somekh, B. (1994) 'Inhabiting each other's castles: towards knowledge and mutual growth through collaboration.' *Educational Action Research*, 2(2), 357–381.

Wenger, E. (1998) *Communities of Practice: Learning, Meaning and Identity*. Cambridge: Cambridge University Press.

Zschokke, S. (2009) 'Web building in Araneus diadematus.' Online. Available at http://www.conservation.unibas.ch/team/zschokke/webconstruction.php?lang=en (accessed 8 September 2009).

Suggested further readings

Coalition of Knowledge-Building Schools. Online. Available at http://www.ckbschools.org (accessed 14 October 2010).

Groundwater-Smith, S. (2005) 'Learning by listening: student voice in research.' Refereed paper presented at the International Practitioner Research/CARN Conference, Utrecht, Netherlands, November.

Groundwater-Smith, S. and Mockler, N. (2002) 'Building knowledge, building professionalism.' Paper presented to the Annual Conference of the Australian Association for Research in Education, University of Queensland, Australia, December.

Groundwater-Smith, S. and Mockler, N. (2009) *Teacher Professional Learning in an Age of Compliance: Mind the Gap*. Dordrecht: Springer.

Groundwater-Smith, S. and Mockler, N. (2011) 'Sustaining professional learning networks – the Australasian challenge.' In C. Day and A. Lieberman (eds) *International Handbook of Teacher and School Development*. London: Sage.

Needham, K. (2011) 'Professional learning in an across school network: an epidemic of passion?' In N. Mockler and J. Sachs (eds) *Rethinking Educational Practice Through Reflexive Inquiry: Essays in Honour of Susan Groundwater-Smith*. Dordrecht: Springer.

CHAPTER 16

MENTORING TEACHER INQUIRY
Lessons in lesson study
Susan Groundwater-Smith

Introduction

Coaching and mentoring are well known in the business literature as strategies for induction and the development of the capacities of those engaged in learning organisations. More recently, those working in school education have turned to these powerful processes as a means of supporting practitioners at various pivotal points in their careers, whether as newly appointed teacher or as experienced school leaders (CUREE, 2005). The focus has been most often upon individual growth and development, however, my intention is to discuss a somewhat different orientation, that of working with a team of practitioners within a context of teacher inquiry. The process could be seen as a blend between coaching for individual development and mentoring for the support of a learning community. Effectively, the process that will be discussed is one where support is given to individual teachers who may be uncertain about the procedure that they might employ when they inquire into teaching and learning in their classrooms, while at the same time assisting a team of teachers in uncovering ways in which they plan for learning; developing, evaluating and enhancing those plans and their delivery.

Thus in this chapter I shall discuss my facilitation of a participatory action research project focused upon lesson study. I shall argue that the role of facilitator is a form of professional research coaching and mentoring with myself, as the academic partner, functioning as a 'knowledgeable other' as outlined by Watanabe and Wang-Iverson (2002). Clearly the role can be satisfied by a number of people such as content coaches, peer coaches and staff development officers and the like. However, in this case, because the process had an emphasis upon inquiry such as designing interventions, collecting and interpreting a range of data and reflecting upon practice, it was conceived that the 'knowledgeable other' for the project should be an academic partner who has had wide experience of teacher research undertaken in practice-based settings such as schools.

Over the years a number of models designed to enhance teacher professional learning have been proposed. Kennedy (2005: 236–7) identified nine such models: training, award bearing, deficit, cascade, standards-based, coaching/mentoring, community of practice, action research and transformative. I shall argue that the project was, in effect, a hybrid of the latter four models in that it worked with a group of teachers who identified themselves as a community of practice, it was supported by an academic partner, it was developed as participatory action research that involves teachers in worthwhile educational change 'through discursively opening up their practice to rational scrutiny by those who have a stake in its outcomes' (Elliott, 2007: 46). Its purpose was to transform practice, moving it from a teacher-centred model to one that gave young people greater agency and autonomy.

Before discussing the project in question and an argument that it was an embodiment of coaching and mentored participatory and transformative action research, it is important to first make a more explicit connection between being the 'knowledgeable other' and the function of these roles as facilitation. As has been indicated, much of the literature concerned with coaching and mentoring, in relation to workplace learning, constructs the activity as individualistic and fulfilling a nurturing function drawing upon the coach/mentor's experience and wisdom as one who can lead by example and provide confidential and secure advice. I would prefer to articulate a more interventionist and critical role. I believed that as a project coach and mentor I was interested in a form of professional community building that liberated participating teachers from the private nature of their classroom practice and developed a generative means for engaging in professional dialogue. Following Warren Little (2002: 918) I desired that the conditions be created that would permit the development of a professional community that would enable learning to result from 'the ongoing encounters that teachers have one with another' in the context of participatory action research and in association with myself as research mentor.

Supporting professional learning through participatory action research is a complex business. As Hoban, Ewing, Herrington, Smith, Kervin and Anderson (2010) have indicated, there are myriad, intersecting factors that are important for sustaining such learning, namely: the school's workplace conditions, the inquiry processes themselves, and the content and focus of the inquiry. Thus, the coaching and mentoring role required a sound understanding of school cultures, across a number of settings, experience in working with practitioners under conditions that may be challenging and unsettling and familiarity with the processes of lesson study and the ways in which these might be captured, reflected and acted upon.

Participatory Action Research and lesson study

Many who write of participatory action research emphasise its transformative and emancipatory nature; the work is seen to require conditions that will allow for genuine dialogue and for social outcomes that are just and equitable. In essence, it is informed by social relations whose intent is to fulfil a desire for

> doing the moral good – The emphasis is on the enhancement of ethically authentic action and the development of situated knowledge rather than on the accumulation of general (generalisable) theoretical knowledge. (Ponte and Smit, 2007: 3)

Those concerned with undertaking action research are familiar with the spiral of observation, reflection, theory building, planning and executing a study, followed by re-observation, further reflection, and so on. Participatory action research (PAR) has in addition a number of other key features identified by Kemmis and McTaggart (2005) as being: a social practice, participatory, practical and collaborative, emancipatory, critical, reflexive and transformative.

The conjunction between PAR and lesson study is seen by Perez, Encarnacion and Servan (2010: 77) as a 'specific form of cooperative or participatory action research specially designed for in-service teacher education' on the grounds that it achieves both change and understanding. In order to make this clear it is important to see lesson study as learning study. Shifting the focus from teachers' actions and planning, important as that focus is, to student learning is challenging and difficult. Wang-Iverson (2002) sees lesson study as a means of making teacher professional collaboration concrete by focusing on specific goals that examine not just teachers at work, but students at work, through the learning that is going on.

In this way teaching can itself become professional learning when the activity is collegial and where the learning arises, principally from the students' engagement and behaviours (Lewis, Perry, Hurd and O'Connell, 2006). In their advocacy for the study of teaching and learning through the study of lessons Fernandez and Yoshida (2004) place their greatest emphasis upon the culture of collegiality that bring teachers together to deeply consider their practice in the context of the classroom and the diverse needs of their students. Similarly, Chokshi and Fernandez (2004) argue for sustained lesson study work as a vehicle for helping teachers build a shared body of professional knowledge.

In essence, lesson study can be characterised as ways of seeing; that is observing how learners respond to a teaching episode that has been prepared collaboratively by a group of teachers with the intention of developing, refining and improving the lesson in the light of such feedback. Just as action research requires participant to engage in cycles of inquiry so too does lesson study as a 'system for building and sharing practitioner knowledge' (Lewis, Perry and Friedkin, 2009: 142). It is a particularly powerful process when the concepts to be taught are problematic for the students and where there is much scope for misunderstanding. Thus the process is based upon the concept of teachers as researchers –where the classroom practitioners are engaged in systematic inquiry regarding what it is that takes place during the teaching episode, which can be characterised as a natural experiment.

Rock and Wilson (2005) see these 'research lessons' as being:

- focused on specific teacher-generated problems, goals or vision of pedagogical practice;
- carefully planned, in collaboration;
- observed by other teachers;
- recorded for analysis and reflection; and
- discussed by lesson study group members. (2005: 78)

They argue that lesson study is based upon principles of learning through social interaction rather than as a result of individual experience; that knowledge is acquired as an adaptive experience; and that knowledge is the result of active mental processing by the individual in a social environment. Much of this takes place in the classroom as the lesson itself is progressing. In effect, the classroom can be conceived of as a learning laboratory for the students as they come into contact with new ideas, principles and practices.

It is clear from the literature that there is no *one* formula for lesson study. As Lewis, Perry and Murata (2004: 3–4) have noted: 'Japanese lesson study is an extremely variable practice that has evolved over a century in tens of thousands of Japanese sites.' However, there are some overarching procedures among them the close observation of students as they engage in learning. Thus lesson study becomes a potent vehicle for teachers to systematically explore learning, on the basis of evidence, with an intention of improving it. It is a process that is described by Lewis (2002) as 'developing the eyes to see children'.

For many secondary school teachers the close observation of learning has not been a matter that has been uppermost in their minds. They are bedevilled by the detail of a crowded curriculum, high stakes assessment, and limited opportunities to know their students well (Ballet, Kelchtermans and Loughran, 2006). As well, they may not be familiar with the participatory action research cycle and may have a somewhat limited view of what constitutes 'research', equating it with a more positivistic set of procedures. In the case upon which this chapter is based, having a facilitator who could both coach and mentor them through the complexities of lesson study was seen as essential to the development of the project.

My role, then, was fourfold and clearly involved both coaching and mentoring by:

- preparing a discussion paper arguing for lesson study as an investigation of pedagogy;
- developing strategies for the collection and interpretation of data;
- acting as a critical friend in lesson study discussions; and
- drafting a final report that would meet the requirements of the funding body; and assisting practitioners in writing papers for professional associations.

The preparation of the discussion paper provided a resource that would create the basis for a dialogue between myself and the participating teachers and clarify the nature of lesson study. Inquiry methods similarly fulfilled a coaching function, by drawing attention to the many creative ways in which information can be gathered, discussed and interpreted, as well as some of the pitfalls and dangers associated with issues of validity and generalisability. Different teachers in the project had different needs and experience and it was often the case that individuals required personalised assistance in understanding processes and procedures.

The latter two practices, being a critical friend and supporting publication and dissemination, moved towards mentoring as the practitioners were encouraged to have greater collective agency, to learn from their shared experience and find ways of making these available to others.

The project – Deeds Not Words

The project, *Deeds Not Words*, involved four schools based in Sydney, New South Wales, and ten experienced teachers who taught two rounds of lessons in semester 1, 2007. The schools involved were diverse in socio-economic terms, gender, secular or religious nature and location.

School A was a comprehensive co-educational, government secondary school with a selective component to cater for students with exceptional ability in sport and was located in Sydney's west.

School B was a faith-based co-educational independent school K-12 to be found in the eastern suburbs.

School C was a faith-based school providing an education for girls, K-12 in the inner west.

School D was a comprehensive girls government secondary school located in Sydney's western suburbs.

The project focused upon planning for learning; observing learning and interpreting learning.

Planning

In their planning the participating teachers operated in teams of three to four that represented the mix of schools and their familiarity with the subject matter in the areas of commerce, economics and business studies being taught across the senior years. In each case the team met and discussed the framework of the lesson to be taught. Planning was based upon the principles of constructivism. This meant that the emphasis in planning was upon designing for learning; that is, focusing upon what the students would do and why. There was a number of elements that had to be considered when designing for learning. These were: problem setting, context, resources, connecting, questioning and explaining, demonstrating learning, and reflection.

Each of these elements needed to be considered in developing an overall unit plan and subsequent lesson plans. They were briefly discussed as a series of questions that had been posed by myself as the action research mentor.

The problem setting

What was the problem that the teachers wished for their students to understand? How did it fit into the overall curriculum in the key learning area?

The context

What was the nature of the context in which the students are learning? The school, the class and the dynamics of the group?

Resources

Along with the teacher, the most significant resource in the classroom was seen to be located in the students themselves: what had been their experiences? How much did they already know? How could they best share their knowledge? How would they evaluate each other's knowledge and understanding? Teachers would also be concerned with the kinds of material resources that could be used to support learning, such as models, graphics, narratives and the like. What media would they employ? What would be the impact of such tools as electronic whiteboards, computers and video?

Connecting

How could the teachers take account of ways to elicit students' prior knowledge and experience and how would they build a bridge between what they already know and what they need to do to achieve the learning goal?

Questioning and explaining

What kind of guiding questions would they formulate to stimulate student thinking and to maintain active learning? How would they accommodate student questions and provide the kinds of explanations that would support learning development?

Demonstration of learning

What processes would they employ that would enable students to demonstrate what they had learned? To what extent did they wish the learning to be individual or group based? How would these demonstrations be authentically assessed?

Reflection

How would they provide opportunities for students to reflect on their learning? What they learned from their teachers? What they learned from their peers? What they learned about themselves and their capabilities?

Observing learning in progress

In most cases in the *Deeds Not Words* study there were two observers in the classroom. It was seen as important that they have a specific brief that would be negotiated between them and the teacher of the day. A number of steps needed to be taken:

- Who would be observed?
- What would be the focus?
- How would the data be collected?
- How would the data be interpreted?

Additionally, it was argued that the learners themselves should be reflecting upon their learning experience. As research mentor I believed it important to outline ways in which these steps could be undertaken.

Who would be observed?

Being able to closely observe all learners in a dynamic and busy classroom was seen as a difficult task. One way to overcome this would be to videotape lessons so that the episode may be returned to at a later point and collectively analysed. Another way to deal with the challenge would be to deliberately select a small number of learners on the basis of contrasts. One might take three learners: one of whom is notably quiet, one who tends to be noisy and highly visible, and one somewhere in the middle. Or one might contrast the learners in terms of the teacher's perception of their motivation and engagement with the subject, or their level of achievement in the subject.

Such observation was seen to require a delicacy and willingness to note even the most obscure of detail – fidgeting, gossiping, turning in the seat, body language and the like; in addition to obvious signs of engagement with the lesson. The greater the detail the more that the account could be used in a subsequent interview with the student, offering him or her a stimulus for recalling the lesson and its impact.

What would be the focus?

Of course the focus of the observations was seen to relate to who is being observed and the purpose of the given lesson. It may be that the focus would be upon turning points in the lesson – when did it become more or less engaging? When did teacher explanations appear to overcome a particular 'roadblock' to learning? When did the insight of a student assist in the development of the lesson? Also, the observer needed to be responsive to unintended moments in the lesson and their consequence – what happened when a student introduces a digression or has clearly lost their way and what was the impact upon other students?

How will the data be collected?

Again, the processes for collecting data would be determined by the overall purpose of the observations. It may be that the observer would maintain a running record, using a time frame that accounted for the introduction to the session, its presentation and its closure. The observer might have some pre-determined categories such as:

- affiliation and rapport with teacher (smiling, nodding, how was attention secured, etc.);
- attitude (engagement – procedural or substantive, indifference, disengagement and distraction);
- approach to problem solving (seeking assistance, independence);
- connection to prior learning;
- curiosity and creativity (dealing with the unexpected); and
- monitoring both formal and informal aspects of the classroom; and so on.

The observer(s) could consider taking digital photographs at agreed intervals and use these to create a timeline of the lesson's development that could be discussed with the target students and later with the class teacher.

Student interviews

It was suggested that a powerful way to supplement observations would be to interview target students, perhaps starting with a general question regarding how they saw themselves as learners in this particular key learning area, what they found to be challenging and puzzling and how they coped with the pacing and sequencing of learning before turning to the specific lesson under observation.

Student reflections

A simple process for gathering student reflections would be for all students in the particular class to complete a minute paper where they could note:

- What went well for you in this lesson?
- What were the main points that you learned during this lesson?
- What puzzled or confused you?
- What would you like to change about this lesson if it could be taught again?

If the participating teacher chose to use the minute paper it was seen as important that it be kept brief and that students had the opportunity to respond anonymously.

Interpreting the data

Teachers saw that as they went about interpreting the data their main purpose would be to identify the strengths and weaknesses of the lesson and the ways in which it could be improved for the next cycle of teaching; always remembering, of course, that they were attempting to look at the lesson through the lens of the learners' experiences. I encouraged them to consider ways of clustering questions together. For example:

- How effective was the initial orientation? How clear were expectations?
- To what extent was attention paid to what the learners brought to the lesson?
- How were learners motivated? How was praise handled?
- How well was the lesson paced? How were digressions handled? Was there information overload?
- How were roadblocks to learning cleared?
- Who seemed to benefit most? Who seemed to benefit least?
- Was learning tailored to individual student needs?
- How helpful were the resources? How accessible were the resources?
- What features of the physical environment supported or impeded learning?
- Were there any specific contextual constraints – are they likely to arise during the next cycle?

Learning from the project

So what could be learned from this project from the perspective of participating teachers and myself as the coach and mentor? Here I wished to address the following questions: Can an approach such as lesson study support collegial professional learning? What support is required to observe and analyse student learning *in situ*? Can a lesson study approach be seen as an opportunity for action learning?

Can an approach such as lesson study support collegial professional learning?

In spite of the logistical difficulties there was a strongly held view among the participants in this project that the processes opened up the classroom doors. The planning, observing and professional conversation following given lessons formed a powerful process of experiential learning. Teachers found themselves in discussions that were related, among other things, to matters of:

- precision and accuracy (how well have we defined the questions that we want the students to pursue?)
- connectedness (how do we use examples from our own and our students' lives such that the content is relevant for them?)
- metacognition (how will we familiarise our students with complex terms and their application?)
- managing impulsivity (how do we acknowledge a student's contribution, but create conditions whereby they are more reflective in providing answers?)

All of these matters and more besides were the basis of discussion and debate.

What support is required to observe and analyse student learning in situ?

This project drew attention to the difficulties experienced in closely observing student learning. The pressures that senior teachers face in meeting school requirements for results in a competitive educational market place meant that teachers have to closely attend to what is a demanding and crowded syllabus in economics, business and commerce classrooms. Nonetheless, the structure of the project allowed for several teachers to be present in the classroom at any one time. They brought to the practice different perspectives and teaching histories. They were able to make more problematic what was familiar to the regular class teacher who was not able to be too comfortable in his or her own 'home'.

Can a lesson study approach be seen as an opportunity for action learning?

In the context of the lesson study project, action learning is the approach that links the world of professional learning with the world of classroom action through reflective and dynamic processes across collegial groups.

In their investigation of the sustainability of professional learning through school based inquiry, Hoban et al. (2010) cited five conditions that can support action learning, these being:

- drawing on local resources and capacities;
- recognising the knowledge and wisdom of teachers;
- demonstrating that teachers are creative and knowledgeable about their environment;
- ensuring that all members of the inquiry team are part of the decision making process; and
- using academic team members (in this case the research mentor) who act as catalysts and who assist the school inquiry team(s) in asking key questions.

It is clear from the data that had been collected that each of these elements were present in the lesson study project. Additionally, the adoption of lesson study itself, as a vehicle, provided a framework for the investigation that gave it force and direction.

In spite of a number of challenges and difficulties and the short time that was available for the project it can be argued that it not only contributed significantly to the discussion regarding learning and teaching in the designated curriculum area and the performance of experienced teachers but also to the notions of coaching and mentored action learning in general and lesson study in particular.

Conclusion

Participatory action research is well recognised as a means for developing teacher professional learning. Its claim to professional knowledge building has been widely argued (Groundwater-Smith and Mockler, 2009). Less well theorised or understood is the manner in which an academic partner may function as a facilitator, coaching and mentoring practitioners in the field. Thus in Rosendahl and Ronnerman's (2006) study we find that there are very different expectations of facilitation arising from the cultural mores of the academics and the school-based practitioners; they argued that the former are looking to support careful and considered reflection, the latter for new ideas and techniques. Working within a collaborative framework itself can be seen to produce many dilemmas in relation to power and authority and the expectations and rewards that go with occupying different roles. Goldstein (2000: 523) in her revealing discussion regarding her project to work collaboratively with an early career classroom teacher observed: 'Any collaboration can be difficult. And when university researchers enter classrooms, some problems are bound to arise because of the issues of power and status inherent in these relations.'

However, I believe that such expectations can be transcended where there is a genuine coaching and mentoring orientation based upon trust and reciprocity, and where the moral intention is to improve teaching and learning practices for the consequential stakeholders, that is to say the young people in our schools. We are not wrestling for control or for status; instead we seek to work together as colleagues who hold each other in mutual regard. Coaching and mentoring the *Deeds Not Words* project certainly meant that I, as academic partner, was well positioned to facilitate the actual inquiry; but equally, I was a learner watching these dedicated teachers and their students struggle with concepts and ideas in ways that gave them agency and power. The opportunities were there for us all to grow and flourish.

References

Ballet, K., Kelchtermans, G., & Loughran, J. (2006). Beyond intensification towards a scholarship of practice: analyzing changes in teachers' work lives. *Teachers and Teaching: Theory and Practice*, 12(2), 209–229.

Chokshi, S., & Fernandez, C. (2004). Challenges to importing Japanese Lesson Study: concerns, misconceptions and nuances. *Phi Delta Kappan*, 85(7), 520–525.

CUREE (2005). *Mentoring and Coaching CPD Capacity Building*. London: DfES.

Elliott, J. (2007). Reinstating social hope through participatory action research. In M. Todhunter (Ed.) *Action Research and Education in Contexts of Poverty: A Tribute to the Life and Work of Professor Orlando Fals Borda* (pp. 33–48). Bogota DC: Universidad de La Salle.

Fernandez, C., & Yoshida, M. (2004). *Lesson Study: A Japanese Approach to Improving Mathematics Teaching and Learning*. Mahwah NJ: Lawrence Erlbaum.

Goldstein, L. (2000). Ethical dilemmas in designing collaborative research: Lessons learned the hard way. *Qualitative Studies in Education, 13*(5), 517–530.

Groundwater-Smith, S., & Mockler, N. (2009). *Teacher Professional Learning in an Age of Compliance: Mind the gap*. Rotterdam: Springer.

Hoban, G., Ewing, R., Herrington, T., Smith, D., Kervin, L., & Anderson, J. (2010). Evaluative inquiry into sustainability of professional learning through school based action learning. In A. Campbell & S. Groundwater-Smith (Eds.) *Action Research in Education: Volume Three* (pp. 103–120). London: Sage Publications.

Kemmis, S., & McTaggart, R. (2005). Participatory action research: Communicative action and the public sphere. In N. K. Denzin & Y. S. Lincoln (Eds.) *The Sage Handbook of Qualitative Research* (3rd ed.; pp. 559–603). Thousand Oaks: Sage Publications.

Kennedy, A. (2005). Models of continuing professional development: a framework for analysis. *Journal of In-service Education, 32*(2), 235–250.

Lewis, C. (2002). *Lesson Study: A Handbook of Teacher-led Instructional Change*. Philadelphia: Research for Better Schools.

Lewis, C., Perry, R., & Friedken, S. (2009). Lesson study as action research. In S. Noffke & B. Somekh (Eds.) *The Sage Handbook of Educational Research* (pp. 142–154). London: Sage Publications.

Lewis, C., Perry, R., & Murata, A. (2004). What constitutes evidence of teachers' learning from lesson study. Paper presented to the Annual Conference of the American Educational Research Association (AERA), San Diego, April 16th.

Lewis, C., Perry, R., Hurd, J., & O'Connell, M. (2006). Lesson study comes of age in North America. *Phi Delta Kappan, 88* (4) 273–281.

Perez, A., Encarnacion, S., & Servan, M. (2010). Participatory action research and the reconstruction of teachers' practical thinking: lesson studies and core reflection. *Educational Action Research, 18*(1), 73–87.

Ponte, P., & Smit, B. (2007). Introduction: Doing research and being researched. In P. Ponte & B. Smit (Eds.) *The Quality of Practitioner Research* (pp. 1–8). Rotterdam: Sense Publishers.

Rock, T., & Wilson, C. (2005). Improving teaching through Lesson Study. *Teacher Education Quarterly, 32*(1), 77–92.

Rosendahl, B., & Ronnerman, K. (2006). Facilitating school improvement. *Professional Development in Education, 32*(4), 497–509.

Wang-Iverson, P. (2002). Why Lesson Study? Paper presented at the Lesson Study Conference. Chicago: November, 20–22.

Warren Little, J. (2002). Locating learning in teachers' communities of practice. *Teaching and Teacher Education, 18*, 917–946.

Watanabe, T., & Wang-Iverson, P. (2002). The role of knowledgeable others. Paper presented at the Lesson Study Conference.

INDEX

Major discussion of a topic is shown by the use of **bold**. 'n' indicates a reference to a note.

Abbs, P. 31
absenteeism 138
accountability 21, 55, 134, 183, 185; *see also* transparency
action learning 67, 197–8
action research: appropriation and technologising of 66–8; characteristics 111; criteria for quality 109–10; large-scale 139–41; researchers 15; structural 43, 73; *see also* participatory action research (PAR)
Action Research Planner (McTaggart and Kemmis) 44
'activist professional' 13
adolescents 84–5
agency, as a concept 17
'*Agora*' 11, 89, 96
Alderson, Priscilla 129
Alford, J. 58
Altrichter, Herbert 51, 54, 109–10, 111
American public schools 18–19
American reform movements 47, 65–6, 108, 125
Anderson, D. 90, 148
Anderson, Gary L. 100, 101, 103, 110
Anderson, J. 190
anonymity, student 127–8, 172–3
Anzaldua, Gloria 118–9, 130
Apple, Michael 32
Arnot, M. 158
Ashenden, Dean 32
assessment reforms 55–6
Atweh, Bill 128, 173
audit culture 186
Australian Bureau of Statistics 37
Australian Government Quality Teaching Program 115, 123
Australian governments 89
Australian Human Rights Commissioner 165
Australian Museum (AM) 143, 144–6, 180, 182
Australian National Schools Network (NSN) 7–8, 46–8, 57, 179, 182
Australian schools 19, 32, 50, 64, 132
Ax, Jan 8

backgrounds, disadvantaged 4, 133, 136–7, 164, 167
Bakhtin, Mikhail 24
Ball, Stephen 113
Beckett, Lori 16
Becoming Critical (Carr and Kemmis) 9, 43, 62, 65–9, 70, 107
behaviour, student 83, 158, 161, 168
Berliner, David 66
Bhatta, Baikuntha 17
Birkett, Dea 120
Bland, Derek C. 128, 173
Blishen, Edward 118
Bodleian library, Oxford 100
Borko, Hilda 102
Bottery, Michael 103
Bottrell, Dorothy 20
Bourdieu, Pierre 17–18
Bowles, Samuel 32
Boyer Lectures 46
boys' schools 152, 181, 182
Bragg, Sara 129, 157, 174
Brandon, M. 165
Brennan, Gerard 174
Brennan, Marie 15

Bristol, Laurette 21–2
British Library Research and Development projects 5
Bullock Report (DES, 1975) 33
bullying 93, 122–3
Burke, Catherine 118, 149
Bush, George W. 65–6, 108

Calvert, G. 165
Cameron, F. 149
Campbell, Anne 14–15
Campbell, Elizabeth 111
CARE (Centre for Applied Research in Education) 5, 139
Carr, Wilfred 9, 34, 70, 73, 109
Carter, Angela 61
case records 5, 6, 30–8
case studies: curriculum-based 5–8, 35; ethical challenges and dilemmas 157–61; professional judgment 48–53, 55, 57; student voice 76, 82, 85, 168–71; *see also* case records
catalytic validity 103, 110
Catholic secondary education 90
Centre for Applied Research in Education (CARE) 5, 34–5, 77, 139
Centre for Practitioner Research (CPR) 156, 178–9
CES (Coalition of Essential Schools) 9
Cherryholmes, Cleo 53
Chesterton, G. K. 91
Chicanos (Mexican-American people) 118–9
Chokshi, S. 191
Christensen, Pia Haudrup 128
CKBS (Coalition of Knowledge Building Schools) *see* Coalition of Knowledge Building Schools (CKBS)
coaching *see* 'Mentoring teacher inquiry: Lessons in lesson study'
coalition government 89
Coalition of Essential Schools (CES) 9
Coalition of Knowledge Building Schools (CKBS): and the Australian Museum 81–2, 143; and David Hargreaves 11; expansion of 177–8; knowledge building 180–2; lessons from 96, 185–6; purpose and adopted processes 16–17, 20–2, 92–4, 121–2, 144; shared purposes 180; strengths and challenges 183–4; sustainability of 184; and University of Sydney 156
Cochran-Smith, Marilyn 15, 51, 184
collaborative mentoring 22
communities of practice 11, 16, 62, 185–6

communities, remote 71, 135, 147, 149, 165
'Concerning equity: The voice of young people' 18–20, **163–74**
confidentiality, student 127–8, 135, 172–3
Connell, R. W. 32
consent, informed 172
consequential stakeholders 82, **118–30**
constructivism 50, 149, 193
Consulting Pupils about Teaching and Learning (British project) 150
consulting with students 124–5
Continuing Professional Development (CPD) 55, 189
contractualism 58
Cook-Sather, Alison 125, 157
Cooke, Bill 67–8
'Cooperative Change Management through Practitioner Inquiry' 15–16, **132–41**
Cordingley, P. 94
Cornu, B. 150
corporate learning portfolio 12
Correas, M. 150
Correia, V. 150
Cossar, J. 165
Cox, Eva 46
CPD (Continuing Professional Development) 55, 189
CPR (Centre for Practitioner Research) 156, 178–9
Crane, B. 82
critical incident analysis 159
critical social science 69–70, 71, 72, 107, 108–9
critique, as a concept 30
Cruddas, L. 166
cultural borders 118–9, 130
cultural diversity 84, 157, 182
cultural institutions 20–1; *see also* libraries; museums
curriculum: hidden 32; perspectives 6, 30–8; reforms 55–6; texts 31; theories 149
Curriculum Issues Project 34–8

Dadds, M. 93
Danby, S. 127
Darling-Hammond, Linda 18–19
data: case records 5; interpretation 196; sets 128, 173
Deakin University, Victoria 44
decision-making, professional 63–4
Deeds not Words (Australian project) 192–8

Deep and persistent disadvantage in Australia (McLachlan, Gilfillan & Gordon) 19
democratic validity 103, 110, 129
Derrida, Jacques 13
descriptive validity 52
'designerly learning' 17
Dessaix, Robert 78
development, as a form of learning 12
Dewey, John 129, 174
dialogic validity 103, 110, 129
Dierking, Lynn 144
'digital natives' 148
digital technology, use of 120, 147
dilemmas, ethical 17, 109, 157–61
Disadvantaged Schools Program (DSP) 4
Divided we stand: why inequality keeps rising (OECD) 19
Dockett, Sue 20
Doherty, Linda 120
Dowsett, Gary 32
DSP (Disadvantaged Schools Program) 4

E-College 147, 150
Eagleton, Terry 24, 68, 78
Ebbutt, David 81
economic disadvantages 4
education, and life chances 19–20
education authorities 64
education policies 55, 67, 86, 91, 113, 132
Education Sciences Reform Act of 2002 (USA) 65–6, 108
educational market place 89–96
educational practices, changes to 134–5
Edwards-Groves, Christine 21–2
Eikeland, O. 109
Eisner, Elliot 52
Eliot, T. S. 25
Elliott, B. 132
Elliott, John 4–5, 10, 15, 183
Eltis, Ken 55
emancipation 41–4, 62
emancipatory-cognitive interests 42, 106, 111, 114
emotional literacy 159
empirical-analytic sciences 5
empirical-rational approach 135
Encarnacion, Soto 191
English schools 34, 64, 82, 85
Enola Gay 99
The Enquiring Teacher: Supporting and sustaining teacher research (with Nias) 6–7
enquiry-based courses 40–4
equality 18

equity 18–20, 19, 34, 71, 128, **163–74**
equity, and ethics 171–2
ethical practice: challenges and dilemmas 17, 109, 157–61; and equity 171–2; issues 13–14, 118, 120, 126, 129, 172; in practitioner research 109–12; principles 72, 111–12, 154–5, 185; responsibilities 51, 129
ethics committees 14, 17, 111, 154–5
'Ethics in practitioner research: An issue of quality' (with Mockler) **106–16**
evaluative validity 52
evidence based practice 93
Ewing, R. 190
exegesis 1
experiential learning 140

facilitator, as participant 83–4
Falk, John 144
Farrell, A. 127
'Father Brown' (Chesterton) 91
Federal Government Initiatives 93
Fenstermacher, Gary D. 8
Fenwick, T. 140
Fernandez, C. 191
Feuer, Michael J. 107
Fielding, Michael: student voice 20, 129, 157, 167, 171, 174; students and research 125, 160
Firestone, William A. 53
Fitzclarence, L. 84
Flannery, Tim 85
Flavian, Heidi 22
Ford Teaching Project 67
Foucault, Michel 31
Frankel, Boris 132, 133
Frankfurt School of Critical Theorists 7, 34; *see also* Habermas, Jurgen
friendship groups 84
fundamentalism 104
Funder, Anna 114
Furlong, John 13, 106, 110
fuzziness, concept of 90–1

Gadamer, Hans-Georg 70–1
Garrick Public School, Australia 136–8
gender, in education (WORDING) 10, 82–4, 85, 93, 152
generalisable validity 52
geomorphology 30–1
Gibbons, Michael T. 11, 90, 101, 102, 107
Gibson, R. 43
Gintis, Herbert 32
girls' schools 93, 122–3, 182
Giroux, Henry 32–3, 34, 55

Gitlin, A. 91, 102
Goethe, Johann Wolfgang von 23
Goldstein, L. 155
Gonski Review of Funding for Schooling in Australia 19
Goodson, Ivor 51
Google Scholar 100
Gore, J. 91, 102
Gorman, Susanna 14, 154
government policies 58, 67, 86, 91, 113, 132
government schools 89, 108, 123–5
governments, and action research 67, 108
Grade 11 Studies Skills Programme 83
Griffiths, Morwenna 73, 140
Grootenboer, Peter 21–2
Grosvenor, Ian 118
Grundy, Shirley 186
Guardian, The 118, 120

Habermas-Gadamer Debate 70–1
Habermas, Jurgen 5, 34, 41–3, 68, 69–70, 70–1
Habermasian ideas 15, 24, 50
Halliday, Michael 31
Hammersley, Martyn 73
Hargreaves, David 11, 92, 125–6, 138, 180–1
Harradine, J. 48
Harvard library, Massachusetts 100
Hasan, Ruqaiya 31
Hattie, John 21
Hawke–Keating Government 7
Hawke, Robert 7
Hechter, M. 84
Herr, Kathryn 100, 101, 103, 110
Herrington, T 190
Heumann Gurian, Elaine 99
Hexter, Jack 2, 9, 10, 61–2, 77–8
Hickey, C. 84
Hoban, G. 190
Holdsworth, R. 119
Holly, P. 42
home environments 83–4, 137–8, 147, 165
home-school relationship 32, 136, 137–8
Hopkins, David 5
hospitality 13
Howard, Sue 120, 128
human research ethic committees 14, 17, 111, 154–5
human rights 14, 164
Human Rights and Equal Opportunities Commission (HREOC) 135
Humanities Curriculum Project 67
Hunter, J. 183

IBPP (Innovation and Best Practice Project) 179
Ideal Speech Situation (ISS) 43, 70
identity, professional 86–7, 179
Ik people 10, 79
Independent Girls' School (IGS) 122–3, 127, 128
indigenous people 71, 79, 135, 136, 165, 181
indigenous students 133
industrial relations 7
inequality 19, 41, 132
informed consent 172
Ingvarson, Lawrence 37
initial teacher education 2, 22, 62, 64
Innovation and Best Practice Project (IBPP) 179
'Innovative Links Between Schools and Universities for Teacher Professional Development' 80–1, 179
instrumentalism 104
intelligent schools 95, 122, 138
interpretative validity 52
interpreting learning 196
interpretive-hermeneutic sciences 5, 106
Isaka, Satoru 91
isolation, geographical 16
ISS (Ideal Speech Situation) 43, 70

Jenson, J. 140
Johnson, Bruce 120, 128
Johnson, Kaye 119, 129
joint enterprise 185
Jordan, P. 165
Judah, Mary-Lee 109

Kass, Efrat 22
Keating, Paul 7
Keats, John 1
Keddie, N. 31, 32, 84, 128
Kelly, Lynda 16–17, 144, 145, 149, 182
Kemmis, Stephen: *Becoming Critical* 62, 65, 68, 107, 109; and educational research 37, 81; key features of PAR 156; knowledge interests 34; 'moral practice' 9; 'Participatory action research and the public sphere' 161, 191; PASP 11, 71, 115, 134, 140; praxis 8; site-based educational development 21–2; 'Understanding professional practice: a synoptic framework' 184
Kennedy, A. 189–90
Kervin, L. 190
Kessler, Sandra 32
Key Competencies Project 49–51, 57

Kids' College 145, 146
KISS principle 115
knowledge: creation 90; from experience 102–3; and information 5; interests 4–5, 106, 114–15; nature of 40–2, 102–3; practical 5; production 101–3, 107; theoretical 5; *see also* Habermas, Jurgen
knowledge building programs *see* CPR (Centre for Practitioner Research); Practitioner Research Special Interest Group (PRSIG); Priority Actions Schools Program (PASP)
Knowledge Creating School, The (Hargreaves) 180–1
Kosko, Bart 90–1

Labbett, Bev 5, 34–5
Lamb, Stephen 19
Laub, Dori 112
leadership, school 119, 140, 164, 174
learning difficulties 135
learning environments: classroom layout 3; 'lesson study' 23, 191–2; museums as 144, 148–9, 182; problematic 84; respite care facility 159–60
learning, experiential 140
learning networks 121–2
learning outcomes: changes to 49, 71; different 83; and equity 132–4; improving 80, 179; NSN (Australian National Schools Network) 46; teaching practices and 92
'Learning outside the classroom: A partnership with a difference' (with Kelly) 16–17, **143–52**
learning portfolios: corporate 12; school 95–6, 134, 135, 136, 138
Learning to Listen: Listening to Learn (with Mockler) 93, 179
Leeds Metropolitan University 14
Lemerise, Tamara 148
lesson study 22–3, **189–98**
Lewin, Kurt 106, 111
Lewis, Catherine 192
Lewis, Ian 42
Lewis, M. 192
libraries 5, 20, 100
life chances, and education 19–20
Lindauer, M. 149
literacy 6, 12, 100, 137
Little, Warren 92, 190
Liverpool Hope University 14, 103
'Living ethical practice in qualitative research' 17–18, **154–61**
local conditions 21–2

Lopez, Ann E. 22
Loucks-Hocsely, S. 151–2
Lundgren, U. P. 30–1
Lytle, Susan L. 51, 184

MacBeath, John 126
MacGilchrist, Barbara 95, 138
McLelland, Margaret 125
McLennan, D. 132
McLuhan, Marshal 3
McNamee, M. 85–6
McTaggart, Robin 80, 101, 156, 191
McWilliam, Erica 151
Maguire, M. H. 158
management, education 8, 65
Managing research ethics: a head-on collision? (Gorman) 14
Marginson, Simon 89
marketisation 65
Marr, David 78
Martin, D. 47
Matson Social Skills Survey 159–60
Maxwell, Joseph A. 52
media, use of 37, 46, 50, 51, 123, 168
Melbourne Declaration on Educational Goals for Young People (2008) 163–4
Menter, Ian 11
'Mentoring teacher inquiry: Lessons in lesson study' 22–3, **189–98**
MEP (Microelectronics Education Program) 35
meritocracy 100
Mexican-American people (Chicanos) 118–9
Mezirow, Jack 37–8
Microelectronics Education Program (MEP) 35
middle classes 85
Mill, John Stuart 161
Mishler, Elliot G. 103, 110
Mitchell, Coral 102
MLC School, Burwood, Australia 179
Mockler, Nicole 13, 20–2, 93, **106–16**, 155, **177–86**
Mode 1 Knowledge 90
Mode 2 Knowledge 90–1, 101, 102, 107
Mohr, Nancy 56
Molotch, Harvey 18
Moor, James H. 127
Moorok Central School, Australia 135–6, 139
moral responsibilities 9, 10, 51, 115, 190
morality 41, 72, 110, 156
Morrow, V. 126
Moss, Peter 171

Mulford, B. 140
multi-media, use of 118, 120–1, 127, 145, 147, 154
multiculturalism 84, 157, 182
Munns, Geoff 157
Murata, Aki 192
Murray-Darling Basin Commission 181
museums 12–13, 16, 82, 99, **143–52**, 181
'My professional self: Two books, a person and my bedside table' 10–11, **76–87**
Myers, Kate 95

narrative, importance of 149
National Academy of Sciences (USA) 66, 108
National College of School Leadership 19
National Government Programs 67
National Partnerships Program 167, 175n5
National Professional Development Program 80
National Project on the Quality of Teaching & Learning (NPQTL) 47, 48, 59n3
Needham, K. 183
neo-liberal conditions 10, 11, 32
network building 7, 92, 156, 177–80
'new scholarship' 100–1
New South Wales education 15–16, 32, 37, 71–2, 89–90, 94
New South Wales Quality Teaching Paper 115
New South Wales State Government Program 94
Nias, Jennifer 35
Nicoll, Viv 4
Nielson, Greg M. 24
Noffke, Susan 15
non-government schools 89–90, 108
normative-reeducative approach 135
Nowotny, Helga 11, 102
Noyes, Andrew 126
NPQTL (National Project on the Quality of Teaching & Learning) 47, 48, 59n3
NSN (Australian National Schools Network) 7–8, 9, 46–8, 57, 179, 182
numeracy 6, 67

Oancea, Alis 13, 106, 110
observation 71, 194–6
Observer, The 118, 120
OECD (Organisation for Economic Cooperation and Development) 19, 100
Ofsted (Office for Standards in Education) 64
Okamoto, D. 84
O'Neil, D. 58

opportunity costs 21, 73, 128, 169, 173
Organisation for Economic Cooperation and Development (OECD) 19, 100
outcome validity 103
OWCHS (Outer Western Comprehensive High School), Sydney 123–5, 128

'Painting the educational landscape with tea: Rereading Becoming critical' (Educational Action Research) 9–10, **61–73**
participatory action research (PAR) 154–61, 156, 165–7, 190–2
participatory capital 20
Participatory research with children and young people (with Dockett and Bottrell) 20
partnerships with schools 94
PASP (Priority Action Schools Program), 11–12, 15–16, 71–2
Pavic, Milorad 61
PBIS (Positive Behavior Interventions & Supports) 158, 182
pedagogy **63–4**; liberatory 12, 95; and mentoring 192; new approaches 134, 149, 159; relevant 136; social 174; visitor 21
peer culture 84, 127
Perez, Angel 191
Perry, Rebecca 192
personal development, health and physical education (PDHPE) 123
personalised learning 125
PETA (Primary English Teachers Association) 181
Piscitelli, B. 148
Placier, P. 134–5
planning for learning 193–4
poetry 3
Polanyi, Michael 40
Ponte, Petra 8, 9, 12
Popkewitz, Thomas 4, 31, 58
positivism 65–6
practical interests 42
practical knowledge 5
practice: before 2–4; understanding 4–8
practice, and theory 69
practice based knowledge 103
practitioner inquiry 13, 14, 80, 80–2, 109–12
practitioner research: as an emancipatory project 107–9; ethical guidelines for 111–12, 185; ethics in **106–16**; funding for 114; issues for 57–8; Stenhouse definition of 79

Practitioner Research Special Interest Group (PRSIG) 143–4, 179
praxis, definition of 8, 18
Prensky, Marc 148
Primary English Teachers Association (PETA) 3, 181
primary schools 32, 37, 54–5, 129, 181
Pring, Richard 67
Priority Actions Schools Program (PASP) 11–12, 15–16, 71–2, 94–6, 132–40, 138–9
privacy, concept of 127
problem solving 22, 53–5, 139, 148, 156
process validity 52, 103, 110
Productivity Commission 19
professional: learning 86–7, 196–7; practice 100–1, 169; self-knowledge 103
professional identity 86–7, 179
professional judgment: case studies 48–53; change process 53–5; curriculum and assessment reform 55–6; evidence and validation 51–3; impediments to change and reform 56–7; methodology 48; practitioner research 57–8
professional knowledge 40–1, 51–2, 90–1, 100–2, 107, 138; *see also* Coalition of Knowledge Building Schools (CKBS); school learning portfolios
'Professional knowledge formation in the Australian educational market place: Changing the perspective' 11–12, 89–96
professional life history 1
PRSIG (Practitioner Research Special Interest Group) 143–4, 179
Pupil Autonomy in Learning with Micro-Computers 15
'Putting teacher professional judgement to work' (Educational Action Research) 7–8

QTIP (Quality Teaching Indigenous Program) 181
qualitative research, and ethical practice **154–61**
quality: and ethics 109–12; of evidence 112–13; of outcome 114–15; in practitioner research 13, 99–104, **106–16**; of purpose 113–14; of teaching 92
Quality Teaching Indigenous Program (QTIP) 181
Quality Teaching Program (Australia) 67, 108
Quality Teaching Projects 148
Queensland Productive Pedagogies 115

'Questions of quality in practitioner research: Universities in the 21st century, a safe place for unsafe idea' 12–13, 99–104

Rankin, Ian 78–9
reasoning: ethical 8; moral 8
Reed, Jane 95
reflection 10, 12, 23; co-operative 139; cognitive 169; critical 34, 40, 80; definition of 37; and learning portfolios 95; public 86, 107, 137; self- 42, 57; student voice 194, 196
reflexive knowledge 30, 90, 101, 107
reform movements 7–8, 47, 65–6, 104, 125
Reid, Alan 20
remote communities 71, 135, 147, 149, 165
'research lessons' 191
research quality 100–4
residential care education programmes 144
respite care settings 159–60
Retallick, J. 95
Richardson, George H. 109
Richardson, V. 134–5
Robinson, Viviane 53
Rock, Tracy 191
Rowe, Ken 92
Rudduck, Jean 5, 77, 119

Sachs, Judyth 13, 111, 113–14, 156, 179, 182
Sackney, Larry 102
Sarason, Seymour 104
Schön, Donald 100–1
school design competitions 118, 120
school funding 133, 135, 148
school-home relationships 32, 136, 137–8
school leadership 119, 140, 164, 174
school learning portfolios 95–6, 134, 135, 136, 138
school reforms 7–8, 80
Schratz, Michael 49
Scott, Peter B. 11, 102
'second record' 9–10, 61–2, 77–8, 79, 85
secondary education 89, 93
self-knowledge 103
Sen, Amartya 19
Servan, Maria 191
SES (socio-economic status) 94
Shambrook Upper School and Community College (England) 82
Shier, Harry 20, 166
Simons, Helen 126
single sex schools 152
sixth forms 5

Sizer, Ted 9
Slavin, Robert 66
Smith, D. 190
Smith, Tracey J. 8
Smithsonian Air and Space Museum 99
Smyth, J. W. 37
social justice 18, 19, 128
social practices 18, 24
socio-economic status (SES) 94, 135, 136, 157, 167, 168
socio-historical factors 31–2, 41, 42
Somekh, Bridget 15, 52, 183
Sontag, Susan 154
Special Forever environmental communication project 181
stakeholders, consequential 82, **118–30**
Stenhouse, Lawrence: definition of research 79, 139; dialogic validity 110; and enquiry-based courses 41; and Jack Hexter 9, 77; and knowledge 33; teacher research 5
student: anonymity 127–8, 172–3; behaviour 83, 158, 161, 168; confidentiality 127–8, 135, 172–3; focus groups 122–3; leadership 122, 123; research programme 122; welfare 137
student-teacher interaction 124, 169
student voice **145–50**, **163–74**; *Deeds not Words* (Australian project) 195–6; different perspectives 128; greater agency for 157–8; school design competitions 118, 120; senior students 83; sustaining 129, 173–4; 'Try Seeing It Through Our Eyes' (video) 37; *see also* 'Concerning equity: The voice of young people'; 'Innovative Links Between Schools and Universities for Teacher Professional Development'
'Student voice: Essential testimony for intelligent schools' 14–15, **118–30**
Students as Researchers (project) 82, 129
Study of Curriculum and Assessment Reform in the Context of Reculturing 49
Sydney Morning Herald 120

TAFE (Tertiary and Further Education Sector) 133
Talking Circles (Key Competencies Project) 49–51, 52, 57–8, 59n5
Taronga Zoo Education Centre 180, 182
Tavani, Herman T. 127
teacher education, initial 2, 22, 62, 64
teacher enquiry 43–4
teacher professional learning 108, 123–5, 134, 151–2, 189–90, 196–7

teacher professionalism 140
teacher retention 135–6
teacher-student interaction 124, 169
Teacher Training Agency (England) 94
technical-cognitive interests 42, 106
Teese, Richard 19, 132, 141, 166–7
Tertiary and Further Education Sector (TAFE) 133
tertiary students 4, 6
theoretical knowledge 5
theoretical validity 52
theory, and practice 69
theory, trivialisation of 68–9
Thomson, Pat 77–8, 84, 157
toilets, provision of 18
transculturalism 24
transparency 79, 103, 112, 164
Tripp, D. 159
trust 104, 110
'Try Seeing It Through Our Eyes' (video) 37
Turnbull, Colin 10, 79
Tyler, Ralph W. 31

unions, teaching 7, 47, 94, 132, 135–6
United Nations Convention on the Rights of the Child (1989) 164–5
universities 7, 12–13, 80, 99–104, 183, 186
University of Sydney 2, 21, 156

Valdecasas, A. 150
validity: catalytic 103, 110; democratic 103, 110, 129; descriptive 52; dialogic 103, 110, 129; evaluative 52; generalisable 52; interpretative 52; outcome 103; process 52, 103, 110; theoretical 52
Values for Australian Schooling 172
values system 110
Van Manen, Max 55–6
Vinson, T. 136–7

Walker, R. 37
Walker, Rob 49
Wang-Iverson, P. 189, 191
Watanabe, T. 189
'Weaving a web of professional practice (Australia) **177–86**
web-based technologies 122, 127, 147
Welsh schools 34
Wenger, Etienne 21
White, Viv 8
Whitlam, (Edward) Gough 4
Wiedel, J. 37
Wilkinson, Jane 21–2
Wilkinson, Marian 78

Willis, Paul 85
Wilson, Cathy 191
Wolfram Cox, Julie 67–8
Wood, Bronwyn E. 20
Woodville Primary School (Australia) 129
work organisation 46
working classes 85
Wyness, Michael G. 166

Yates, Lyn 66, 108
York Outstation Program 42
Yoshida, M. 191

Zschokke, Samuel 177